THE AXMANN
CONSPIRACY

THE AXMANN CONSPIRACY

THE NAZI PLAN FOR A FOURTH REICH

AND HOW THE U.S. ARMY DEFEATED IT

SCOTT ANDREW SELBY

BERKLEY CALIBER, NEW YORK

BERKLEY BOOKS
Published by the Penguin Group
Penguin Group (USA) Inc.
375 Hudson Street, New York, New York 10014, USA
Penguin Group (Canada), 90 Eglinton Avenue East, Suite 700, Toronto, Ontario M4P 2Y3, Canada
(a division of Pearson Penguin Canada Inc.) • Penguin Books Ltd., 80 Strand, London WC2R 0RL,
England • Penguin Group Ireland, 25 St. Stephen's Green, Dublin 2, Ireland (a division of Penguin
Books Ltd.) • Penguin Group (Australia), 250 Camberwell Road, Camberwell, Victoria 3124, Australia
(a division of Pearson Australia Group Pty. Ltd.) • Penguin Books India Pvt. Ltd., 11 Community
Centre, Panchsheel Park, New Delhi—110 017, India • Penguin Group (NZ), 67 Apollo Drive,
Rosedale, Auckland 0632, New Zealand (a division of Pearson New Zealand Ltd.) • Penguin Books
(South Africa) (Pty.) Ltd., 24 Sturdee Avenue, Rosebank, Johannesburg 2196, South Africa

Penguin Books Ltd., Registered Offices: 80 Strand, London WC2R 0RL, England

This book is an original publication of The Berkley Publishing Group.

First Edition: September 2012

Library of Congress Cataloging-in-Publication Data

Selby, Scott Andrew.
The Axmann conspiracy : the Nazi plan for a Fourth Reich and how
the U.S. Army defeated it / Scott Andrew Selby.
p.   cm.
Includes bibliographical references and index.
ISBN 978-0-425-25270-3
1. Germany—Politics and government—1945–1990.   2. Germany—History—1945–1955
3. National socialism.   4. Conspiracies—Germany—History–20th century.   5. Axmann, Artur,
1913–   6. Axmann, Artur, 1913—Political and social views.   7. Nazis—Biography.   8. Hunter, Jack.
9. United States. Army. Counter Intelligence Corps—Biography.   10. Espionage, American—
Germany—History—20th century.   I. Title.
DD257.4.S38 2012
943.087'4—dc23
2012001998

PRINTED IN THE UNITED STATES OF AMERICA

10   9   8   7   6   5   4   3   2   1

Dedicated to those who fought against the Nazis—before, during, and after the war.

The [Counter Intelligence Corp] has more adventure stories buried in its secret files than a month's output of blood and thunder comic books. Unfortunately for the reading public, these bona fide cloak and dagger stories are not for publication.

WILLIAM ATTWOOD IN THE *NEW YORK HERALD TRIBUNE* (1947)

CONTENTS

CONTENTS

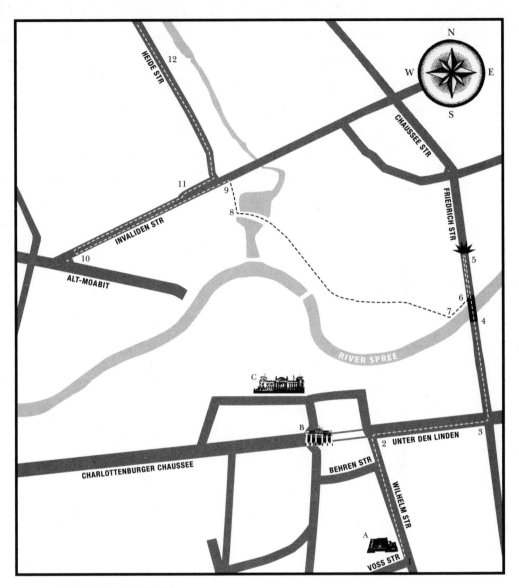

AXMANN'S BREAKOUT

A Bunker Area
B Brandenburg Gate
C Reichstag Building

1 Exit and head left
2 Turn right (see Russians to the left)
3 Turn left
4 Stop at Weidendammer Bridge
(Russians on other side)
5 Cross the bridge alongside a tank, the
tank explodes

6 Retreat, then walk along Spree River
7 Take the train tracks
8 Bump into Russian soldiers
9 Turn left
10 Head back
11 Run into Bormann's body
12 Take Heidestrasse

Illustration by Johan Stenbeck

CHRONOLOGY OF BACKGROUND EVENTS
APRIL 1945 TO APRIL 1946

1945:

APRIL 12 U.S. President FDR dies; Harry Truman becomes President

APRIL 16 Battle of Berlin begins—the Soviets vs. the Germans

APRIL 20 Hitler's fifty-sixth birthday—this includes an awards ceremony with Hitler Youth

APRIL 25 American and Soviet forces meet at the River Elbe in Germany

APRIL 28 Italian partisans kill Mussolini

APRIL 30 Hitler and Eva Braun commit suicide

MAY 1 Joseph Goebbels and his wife commit suicide; Hitler's death is announced

MAY 1–2 Breakout from Hitler's bunker

MAY 2 Surrender of German forces in Berlin to the Soviets

MAY 7 The Flensburg government agrees to an unconditional surrender

MAY 8 Victory in Europe Day (V-E) Day

MAY 23 The Allies disband the Flensburg government and arrest its leaders

MAY 23 *Reichsführer-SS* Heinrich Himmler commits suicide

JUNE 5 The Allies officially take over governmental control of Germany

JULY The Americans and British occupy their zones in Berlin (and the French Zone) and withdraw from territory they hold in the Soviet Zone in East Germany

JULY 16–AUGUST 2 The Potsdam Conference

JULY 26 The Potsdam Declaration is issued (re: Japan)

AUGUST 2 U.K., U.S.S.R., and U.S. issue the Potsdam Agreement

AUGUST 6 U.S. drops an atom bomb on Hiroshima (Japan)

AUGUST 9 U.S. drops an atom bomb on Nagasaki (Japan)

AUGUST 12 The French occupy their zone in Berlin

AUGUST 14 Japan agrees to an unconditional surrender

SEPTEMBER 2 Victory over Japan (V-J) Day (Japan signs surrender document)

OCTOBER 19 Nuremberg Trials indictments served

OCTOBER 24 United Nations officially is formed

NOVEMBER 11 George Patton replaces Dwight Eisenhower as military governor of the American Zone

NOVEMBER 20 The Nuremberg Trials begin

NOVEMBER 26 Joseph McNarney becomes military governor of the American Zone

NOVEMBER 29 Images of concentration camps shown at the Nuremberg Trials

DECEMBER 24 Berlin's curfew ends

1946:

JANUARY 5 Adolf Eichmann escapes U.S. custody

JANUARY 7 Using its old borders, Austria is recognized and divided into four zones

JANUARY 14 Agreement on Reparation from Germany is signed

JANUARY 27 Local elections are held in the American Zone of Germany

FEBRUARY 9 Stalin gives a major speech against capitalism

MARCH 5 Churchill gives his famous "iron curtain" speech about the U.S.S.R.

MARCH 11 Auschwitz commandant Rudolf Höss is caught

MARCH 13–22: *Reichsmarschall* Hermann Göring testifies at Nuremberg

APRIL 15 Rudolf Höss testifies at Nuremberg

APRIL 18 The International Court of Justice meets for the first time

APRIL 28 The International Military Tribunal for the Far East indicts ex–Japanese premier Hideki Tōjō for war crimes

APRIL 28 First postwar county-level elections held in the American Zone of Germany

DRAMATIS PERSONAE

Counter Intelligence Corps ("CIC") Agents

BRUCE HAYWOOD British Intelligence, but worked with the CIC

GEORGE HOCHSCHILD 307th CIC detachment, Seventh Army

JACK HUNTER Case officer in charge of Operation Nursery

WALTER KAUFMAN Rosenheim CIC, ran informant Ebeling

IRVING J. LEWIS Rosenheim CIC, ran informant Ebeling

WERNER D. NORDHEIM 307th CIC detachment, Seventh Army

TIMOTHY REIS 307th CIC detachment, Seventh Army

Informants

GÜNTER EBELING, CODENAME SLIM *HJ Oberstammführer*[1]

HANS GARMS Black marketer, partner in Tessmann

SIEGFRIED KULAS, CODENAME KARL Former HJ and SS officer

KURT POMMERENING, CODENAME PAUL Dispatcher at Tessmann

Hitler Youth Leaders/Christian Tessmann & Sons/Nazi Personnel

ARTUR AXMANN *Reichsjugendführer* (head of the Hitler Youth)

WALTER BERGEMANN HJ and then Tessmann's head of legal matters

KURT BUDÄUS HJ district leader, a leader of the northern group

WILLI HEIDEMANN *HJ Oberbannführer*, in charge of economics

GISELA HERMANN Berlin BDM leader (*Obergebietsführerin*)

ERICH KEMPKA Hitler's chauffeur

MAX LEBENS SS officer directing Werwolf in Bavaria

ARMIN LEHMANN Axmann's courier in Berlin

WILLI LOHEL HJ district leader, a leader of the northern group

MELITA MASCHMANN BDM officer who was in Berlin, then with Rüdiger

GUSTAV MEMMINGER *HJ Hauptbannführer*, HJ propaganda chief

ERNST OVERBECK *HJ Hauptbannführer*, HJ Organization Office chief

HANS-ADOLF PRÜTZMANN *SS Obergruppenführer*, head of Operation Werwolf

DR. JUTTA RÜDIGER *Reichsreferentin des BDM* (head of the BDM)

GERHARD "GERD" WELTZIN Axmann's adjunct

SIMON WINTER *HJ Oberbannführer*, head of HJ Agriculture

OTTO WÜRSCHINGER *HJ Hauptbannführer*, working for Ernst Overbeck

THE AXMANN CONSPIRACY

HITLER'S BUNKER

Whereas Socialism, and even capitalism in a more grudging
way, have said to people "I offer you a good time," Hitler has
said to them "I offer you struggle, danger and death," and as
a result a whole nation flings itself at his feet.

GEORGE ORWELL[1]

BERLIN, APRIL 30, 1945

For those of Hitler's men still in the heart of the city's government sector, the Battle of Berlin was almost lost.

Shell after shell sent deafening explosions through the Reich Chancellery garden above Hitler's bunker, kicking up debris and shrapnel.[2] Artur Axmann, to get from his command post in the cellar of the Party Chancellery at Wilhelmstrasse 64 to Hitler's bunker, was forced to run across exposed territory.[3] En route, he passed the skeleton of a horse whose body had been stripped of meat by people hungry enough to risk enemy fire in search of food.[4]

Axmann wore a moistened bandana across his mouth and nose, like a bank robber in a Western—not to conceal his identity, but rather to make the noxious air, full of fumes produced by the Soviets' white phosphorus shells, marginally more breathable.[5]

He wet his bandana with wine, as it was more plentiful than water—the only running water was in the bunker itself.[6] Even with the bandana, the air still smelled of ash and of death.

Axmann reeled from exhaustion. He was dirty, and a scruffy beard was growing on his chin. Before these last days of the war, he was always meticulously dressed in his uniform and clean-shaven.

Of slight build, Axmann stood just over five and a half feet.[7] He was young and handsome, with dark blond hair that flowed over his scalp in waves. His sharp chin and sculpted cheeks offset his piercing gray-blue eyes.[8] His most noticeable feature, though, was the result of an earlier war injury—Axmann had no right forearm, which meant that he was also missing a hand. Where it used to be, he now managed instead with a prosthetic device he partially covered with a glove.

The scream of the explosions rocking the cellar he employed as his command post, combined with the fatigue of fighting a battle he knew was lost, had culminated in a bad case of insomnia.[9] Moreover, without running water in his command post, he could not properly bathe. Once in the bunker, Axmann asked Hitler's forgiveness for not being presentable, to which Hitler replied, "You look like I did during the First World War."[10]

Axmann's soiled uniform bore the insignia of a *Reichsjugendführer*—head of the Reich's young people—a position he'd occupied for five years. This meant Axmann was in charge of the Hitler Youth (*Hitler Jugend*, "*HJ*") and its female counterpart, the League of German Girls in the Hitler Youth (*Bund Deutscher Mädel*, "*BDM*").[11]

As *Reichsjugendführer*, thirty-two-year-old Axmann reported directly to Adolf Hitler himself. This was an enormous step up from his humble working-class origins.

Axmann commanded Hitler Youth—some as young as twelve

years old—to defend Berlin to the death, despite the fact that the fight against the Russians was futile, as even the most dedicated Nazi could now see.[12] The Red Army encircled the city, and were so near the Führerbunker that Russian snipers could fire upon anyone brave or foolish enough to go outside.

Even so, Axmann ordered HJ members to continue the fight against the better equipped, trained, and experienced Russian troops. In the weeks leading up to the Battle of Berlin, he'd put together an antitank brigade comprised of HJ members.[13] These boys used throwaway, portable grenade launchers called *Panzerfaust* ("tank fist") to take out Soviet tanks.[14] To successfully blast an enemy tank, the boys had to venture dangerously close to it. Sometimes they succeeded, but in the process, they were killed in large numbers.

In late March, Axmann announced these HJ anti-tank groups in the official Nazi newspaper: "From the Hitler Youth has emerged a movement of young tank busters. . . . There is only victory or annihilation. Know no bounds in your love to your people; equally know no bounds in your hatred of the enemy. It is your duty to watch when others are tired; to stand when others are weak. Your greatest honor, however is your unshakeable faithfulness to Adolf Hitler."[15]

Many of the boys who survived this fighting were badly injured. The same day that Axmann's article came out, the leader of a group of HJ fighting in Vienna, Austria, wrote in his diary: "Here they are, Willi with his artificial lower leg, Hubert with his shot-off thigh, Hannes with his damaged foot, Schorschi with a prosthesis and head bandage, Karl with his empty sleeve, and all the others, those already recuperated or barely so."[16] And these were the boys who were considered fit enough to fight.

The goal of these boys' fighting and dying was not to stop the Russians from conquering Berlin, which was not even remotely possible.[17] They died to buy Axmann and the Führer a little more time and keep open the possibility of their escape. Axmann had previously offered to lead two hundred HJ boys in a desperate maneuver to evacuate the Führer from Berlin, using them as a human shield.[18] Hitler had turned down Axmann's offer, then "shook Axmann's hand and thanked him for his loyalty."[19]

The day before, Axmann and Hitler had had a long, personal talk. Shortly before this conversation, Hitler received the distressing news that the Soviets were about a mile away and that Communist partisans had executed his former ally, Italian dictator Benito Mussolini. His corpse had been mutilated and hung upside down in front of jeering crowds in Milan. Axmann attended a military conference in the bunker in which "it was once touched upon . . . that Mussolini's body had been hanged by its feet in Milan and I felt immediately that that had impressed Hitler very profoundly."[20]

Axmann knew that his Führer planned to kill himself rather than risk the Soviets taking him prisoner.[21] Hitler thought Stalin would especially love to capture him the next day, May 1, the biggest holiday of the Communist calendar. Known as May Day, or International Workers' Day, this was the day that leftists all over the world commemorated the 1886 Haymarket Massacre in Chicago. In the Communist U.S.S.R., May Day was an official state holiday accompanied by a massive military parade in Red Square. May Day 1945 would mark the first time Moscow had held a military parade since the war started.[22] On this day, Stalin planned to extol to the Soviet citizens all the many victories the Red Army had scored thus far. If he could also declare Hitler's capture, that would be a most impressive announcement.

Ironically, Axmann first met Hitler in person and shook his hand as part of a May 1 ceremony in the once magnificent Congress Hall of the Old Reich Chancellery in 1933.[23] Hitler had been appointed Germany's chancellor that January and the twenty-year-old Axmann was then a rising star in the Hitler Youth organization. Now this building, which had been a centerpiece of German governmental power, was heavily damaged and Hitler had been reduced to holding meetings in a crowded room in an underground bunker.

The mood in the bunker that day was grim, as it was generally believed that Hitler would not live another full day. There was no official announcement that the Führer was going to take his life, but the opportunity for a safe escape had passed and it was known that the leader was not willing to risk being captured.

Along with his adjunct, Gerhard "Gerd" Weltzin, Axmann was in the bunker during the night of April 29 and into the early hours of April 30.[24] They waited in the antechamber to Hitler's living quarters. Axmann felt despondent, with it now being abundantly clear that there was no hope for those left in the bunker to repel the Russians.

Axmann and Weltzin were alone when Hitler came out and welcomed them.[25] As Axmann later wrote, Weltzin left to give them privacy while Hitler "went towards the bench and gestured with his hand to welcome me to the place beside him. First, we sat in silence beside each other. I had so many questions, but I wasn't able to start the conversation. In those minutes of silence, I remembered March 13, 1942. Hitler welcomed me after my injury in a barrack of his headquarters [known as the "Wolf's Lair"] in Rastenburg. . . . After the first month of the campaign against Russia, Hitler was quite optimistic, full of vitality and strength."[26]

"Now, a beaten man sat beside me, who had once ruled over Europe. And I knew that he would be dead tomorrow. I could not speak. I felt like my throat was choking. Finally, Hitler broke the silence. He asked about my background and my family. I talked about my difficult childhood and my mother who had gone to work for us three sons in a factory for 16 years. 'Yes, adversity is always the greatest teacher in life,' said Hitler. Now that the talks were under way, I found it easier to ask my questions and I began: 'What will happen to our people?'"[27]

Axmann added, "We cannot be at the end of our history, this cannot be the end!"[28]

Hitler answered Axmann that "I am filled with horror when I think of our enemies destroying our unity and how the Reich is being cut into pieces. It now goes to the very survival of our people, mere survival. The people now have to undergo so much suffering. If the suffering which will now follow is endured with a sense of fate and national community, then there will be an uprising again."[29]

Hitler then paused for a moment before adding, "Ideas continue to live according to their own laws. I think something completely new will come."[30]

"We still were alone in the anteroom. All the time nobody passed by. You could only hear the monotonous sound of the ventilator." Axmann recalled that he offered to end his life with his Führer, but Hitler "refused, saying that your place is among the living. Then he got up and said goodbye. . . . Twelve hours after this talk he was dead."[31]

Despite his exhaustion, Axmann slept poorly that night while feeling that all hope was gone.[32] He dwelled on how he might escape alive from the Soviet positions that surrounded the bunker. He had given away his "poison lighter"—a functioning lighter carried by Nazi spies that contained a secret compartment for a cyanide pill—to Magda, wife of the notorious minister of propaganda, Dr. Joseph Goebbels.[33]

An HJ doctor had given him this lighter more than a year before and he'd kept it as a novelty.[34] In March, Axmann had visited Dr. and Mrs. Goebbels in their apartment near the Brandenburg Gate. When he lit a cigarette for Mrs. Goebbels, she asked about his unusual lighter and Axmann told her about its use for secret agents. She asked him for it, and as he did not intend to ever use it, he gave it to her.[35]

In the afternoon of April 30, during the daylight hours, Axmann rushed across the exposed ground to the bunker. He moved fast and stayed low to the ground to elude Russian snipers perching in the nearby ruins of the Hotel Kaiserhof, which had "collapsed like a house of cards."[36] Bodies, many of them burned, littered the bombed out landscape. Axmann's courier, Armin Lehmann, who had to run this same gauntlet on many occasions, described the strong odor emanating from those bodies that had been burned by flamethrowers, as an unforgettable "particularly nauseating, sickly sweet smell."[37]

It was a dangerous journey from Axmann's command post to Hitler's bunker. With the Russians so close, Axmann wrote of this journey, "It was every time a matter of life and death. To my leader of Berlin's HJ [*Gebietsführer*] Otto Hamann and his BDM leader [Gisela Hermann], I gave the advice to watch out outside when they left the basement [command post]. Both were laughing. Two hours later, I found out that they had been heavily wounded by grenade fragments. They had lain a long time on the street until they were found. Now they lay in the crowded [New] Reich Chancellery military hospital on mattresses in between the boxes of the bunker pharmacy. . . . There I sat beside my friend Hamann. When I lifted the blanket, I saw that his thigh was already black. . . . A short time later, he died due to his injuries. During a pause in the fighting, he was buried in the garden of the Reich Chancellery, which was marked by bombs and grenades. This garden was now a battlefield and cemetery in one."[38]

When Axmann descended into the bunker on April 30, Hitler was probably still alive. Axmann first talked to his friend Goebbels, who told him that he believed Hitler was still alive, but not for much longer as he "had already locked himself in and that he had decided to depart from life that day."[39] Axmann then rushed through the bunker to try to say a final good-bye to Hitler.[40]

Hitler had instructed the guard at the door, his personal adjutant *Schutzstaffel* ("SS") Major (*Sturmbarmführer*) Otto Günsche, to not let anyone in and to wait ten minutes before going in himself. When Axmann reached the antechamber outside Hitler's study, Günsche refused to let him in despite their friendship. Günsche had been a leader in the HJ and got along well with Axmann. He told Axmann that it was "too late—too late for anyone."[41]

The time moved slowly, as Günsche later explained: "The last instruction both [Hitler's valet Heinz] Linge and I had—directly from the Führer—was to wait ten minutes and then, and only then, to enter the room. This is just what we did. I kept glancing at my watch. I thought it must have stopped; they were the longest ten minutes in my life."[42]

Those waiting breathed in the fetid, stale air of the bunker in silence. Despite later reports of some inside the bunker being able to hear Hitler shoot himself, because of the thickness of the sealed double doors, the sole noticeable noise was the whoosh of the ventilation system.[43] Axmann later said that "I was standing right there, as close to the door as possible, but I certainly heard no shot."[44] In fact, Axmann explained that "no sound could be heard through those security doors."[45]

As soon as the ten minutes were up, Joseph Goebbels and Axmann entered the room.[46] Inside, they found Hitler dead on a small sofa, where he had shot himself in his right temple with his 7.65mm Walther PPK pistol.[47]

Next to him, Eva Braun Hitler leaned on Hitler's body, looking as if she were asleep.[48] Having bitten down on a glass cyanide capsule, she left behind an unblemished corpse. A day and a half before, she'd married Hitler in a ceremony in the bunker presided over by a low-level local government official. As part of this civil ceremony, the official followed government protocol by having the bride and groom certify, "that they were of pure Aryan descent and were free from hereditary disease."[49]

Axmann was not present at the wedding, but he did stop by afterward to congratulate the newlyweds.[50] Now Axmann had gone in a short time from being one of only eight guests at their post-wedding party to standing over their dead bodies.[51]

No one spoke—choked silence filled the room for around ten minutes as others filed in, until finally Axmann left the room with Goebbels. After the initial shock wore off, Goebbels dramatically proclaimed, "The heart of Germany has ceased to beat. The Führer is dead."[52]

One of Hitler's personal secretaries, Traudl Junge, had written in her journal four days before, "The thought that [Hitler] intends to commit suicide, while young boys are fighting for him to their last breath, this fact is demoralizing."[53] She planned on speaking to Hitler about this, hoping to convince him to stop these boys from fighting, but now it was too late.[54] Hitler was dead and those boys who were still able to continue to fight.

While Russian artillery shells landed nearby, the bodies of Hitler and his new bride were carried out of the bunker and into the Chancellery's garden. Hitler had lived in his underground bunker for 105 days, since January 16, 1945. His meteoric rise to power and subsequent plunging of the world into war had culminated in his body being laid to rest in the shelled ground of what had once been a fine garden.

In the garden, these two bodies were doused in gasoline and set on fire.

The ceremony surrounding what came to be called the "Viking Funeral" was in stark contrast to the elaborate rituals that celebrated Hitler during his reign. There was no pageantry, no music, no film cameras, no masses: a handful of his last followers gave a brief "Heil Hitler" raised arm salute, and then left him and his wife to burn alone. It was too dangerous to linger aboveground, even for the funeral of the Führer himself.

Axmann stayed inside the bunker as he "did not want to watch the burning, the cremating of the bodies."[55] He later explained to an interrogator that it was "too horrible for him to witness."[56]

Günsche gave Axmann the handgun with which Hitler had shot himself.[57] He also gave him the 6.35mm pistol that Hitler used to carry on his person, which they had found unfired near Eva Braun Hitler.[58]

According to Traudl Junge, Günsche told her that Hitler's "ashes were collected into a box, which was given to the Reichsjugendführer Axmann."[59] However, Axmann claims that he was never given Hitler's ashes.[60] In 1965, Axmann wrote, "Later on it could be read in the newspaper that they had passed Hitler's ashes in a metal container to me. This is speculation and not true."[61] As for why Traudl Junge thought that Günsche had given him a container with Hitler's ashes in it, Axmann speculated in his memoirs that she might have somehow confused Günsche giving him the pistol Hitler had used to kill himself with Günsche giving him an urn holding Hitler's ashes.[62]

Hitler's burned body was left behind in the Chancellery garden, accompanied by the body of his bride. His last known words had been to his valet, Heinz Linge: "Linge, old friend, I want you now to join the breakout group."

"Why, my Führer?" asked Linge.

"To serve the man who will come after me," said Hitler enigmatically.[63]

By "the man who will come after me," Hitler may have meant the next Führer. He did not say explicitly who this man would be and it was not clear whom he meant. However, from his early to his final days, Hitler encouraged a form of social Darwinism among his subordinates whereby competition resulted in the strongest seizing power. Even in anticipation of events after his death, this strategy appears to have remained the same.

Hitler's last will and testament, which he had transcribed to Traudl Junge the day before, did not name the next Führer. Instead, it divided up the positions of power of what little was left of Nazi Germany from one into three. Joseph Goebbels, the propaganda minister, would replace Hitler as Reich chancellor; Grand Admiral Karl Dönitz (who was safely far from Berlin in unconquered Flensburg) would become Reich president; Martin Bormann would be party minister. Bormann and Goebbels were both still in the bunker; of these three, only Dönitz was not in danger of being captured by the Russians.

It would be up to Axmann to secure his own position in what little was left of the Nazi hierarchy after Hitler's passing. While he had believed in Hitler and stayed with him in the bunker until the end, Axmann had prepared for the possibility of defeat by putting a plan into motion only a month before. Although Axmann remained trapped in the ruins of Berlin, those loyal to him gathered in Bad Tölz (about four hundred miles to the south), which was still German-controlled territory. Now all that remained was for Axmann to find a way to join them, which would be a considerable challenge.

ONE

BREAKOUT

In the presence of this blood banner, which represents our Führer, I swear to devote all my energies and my strength to the savior of our country, Adolf Hitler. I am willing and ready to give up my life for him, so help me God.

OATH TAKEN BY TEN-YEAR-OLD BOYS ON JOINING THE HJ[1]

Hitler was dead by his own hand. The Soviets had encircled what little was left of the Nazi forces in central Berlin.

The two sides now fought for control of the ruins of the Reichstag building, just across the large square (the Wilhelmplatz) from the Reich Chancellery and the bunker. Once home to Germany's parliament, it had been abandoned since being set on fire in 1933, yet it retained its symbolic value. Stalin very much desired its capture in time for May Day (May 1).

The Russians launched their attack on the building during the morning of April 30 but were unable to gain entry until that evening. Nazi defenders took advantage of the building's rubble to force the incoming Russians to fight a fierce battle waged not in terms of meters gained or lost, but rooms.

Even with Axmann's child soldiers of the Hitler Youth, the fighting in Berlin could not go on much longer. Eventually, the Russians would capture what remained of Nazi Berlin and those who stayed in it. Those still living had to take action.

Axmann did not allow the boys of Hitler Youth on the front lines to decide whether to break out or stay.[2] They were commanded to fight in order to keep open the possibility of escape for those left in the bunker. As Axmann was fond of telling them, "There is nothing but victory or annihilation."[3]

While Axmann himself was a devoted Nazi and loyal follower of Adolf Hitler, many Hitler Youth boys who joined in the early years, before the Nazis had seized power, had done so for small benefits like camping and camaraderie. But the boys fighting in Berlin had been required to join HJ.[4]

HJ proper was for boys aged fourteen to eighteen, but it had a junior section called *Deutsches Jungvolk* (German Youth) for those ten to fourteen. Even some of these *Deutsches Jungvolk* fought toward the end of the war. Hitler, with Axmann nearby, had awarded boys as young as twelve the Iron Cross just a week and a half before his suicide in the bunker.[5]

On the afternoon of his fifty-sixth birthday, April 20, Hitler left the bunker to appear in public for the last time. He ascended into the open air of the nearby Reich Chancellery's garden to honor soldiers from an army group, a *Waffen* SS panzer division, and assorted Hitler Youth.

The once magnificent headquarters of the Nazi regime had been badly damaged by Allied air raids, but the gardens could still be used for ceremonies. Hitler was accompanied by a veritable who's who of the remaining key figures of the Third Reich, including the minister of propaganda, Joseph Goebbels; the head of the Party Chancellery and Hitler's personal secretary, Martin Bormann; the chief of the German Police and leader of the SS, Heinrich Himmler; and the minister of armaments and war production, Albert Speer.[6] The head of the air force, Hermann Göring, had met with Hitler earlier, but left before the ceremony.[7]

During this ceremony, Axmann used his left arm to give the Nazi salute, as he was missing his right forearm. He then announced, "My Fuhrer! In the name of Germany's youth, I congratulate you on your birthday. I am proud once again to introduce you to the young fighters whose courage and valour is typical of the readiness for action of the Hitler Youth. They stand the test on the home front with an iron will to achieve the final victory."[8]

Hitler then answered him with "Thanks, thanks, Axmann. If in battle only all were as brave as these boys."[9]

With Axmann at his side, Hitler pinched cheeks and shook hands with uniformed boys like a kindly old man proud of the soap box derby trophy his grandson had won. His hands trembled, his back was slightly bent, and he looked older than he actually was.[10] One person who observed him that day said that "He seemed closer to seventy than fifty-six. He looked what I would call physically senile."[11]

Hitler then gave a short speech saying, "On all fronts heavy fighting is taking place. Here in Berlin we are facing the great, decisive battle. Germany's destiny will be decided by the performance of the German soldier: his exemplary steadfastness and his unbending will to fight. You are witnesses to the fact that with dogged resistance even an enemy that outnumbers us can be repelled. Our belief that we will win the battle for Berlin has to remain unbroken. The situation can be compared with that of a patient believed to have reached the end. Yet, he does not have to die. He can be saved with a new medication, discovered just in time to save him, which is now being produced. We just have to be determined to hold out until this medication can be applied, to achieve final victory. That is what counts, to keep on fighting with an iron will!"[12]

When a visibly haggard Hitler gave a weak Nazi salute with "*Heil*

Euch" (hail to you) no one responded. Those present had been instructed earlier to respond with "*Heil, mein Führer*" (hail my leader)—these salute expressions and responses were different now that they involved the actual leader of Nazi Germany.

But instead of a reply of "*Heil, mein Führer*," there was a very awkward silence. It could have been a reaction to Hitler's poor health, or it could have been what he had said, but regardless of the explanation, no one responded. Axmann later recalled, "All you could hear was the distant rumbling from the front, now scarcely nineteen miles away."[13]

One of those awarded the Iron Cross by Hitler that day, sixteen-year-old Armin Lehmann, later wrote that "it was crystal clear to me that Axmann wanted to ingratiate himself with the Fuhrer by demonstrating how loyal and brave the Hitler Youth were."[14] Lehmann soon became Axmann's courier.

Afterward, Hitler slowly shuffled off to descend into his bunker for the last time. From then until his death, he remained underground, safe from Russian bombardments.

Axmann understood the mind-set of the boys he commanded because he had once been a member of HJ himself. In 1928, when Axmann was fifteen years old and still in high school, he heard a speech by Joseph Goebbels that inspired him to join the Nazi movement. He joined the National Socialist Schoolchildren's League and later the HJ. Full of ambition and hardworking, he started by organizing his fellow students in the Wedding district of Berlin. At that time, Wedding was a tough neighborhood for a Nazi, since it was then a working-class bastion of their leftwing opponents.

His family had lived in Hagen, Germany, where he was born on February 18, 1913. In 1916, the family moved to Berlin. Soon after this move, Axmann's father, Aloys, an insurance clerk, died from diabetes at the age of thirty-two. His mother, Emma, was left to take care of the family on her own. Axmann was the youngest of three brothers (the others were Kurt, born 1907, and Richard, born 1910). He also had two older sisters, who both died young, before he was old enough to remember them.[15]

After graduating high school, Axmann went on to study law, economics, and government at Berlin University. In 1931, when his mother lost her factory job, he quit school so that he could work full-time and support the family.[16] That year he officially joined the Nazi Party—at the time, one had to be at least eighteen years old to do so.[17]

On January 30, 1933, Hitler became the chancellor of Germany. Five months later, Axmann was promoted to run the Social Office of the Reich Youth Leadership.[18]

While Axmann had become a Nazi early on in their struggle for power, now the floodgates opened. Germans flocked to join the Nazi Party in large numbers. Hitler solidified his position, and the party continued to grow. HJ membership increased as well, with other competing youth organizations eventually banned and participation in the HJ made mandatory.[19]

A *Time* magazine article in 1934 wrote of the disbandment of the German Boy Scout Organization: "The last of the German Scouts laid away their fleur-de-lis Scout badges. Presently they will be issued the swastika emblems of Hitler Youth."[20] These emblems used by the HJ featured a swastika in an elongated diamond pattern. While the Boy Scouts motto was the bland "Be Prepared," HJ used the dramatic and warlike "Blood and Honor."

In addition to his work in the HJ, Axmann served in the military. He joined the infantry and moved into a barracks for his training in 1938. Even during basic training, he continued to do his job as head of the Social Office of the Reich Youth. Subordinates visited him at the barracks, and he snuck off base for meetings from time to time.

In September 1939, Germany invaded Poland, which set off World War II. Axmann was called up from the reserves to serve in an infantry regiment.[21] He was happy to find one of his HJ comrades from the national office serving with him, Walter Bergemann.[22] Bergemann worked in the legal department of the HJ head office in Berlin, and their paths would cross again after the war.

Axmann served on the Western Front between Germany and France from September 1939 through April 1940.[23] It was during this time that he first saw action. As Axmann later put it, "on the heights of Spicherer, I received my baptism of fire."[24] A shell from French artillery almost killed him; he barely managed to jump into a crater in time to save himself.[25]

He survived another close call while part of a reconnaissance mission into French territory. It was during the winter, with heavy snow covering up the mines that littered the no-man's-land separating the French from the Germans. At the start of this mission, they found a mine entangled in a barbwire fence. When they entered a small French village, a barking dog drew unwanted attention to them. The reconnaissance team killed it quickly so as not to risk discovery.

When a much larger French group showed up to investigate the barking dog, Axmann's team hid in a rectory, and although the French walked right by, none of them went in. If the Germans had been discovered, Axmann believed that the French would have quickly won the resulting firefight. All the French had to do was throw some hand grenades into the rectory, and they would have likely killed Axmann and his fellow Germans.[26]

Axmann left active military duty and returned to Berlin to serve as deputy to the first *Reichsjugendführer*, Baldur von Schirach, starting in May 1940.[27] That August, when Hitler appointed Schirach to be the district leader (*Gauleiter*) of Vienna, Schirach recommended Axmann to Hitler as his replacement.[28] And so, Axmann became the second and final *Reichsjugendführer* at the age of twenty-seven, in August 1940.[29]

In June 1941, after a visit to Rome to meet Mussolini, Axmann rejoined the infantry as a lieutenant while retaining his position in the HJ.[30] At 3:15 A.M. on June 22, Germany broke its treaty with the Soviet Union by invading it. Codenamed Operation Barbarossa, this massive German invasion took Stalin by surprise. The first day of the invasion, when Axmann was on the front lines, enemy fire hit him immediately above his left elbow and in his right arm, about half of which had to be amputated. The injury to his left arm though was relatively minor.

Axmann's right arm had been his dominant one, so this was a serious loss. He had to adapt to writing with his left hand and greeting colleagues in the inverse.[31] The Nazi salute usually involved the raising of one's right arm, but the disabled could use their left arms.

Below the elbow, a prosthetic was fitted, which Axmann came to wear proudly, like a badge, proof of the weight of his military sacrifice. On the hand portion of his false arm, Axmann became known for placing a pristine white glove. In this way, he wielded his injury with regality and pomp.

Axmann spent much of his convalescence with his wife, Ilse Bachstein. During their marriage, they had only one child, a son, but he was too young to ever join the HJ. Ilse herself never joined the BDM or the Nazi Party. In fact, her father was a Social Democrat (a liberal party which had been banned and its leaders persecuted by Hitler).[32]

In December 1941, he completed his recuperation and returned to his job as *Reichsjugendführer*.

As the head of Hitler Youth, Axmann came to take a certain pride in his working-class background. A BDM officer, Melita Maschmann, wrote regarding what she called Axmann's "humble beginnings" that "he was in a certain sense the proletarian showpiece of the youth leadership corps: he was proof to us that every German boy had a field marshal's baton in his knapsack. One was always hearing how he and his brothers had been brought up by the widow of a factory worker who had had to earn her living during the depression by taking in washing."[33]

Now, at the end of April 1945, after Hitler's death, Artur Axmann was stuck in Berlin's government district along with many other Nazis. For those in this shrinking pocket of German-controlled territory, few options remained available. Those too injured to walk, who were housed in the emergency hospital in the basement of the New Reich Chancellery, had only two choices: suicide or surrender to the Russian forces. The rest, however, had the option of trying to break through the Soviet lines. Once they broke out, they could either go into hiding or head west to surrender to the Americans.

Those left in Berlin's government center considered surrender to be a hazardous option. If captured by the Russians, who were still raw from the mass slaughters and other atrocities committed by the German Army during the failed invasion of the Soviet Union, they would likely suffer tremendously and perhaps even be killed.

However, surrendering to the Americans carried its own risks. They were far away, across the Elbe River to the west. It would be a treacherous journey through territory controlled by the Russians, with active fighting still going on between the Germans and Russians. For example, some other nearby German forces had already given up on coming to Berlin's rescue and were instead fighting their way west to the Americans.

The Western Allies had stayed on the west side of the Elbe River, instead of invading Berlin. General Dwight D. "Ike" Eisenhower, the supreme commander of the Allied Forces in Europe and future president, had decided to let the Soviets take Berlin. He had made this still controversial decision in part because the Allies had already agreed to divide Berlin. Eisenhower thought it pointless to waste an estimated one hundred thousand of his troops' lives to take Berlin, only to have to give part of it back to the Soviets later.[34] Other factors that influenced this decision included the fact that the Russians were already much closer to Berlin than the Americans, and "the fear of a prolonged guerrilla campaign in Germany, directed from an alpine fortress."[35]

The year before, in August 1944, Eisenhower had written in a letter that "there has developed in my mind some suspicion that the fanatics of that country may attempt to carry on a long and bitter guerilla warfare. Such a prospect is a dark one and I think we should do everything possible to prevent its occurrence."[36] By the time the war in Europe was nearing its end, Eisenhower's fear had a specific focus—a possible national redoubt in the Bavarian Alps.

While Axmann was in charge of the remaining HJ, the overall defense of Berlin's central government area was in the hands of Brigadier General (SS *Brigadeführer*) Wilhelm Mohnke. This area "included the Reichs Chancellery, Führerbunker and Reichstag."[37] The two knew each other well.

Mohnke had previously commanded the 26th SS Panzergrenadier Regiment in the 12th SS Panzer Division *Hitlerjugend*. This was a *Waffen* SS armored division formed with inexperienced and quickly trained HJ serving under veteran noncommissioned and commissioned officers.

Albert Speer, the ex-minister of armaments and war production for Nazi Germany, explained when he was being interrogated after the war, "The 'HITLER YOUTH' Division of the Waffen SS consisted of the cream of the German Youth. Without having a skeleton staff of old soldiers experienced at the front, they were relentlessly sent into action, which meant a steady blood-letting of the best German youth, without any military advantage."[38]

On April 16, Mohnke had started the Battle of Berlin with over two thousand soldiers. By the afternoon of April 30, he had amassed around ten thousand fighters. His command had grown as soldiers retreated into the center of what remained of Nazi-controlled territory in Berlin. They then joined his forces. These ten thousand faced an enemy of about one and a half million soldiers. There were roughly another million Soviet fighters positioned outside the city.

The breakout itself fell under Mohnke's command as well. Hitler had previously given permission for everyone who remained to break out of Soviet lines. Around 7 P.M. (about three and half hours after Hitler's death) on Monday, April 30, 1945, Mohnke announced that the breakout would not happen for at least twenty-four hours. For those still in the bunker who were not part of its defense, the only thing left to do was rest and wait until Mohnke decreed that the time was right.

The mood in the bunker was a strange one. Axmann later said "the subject [of Hitler's suicide] was a kind of taboo that night. No one spoke of Hitler, not of Hitler as a dead man, a mortal corpse. It was perhaps beyond our ken. His death may have been on everybody's mind, but it was pushed into the subconscious. Goebbels, for example, talked on and on about his first meeting with Hitler, about the great triumph of 1933, about pleasant days in Berchtesgaden [in the Bavarian Alps]. He managed to transport us all out of the bunker and off to the magnificent Alps. Once upon a time . . ."

Some in the bunker decided that they didn't want to live without their Führer and so took the only certain path to avoid capture by the Soviets—suicide. Most notably, for the first and last time in his life, Joseph Goebbels, the charismatic propaganda minister for the Third Reich, disobeyed a direct order of his Führer.[39] Hitler had wanted him to escape Berlin and become Reich chancellor of what remained of the Third Reich.

However, Goebbels and his wife, Magda, decided to stay in Berlin to kill themselves and their six children—one boy and five girls, ages four to twelve years old.

While Goebbels intended to die in the bunker before the Russians could reach it, Axmann and the vast majority of those who remained wanted to live.

On the evening of Tuesday, May 1, Axmann once again ran across the exposed ground between his cellar command post and the bunker. As he later explained, he "wanted to say goodbye to both the Goebbelses. I found the couple sitting at the long conference table with Werner Naumann, Hans Baur, Walter Hewel, General Krebs, three or four others. Goebbels stood up to greet me. He soon launched into lively memories of our old street-fighting days in Berlin-Wedding, from 1928 to 1933. He recalled how we had clobbered the Berlin Communists and the Socialists into submission, to the tune of the 'Horst Wessel' marching song, on their old home ground. . . . But there was not a word about his family. Magda Goebbels just sat there, saying little, head high. She was chain-smoking and sipping champagne. I did not ask about the children because someone, either Baur or Hewel, had whispered to me that they were already dead."[40]

Later that night, Joseph and Magda Goebbels committed suicide and their bodies were burned. Unlike Adolf and Eva Hitler, they killed themselves aboveground, in the Reich Chancellery garden itself. This way they spared those who survived them from having to carry their corpses upstairs. Their children's bodies were left where they lay in their room, to be discovered by the Soviets.

Mohnke had been formulating a plan for the escape. He later explained, "I spent the whole long afternoon working out the details of the breakout with Colonel Klingemeirer and my staff. We established the march route, organized the separate groups, calculated, and synchronized the timing."[41]

The time had come for those left who were still able to walk and didn't want to commit suicide or be captured by the Soviets to flee through the ruins of Berlin. Once the glorious capital of a Nazi empire that had recently presided over most of Europe, the city was now a mess of rubble that provided both snipers and those escaping with cover in which to hide. Albert Speer, who had been Hitler's favorite architect as well as the minister of armaments and war production, said that "Berlin was, in April 1945, more ruins than a town, one could find almost no building which was still intact."[42]

Those left in the government district were well aware of the grave danger of their escape plan. As Traudl Junge recalls feeling before attempting escape: "There was no hope to come through these lines alive, but it was still better to die in the open air by a bullet, than to swallow in this shelter the poison, before the Russians would break down the door."[43]

To prepare for their escape, those who could find civilian clothes put them on and left behind their military uniforms. For the rest, including Axmann, the best they could do was remove insignia of rank and destroy their papers—the hope was that if stopped, one could pretend to be a civilian or low-level soldier. Some of the women disguised themselves as men by wearing *Wehrmacht* uniforms. As an added precaution, they used makeup to create the appearance that they suffered from a highly contagious disease—smallpox. The same makeup they'd once used to look their best, they now employed to look diseased. The women hoped these measures would prevent Russian soldiers from raping them.

Axmann was a wanted man. His high rank meant that he fell into the automatic arrest category for Allied troops. Before Germany was even conquered, the Allies determined whole categories of persons to be arrested as soon as troops came across them, without regard to their individual circumstances, but based solely on the position they had held as part of the Third Reich. For instance, the military command of the Allied Forces on the Western Front "had long ago worked out automatic arrest categories ranging from the top Nazi leadership to the local *Ortsgruppenleiter,* from the top *Gestapo* agents to leaders of the Hitler Youth, the Peasants' League, and the Labor Front. . . . They were all presumed to be confirmed Nazis and, with some allowance for excessive zeal on the part of the Counterintelligence Corps (CIC), the vast majority doubtless were. Usually, of course, they did what they could to conceal their identities and their pasts. Some succeeded no doubt, but most were not hard to find."[44]

Moreover, as *Reichsjugendführer,* the U.S. War Crimes Office considered him responsible for the Nazification of German youth. In addition, he had directly commanded young boys to their deaths toward the end of the war.

He also bore responsibility for the roundup of "Swing Kids" from Hamburg, many of whom were sent to concentration camps.[45] The "crime" committed by these German youths was that they had rejected the HJ in favor of a subculture based on American jazz and swing music. Three years before, Axmann had written to the head of the SS, Heinrich Himmler, that "I would very much appreciate an order to your Hamburg offices to the effect that the 'Swing Youth' will be proceeded against as severely as possible."[46]

Fortunately for him, Axmann was much less known among enemy troops than some of the other high-ranking Nazis in the bunker. Despite his impressive medals and position, it was unlikely that any non-Germans who encountered him would know who he was. His use of a sophisticated prosthetic device might have been a giveaway to certain Germans, but the average Russian soldier would not be able to spot him, even with this telltale sign.

The harsh conditions of the end days in Berlin helped mask his high status—he was dirty, unshaven, smelly, and sleep-deprived. Instead of looking like an important Nazi official, he more closely resembled an ordinary soldier or, with his injury, a war invalid.

A few days before, Hitler had awarded him the highest medal of the Nazi Party—the Gold Cross of the German Order of the Great German Empire—for his use of the HJ to defend the Third Reich.[47] This medal was only given eleven times in total (most often posthumously). Axmann was one of only two recipients to survive the war and its immediate aftermath.[48] Those awarded it were supposed to form an elite fraternity, but it was destined to be a co-fraternity of two— Axmann and the Reich labor leader, Konstantin Hierl.

At the ceremony, Hitler also awarded Axmann with the Iron Cross First Class "for his personal gallant efforts." In order to be qualified to receive this medal, one had to have previously received the Iron Cross Second Class—Axmann got his in 1941. Axmann also had a wound badge (silver) for the lost right hand, a Golden Party Badge (which looked like a Nazi Party Badge surrounded by a golden wreath), a Hitler Youth Golden Medal (with oak leaf), the Service Award of the NSDAP (in silver), and two War Merit Crosses (second and first class, both without swords).

When Hitler gave Axmann the German Order, he proclaimed, "Without your boys, the struggle could simply not be carried, not only here in Berlin, but throughout Germany." Axmann then answered enthusiastically, "They are your boys, my Fuhrer!"[49] Hitler's hands trembled too much for him to pin the award himself, so Hitler's personal adjutant Major Otto Günsche pinned it on Axmann instead.

The German Order itself was a large, gaudy medal with a Golden Party Badge in its center, surrounded by a black-and-gold Iron Cross. A gold eagle sat between each pair of the four points of the cross. Above the cross lay a laurel wreath with two crossed swords. On top of the swords were two small oak leaves below an eagle with spread wings holding a swastika encircled by an oak wreath. On the back was a copy of Hitler's signature.

Of course, Axmann could not wear such a medal during his escape.

The plan approved by Mohnke was for a staggered exit from the bunker in groups, rather than a mass escape. As Axmann later recalled, "I consulted with my comrades regarding all the possibilities of the breakout. We were united in the fact that only in small groups or individually could we escape through the Russian lines."[50]

Everyone except Axmann's group planned on descending into Berlin's extensive subway tunnels and heading northwest until they bypassed the Soviets. It was a formidable task—most of those attempting to escape from the government center would be captured within a day or two.

The first group, lead by Mohnke himself, was to start at nine that night, but they were delayed until 11 P.M. Before the breakout began, everyone who was leaving gathered in the underground portion of the New Reich Chancellery. From there, as Lehmann recalled, they could exit from "one of the underground garages that faced Wilhelmstrasse. It had once housed the Chancellery fire brigade but was now home to a fleet of shiny black government limousines. . . . The cars had been shunted in an untidy pile to the side of the vast garage to make way for the army of escapees. There were about 1,000 people to be evacuated in all."[51]

Hitler's chauffeur, Erich Kempka, described what happened next: "The men and women singly left the Chancellery through a narrow hole in the wall along Wilhelm-Strasse near the corner of Wilhelm-Strasse and Voss-Strasse. Because of the heavy artillery-fire everyone ran as quickly as possible to the next entrance of the subway in reach."[52]

"The next entrance of the Kaiserhof-stop about 50 [meters] from the building of the Reichs-Chancellery had collapsed after a direct artillery-hit. Therefore, we went to the entrance approximately 200 [meters] distant from the Reichs-Chancellery which was located opposite the Hotel Kaiserhof. This entrance was open. At the subway-station the single groups gathered again and went to the subway-station Friedrichstrasse along the tracks of the subway."[53]

This was as far as the breakout groups could get via the subway tunnels; further progress underground was impossible owing to damage to this tunnel. When they emerged from the Friedrichstrasse station, they took cover with German troops in the surviving structures in the Mitte district, such as the Admiralspalast Theater. The Spree River still stood between them and the possibility of freedom.

As the Prussian General Helmuth von Moltke once famously stated, "No battle plan survives first contact with the enemy."[54] Here the plan fell apart even before reaching the enemy lines, when those escaping the bunker discovered that the subway tunnel under the Spree River was blocked.

Axmann was in charge of the hundred or so Hitler Youth left in the government center.[55] Unlike the other groups, he chose to stay aboveground, avoiding the subway tunnels. It was a calculated decision— there were dangers to going underground like the other groups, as no one really knew what the conditions were like in the subway tunnels, and there were rumors of flooding, barriers, and enemy troops. Also, Axmann had an advantage over some of those escaping as he knew Berlin especially well, having grown up there. He was more comfortable navigating these streets than slogging his way underground.[56]

Armin Lehmann was part of Axmann's escape group. He believed that Axmann decided to avoid the subway in part because "he was . . . a brave man. Hiding from the enemy was not the sort of notion he was comfortable with. Running away down the subway lines like a rat did not appeal. If he had to face the enemy, then he would face him head on. I think Mohnke also wanted above-ground activities to divert attention from the underground escape attempt. . . . It occurred to me to ask Axmann what the plan was if we did manage to break through the Russian lines. 'Keep on fighting as ordered by the Fuhrer!' he replied simply."[57]

Axmann's group left the relative safety of the New Reich

Chancellery shortly before midnight on May 1.[58] It was mostly men but included three women—the BDM doctor Gertrud Huhn and two of her nurses.[59] The wounded that could not walk, including HJ boys and BDM girls, had to be left behind. Axmann gave the badly wounded leader of the Berlin BDM, *Obergebietsführerin* Gisela Hermann, Hitler's 6.35mm gun so she would have something with which to protect herself. This was the gun that had been found unfired near Eva Braun Hitler.

Before committing suicide, Eva Braun Hitler had given Gisela Hermann the bridal gown she had worn during her wedding to Adolf Hitler.[60] So Gisela Hermann now had two relics of the dramatic end of the Third Reich.

Axmann left her in the emergency hospital beneath the New Reich Chancellery. He held on to the gun with which Hitler had killed himself.[61]

The stink of urban warfare was overwhelming. Berlin reeked of a mixture of decomposing bodies, blood, gunpowder, dust, particles from collapsed structures, burned ash, gasoline, and smoke. The remnants of buildings littered the streets—broken glass, pieces of brick, concrete chunks, and shattered wood lying on ground chewed up first by bombs and now by artillery fire.

Lehmann recalled that "Axmann gave the word and we were all to go, one by one, walking single-file and as close to the walls as was possible. . . . It was a great relief to me when we first emerged on Wilhelmstrasse because it was quieter than I had thought it would be. In the background, the noise from Stalin's guns rumbled on as much as ever, but the Wilhelmstrasse at that moment wasn't the shooting gallery it had been during the day. It was suspiciously quiet, thankfully. Nevertheless, it was nerve-wracking when the odd shot did ring out and it made one duck involuntarily. Fortunately, none of us was hit."[62]

Axmann later described what happened next: "We were moving

silently along what was left of the walls, like shadows, single file. Just before we turned right and east, into Unter den Linden, we suddenly saw the giant hulk of the old Reichstag, which was still smoldering. Even closer, we could now spot Russian infantrymen and tankers in bivouac, directly around—and under—the Brandenburg Gate. Other Russians were roasting an ox on a spit set up in the middle of the Pariser Platz, halfway between the ruined mansions of the American and French embassies. The Russians seemed rather keen about minding their own business, which suited us desperate Germans perfectly. It was all like a dream, the kind one has after falling asleep while reading one of those epic Russian novels. We moseyed silently past the Adlon Hotel and the Russian embassy, under cover of dark. The Russians simply did not see us. Many of them were singing. We were not."[63]

Lehmann had a hard time believing that the Russians didn't see them. He latter considered it "inconceivable," but whether they saw the fleeing Germans and decided to ignore them or didn't see them, "no shots rang out."[64]

Axmann recalled that "there was still no fighting as we moved now, as fast as possible, down the once-fashionable Unter den Linden. It was only after we turned north again, entering the Friedrichstrasse, that we landed plumb in the middle of a very brisk skirmish. What we saw before our astonished eyes was a kind of SS international brigade—very few Germans but a lot of Danes, Swedes, Norwegians, Dutch, Belgians, Latvians and that French group called Kampfgruppe Charlemagne."[65]

When Axmann's group ran into all these other Nazis trying to fight their way free, they joined up with them. Their walk aboveground had led to the same place as the other groups' route through the subway tunnels. Now this mass of escapees had to get across the Spree River. The main way across was the Weidendammer Bridge. Many of the bridges across the Spree had been destroyed, and this was one of the few still intact.

The Russians were on the other side of the bridge though, behind an anti-tank barricade and in "the houses and basements to both sides of the Friedrichstrasse north of the Weidendammer bridge," according to Kempka.[66] A few of the Germans, including Mohnke, Kempka, and Hitler's female secretaries had already bypassed this dangerous bridge and taken a small nearby footbridge instead. Most, including Axmann, did not know about this alternative. Mohnke had no way of communicating with the other escapees, so he and his group could only hide in the rubble and watch as the others tried to fight their way across the River Spree.

Axmann had no problem with using the boys of HJ to enable him and his fellow high-ranking Nazis to escape. He considered the Hitler Youth to be "the center of national resistance" against the Allies. Two weeks before, he had unexpectedly shown up at General Helmuth Weidling's command post to volunteer the use of HJ boys to help defend Berlin. General Weidling told Axmann with "extremely coarse language" that he could not "sacrifice these children for a cause that is already lost."[67] Weidling went on to say in no uncertain terms, "I will not use them and I demand that the order sending these children into battle is rescinded."[68] Axmann pretended to accept this order and then disobeyed it, commanding the HJ to fight the Russians.[69]

A colonel who was at Weidling's headquarters later wrote that "shortly afterward while the fighting troops were withdrawing to Strausberg, Hitlerjugend tank-hunting units were roaming about the countryside and in the Buckow woods, inadequately trained and sent into action by inexperienced leaders in a manner both unrealistic and unwarlike, to find their fate in death or captivity."[70]

Axmann's courier, Armin Lehmann, wrote of this dispute over the use of the HJ, "There was a growing row between Axmann and

General Weidling. Weidling wanted to disband all of the Volkssturm Hitler Youth troops. He wanted to send the boys home and save their lives. Not so Axmann. He was intent on holding out until the bitter end. He was determined to prove to his Führer that the HJ would keep on fighting and remain loyal until victory or death. Axmann had expressed frequently in my presence that 'the Führer can depend on the Hitler Youth.' In Axmann's eyes our lives belonged to him and whatever he asked of us, we had to fulfill. Yet, Axmann must have known by then that there was no new miracle weapon ready to be deployed. There was no future but death, disgrace or misery. Somehow or other Axmann won the day. It was he, not Weidling, who had won Hitler's ear."[71]

Axmann had ordered the HJ to protect key bridges so that hoped-for German reinforcements would have a way into the city and so that important Nazis could flee. The first reason was the one Axmann discussed with Hitler, but the reinforcements that Hitler expected to arrive and save the day were not coming. While Hitler had talked about miracle weapons that were going to turn the tide of the war (such as during his birthday speech), according to Axmann, Hitler's hopes changed from new technologies to the Twelfth Army (commanded by General Walther Wenck) rescuing them.[72]

Axmann had a large group of HJ boys available to him at the Reich Sports Field in Berlin. This massive sports complex had been built for the 1936 Summer Olympics at which the Third Reich had hosted the world's premier sporting event. It was here that the African-American runner Jesse Owens famously won four gold medals.

On April 19, 1945, the day before Hitler's final birthday, Axmann had addressed a crowd of HJ and BDM during one of the last large ceremonies of the Third Reich. The occasion for this event was the induction into the lowest ranks of the HJ and the BDM of ten-year-old children (the *Deutsches Jungvolk* and *Jungmädelbund* respectively).[73]

Such induction ceremonies normally took place on Hitler's birthday throughout the Third Reich.[74] These were not normal times though, and it was held a day early this time.

Members of Axmann's HJ Division had been training at the Reich Sports Field in how to get close to tanks and then blow them up using *Panzerfaust*. So, they too were there that day to hear Axmann speak. He used his trademark line that "There is only victory or annihilation."[75]

The Battle of Berlin had begun three days before, on April 16. Despite the hopelessness of their current situation, Axmann told the gathering of his young followers, "The youth in the enemy-occupied territories has become the soul of the resistance. Our boys and girls will never surrender."[76]

BDM *Bannführerin* Melita Maschmann was in Berlin in April 1945 and later wrote of the response of Hitler Youth to rhetoric like that used by Axmann. "I shall never forget my encounters with the youngest of them, still half children, who did what they believed to be their duty until they were literally ready to drop. They had been fed on legends of heroism for as long as they could remember. For them the call to the 'ultimate sacrifice' was no empty phrase. It went straight to their hearts and they felt that now their hour had come, the moment when they really counted and were no longer dismissed because they were still too young."[77]

Axmann had encouraged this kind of reaction in his charges for some time now. For example, on September 3, 1944, Axmann used strong language in a newspaper article to motivate HJ to fight: "As the sixth year of war begins, Adolf Hitler's youth stands prepared to fight resolutely and with dedication for the freedom of their lives and their future. We say to them: 'You must decide whether you want to be the last of an unworthy race despised by future generations, or whether you want to be part of a new time, marvelous beyond all imagination.'"[78]

BDM *Bannführerin* Melita Maschmann thought back on what it must have been like for the youth who fought in Berlin. "I dread to think what despair and misery must have overcome them as they saw their comrades bleeding to death beside them and when their own intoxication gave way to sober consciousness. None of us who led those young people can remember, without feelings of guilt and horror, how they were smashed at the war front. In the state of blind frenzy to which they had been incited, how could they have recognized the contradiction between those human values (patriotism, loyalty, courage, obedience) to which they believed they were sacrificing themselves, and the inhumanity of the 'Führer' they worshiped? Drunk with power, he cynically let whole hecatombs of young people bleed to death. If there is anything that forces us to examine the principles on which we operated as leaders in the Hitler Youth . . . it is this senseless sacrifice of young people."[79]

Maschmann went on to say that "if Axmann had not learnt to idolize the German nation he would not have sent out those fifteen- and sixteen-year-olds to defend Berlin on April 23, 1945. He was these boys' supreme leader—but their lives and wellbeing meant less to him than National Socialist Germany, which was even then in its death throes."[80]

A member of Hitler Youth, Axel Eckenhoff, who fought to hold the Schilling Bridge in Berlin, was so upset by how HJ were slaughtered that he thought Axmann's sending out boys to defend the city and the bridges "was criminal."[81] Having survived that bloodbath, he felt that he "could shoot that Axmann."[82]

Reinhard Appel, who also fought in Berlin as a member of Hitler Youth, later said in response to Axmann's justifications after the war: "It was such a deceitful thing for [Axmann] to say, that the lads had successfully defended the bridges over the Havel and thus given many people the chance to escape beyond the Elbe. But it was all fairy-tales.

For whom and for what did we defend those bridges? So that someone like [head of the SS Heinrich] Himmler, the murderer of the Jews, could escape. And for that we were meant to give our lives, for men who killed Jews? It sickens me!"[83]

Only later in life did Appel come to the understanding he expressed above. During the fighting for Berlin, he was still an indoctrinated HJ member who was willing to die for his cause. He almost lost his life in the fight for Berlin when he tried to lob a grenade at a group of Russian soldiers just before his position was overrun. His sergeant had to physically stop him from this suicidal gesture. The Russians would have responded by killing all of them. Instead, they surrendered and so survived.[84]

Having successfully fled the government area around the bunker, Axmann and his fellow escapees now needed to make their way across the Weidendammer Bridge somehow. It was only 240 feet long, but as it was under constant enemy fire, anyone trying to run across it would be dead long before they made it to the other side. Even crossing in a large group would be suicidal without armored support.

At seventy-four feet wide, the ornate cast iron bridge was big enough for a tank to drive onto it. Mohnke had recalled a Tiger tank from the SS *Nordland* Division (the foreign SS volunteers Axmann ran into) the afternoon before for just such a purpose. There was now a large mass of people waiting to try to break out here, including foreign SS members, ordinary soldiers (*Wehrmacht*), and refugees from Hitler's bunker.

There were also members of the *Volkssturm* (People's Storm), the catchall group for males from sixteen to sixty who were not already serving in the military. It mostly consisted of boys from HJ, the wounded, those previously considered unfit for military service, and old men. There was no standard uniform for the *Volkssturm*. Its members could wear whatever uniform-like clothing they had and merely add a black armband that said *"Deutscher Volkssturm Wehrmacht."*[85] Old men wore their uniforms from the last world war, while some wore their uniforms from their civilian jobs. No one knew if those out of military uniform would be executed if caught by the enemy. The Geneva Convention's protections applied only to those who wore military uniforms. People out of uniform who fought could legally be shot as spies.

Although night had fallen and it should have been dark out, those fleeing Berlin were lit up by the flames of the buildings burning all around them. The city was on fire, and a large group of Germans trying to flee were easy targets for the Russians to spot.

The Tiger II tank, which Mohnke had procured, led the Germans in their attempt to get across the Weidendammer Bridge. It was a giant, heavily armored machine weighing more than 150,000 pounds, with a width of twelve feet, a height of ten feet, and a length of more than thirty-three feet (including its formidable front gun).[86] Among other names, it was also known as the "King Tiger."[87]

Axmann, along with many others, crossed the bridge behind the cover of this massive tank. It was a nerve-wracking journey, made under heavy enemy fire. The tank successfully made it to the other side of the Spree River and pushed back the Soviet soldiers there. Following this tank, the escapees made it one block north of the bridge to the Ziegelstrasse, when the Soviets succeeded in hitting the tank with a rocket-propelled grenade.[88]

The tank (and its ammunition) blew up in a blinding, deafening roar. As Axmann later wrote, this blast threw him "through the air. I was not knocked unconscious and was only slightly wounded by a sliver of shrapnel in the calf of my leg. Five minutes later, when I recovered my bearings, I crawled into the nearest shell hole. It was here that I first met up with [Martin] Bormann, [Werner] Naumann, [Hans] Baur, [Günther] Schwaegermann [who was Goebbels's adjutant], Guenther Dietrich (another Goebbels aide) and [Dr. Ludwig] Stumpfegger."[89]

Hitler's chauffeur, Erich Kempka, testified at Martin Bormann's trial by the International Military Tribunal at Nuremberg that Bormann died as a result of this explosion. Kempka, like Axmann, had crossed the Weidendammer Bridge behind the Tiger II tank. He testified that "the leading tank, beside which Martin Bormann was walking along about at the middle of the tank on the left-hand side, suddenly received a direct hit, I imagine from a bazooka fired from a window, and was blown up. A flash of fire suddenly shot up on the very side where Bormann was walking. . . . The tank was blown to pieces right there where . . . Bormann was walking. I myself was flung to one side by the explosion."[90]

Although Kempka was knocked out and temporarily blinded, and did not actually see Bormann's body, he believed "that the strength of the explosion was such that it killed him."[91]

Kempka was wrong. Bormann, like Axmann, was just knocked down.

Others were not so lucky as Axmann and Bormann; this same blast killed or seriously injured many of those trying to escape. The Russians quickly shot at the escapees who remained behind and retook control of the north side of the Weidendammer Bridge. The Germans still stuck on the south side of the Spree River needed to fight their way across the bridge again if they were to escape.

While Axmann had succeeded in getting across the bridge alive, according to his HJ courier Armin Lehmann, "almost every single Hitler Youth on the Weidendamm Bridge was wiped out."[92] The breakout group Axmann commanded had started with a large number of HJ; now they were dead, injured, captured, or otherwise unable to continue the escape attempt with their *Reichsjugendführer*.

Once they recovered from the shock of being knocked to the ground by an explosion, Axmann and his new companions slipped away in the resulting confusion. Axmann's senior aide, HJ *Oberbannführer* (Major) Gerd Weltzin, accompanied them.

Bormann was an undesirable escape companion. After the deaths of Hitler and Goebbels, he was one of the most wanted men left alive, and so a bigger target than Axmann. It did not help matters that Axmann, like almost everyone who knew Bormann, didn't like him. Moreover, during the breakout attempt, Bormann was drunk.

First, they retreated toward the north side of the Weidendammer Bridge. They then walked southwest about eight hundred feet along a street called Schiffbauerdamm, which ran along the right bank of the Spree River, until they hit the railroad tracks.

This group left Schiffbauerdamm and headed northwest along the railroad tracks toward the main Berlin train station. It was around a half-mile walk and involved crossing another bridge, a small railway crossing over the Humboldt Harbor of the Spree. They kept to the railroad tracks. They hoped that by avoiding streets, they could slip through Russian-controlled territory undetected.

Axmann later related how after crossing the Humboldt Harbor, "several of us jumped down from the bridge and found, to our chagrin, that there was a whole Russian infantry platoon in bivouac under it. They promptly surrounded us. But to our amazement and joy they simply kept announcing in a boisterous chorus, 'Hitler kaputt, Krieg aus!'"[93] By this, the Russians meant that Hitler was dead and they had won the war (even though it was not quite over). So they were in a celebratory mood.

It had been almost four years of bloody fighting since Germany attacked the U.S.S.R. on June 22, 1941, when Axmann lost part of his arm. He needed to keep his cool to survive this strange encounter.

"Next, they engaged us in a very pleasant chat in broken German.

All seemed to be fascinated by my artificial arm, and I kept showing it to them as if it were the latest product of some Nuremberg toy factory. Then they graciously offered us papirosi, cigarettes with paper mouthpieces. Apparently they thought we were simple Volkssturm men returning from a long, hard evening at the front."[94]

Despite the immense power that Bormann had wielded in the Third Reich, few knew who he was, and the odds of a Russian soldier recognizing him were very, very low.[95] Hitler had ordered his personal pilot, Lieutenant General (SS *Gruppenführer*) Hans Baur, to guard Bormann during the breakout.[96] However, Baur had lost him early on. Baur later recalled that Bormann "wore a simple brown public officials' uniform without insignia. . . . His face was little known in those days. No one would have recognized him."[97]

Axmann was wearing his uniform, but he had wisely removed his insignia.[98] The other escapees had done the same by now. Otherwise, the celebrating Russian soldiers would have known these were no common *Volkssturm* men, but high-ranking Nazis.

Axmann went on to explain, "What spoiled this bit of fraternization was a psychologically false move by the tipsy Bormann and Dr. Stumpfegger. They began to edge away and finally broke out running. This made the Russians suddenly suspicious, but Weltzin and I were now able to shuffle off as casually as possible without being noticed."[99]

Although relatively unknown to citizens of the Third Reich, Bormann was a consummate bureaucrat and one of the most powerful officials in Nazi Germany. He looked the part of a stereotypical bureaucrat—a baby-faced bulldog with a receding hairline.

As Hitler's personal secretary, Bormann's power derived from his control of access to the Führer. He had also been head of the Party Chancellery. Many among the Allies considered him the second most powerful man in Nazi Germany. He, along with Dönitz, was now one of two named successors to Hitler's power still alive—Goebbels having killed himself. Bormann carried with him a copy of Hitler's last testament that named him party minister (*Parteiminister*). He hoped to make it through enemy territory to join Dönitz's government in Flensburg.

SS Lieutenant Colonel (*Obersturmbannführer*) Dr. Ludwig Stumpfegger had been with them in the bunker, where he had served as the Führer's final personal doctor. As an orthopedic surgeon, he had previously worked for the German Olympic team, but he had also committed crimes against humanity by performing medical experiments on female concentration camp inmates at Ravensbrück. He and Martin Bormann must have looked like a comically odd pairing as they fled along the railroad tracks toward a railway station in Berlin's Mitte district, Stettiner Bahnhof. Bormann was a short, obese man, while the skinny Stumpfegger stood more than six and a half feet tall.

With the Soviet Army all around them, the escapees from the bunker had to hide, bluff, and otherwise make their way across the ruined city. Werner Naumann, accompanied by Goebbels's aides Schwaegermann and Dietrich, stayed on the left side of the Invalidenstrasse (a major Berlin street), while Axmann and Weltzin walked down the right.[100] They were all heading southwest toward the street Alt-Moabit.

In his testament, Hitler had named Naumann as Goebbels's successor for propaganda minister of what little was left of the Third Reich. He had been state secretary of the Propaganda Ministry, directly under Goebbels.

It was during this walk down Invalidenstrasse that Axmann and his aide became separated from Naumann's group. The *Reichsjugendführer* had gone from being in charge of millions of members of Hitler Youth to a single aide. After having walked a few blocks, Axmann and Weltzin turned around without Naumann's group and headed back "on account of finding strong Russian patrols and sentries ahead."[101]

Meanwhile, Bormann and Stumpfegger had panicked while they

were on their own. They decided to kill themselves with cyanide rather than risk capture. As Bormann bit down on his blue-glass cyanide capsule, fragments of it became embedded into his jawbones.[102] These fragments were discovered when his remains were located decades later.

They had to bite the capsules first; if swallowed whole, the poison might pass through their systems without killing them.[103] As an expert on forensic toxicology, Professor M. David Osselton explained in 2011, "The container would have to be broken to release the poison for subsequent absorption into the body tissues. If not broken, it is likely that the capsule would pass through the alimentary tract undamaged and the poison would not be released to exert its intended effect."[104]

Professor Osselton went on to describe what this poison did to Bormann and Stumpfegger. "Inhalation of cyanide fumes produces the most rapid effects that may be characterised by flushing, headache, abnormal breathing progressing to coma and death within approximately 10 minutes if not treated. . . . This process is exemplified by comparison to individuals who smoke drugs such as crack cocaine or heroin rather than taking the drugs orally. An almost immediate effect is noted when these drugs are smoked as they enter the blood circulation without first having to pass through the liver where a proportion is removed and so get to their site of action faster."[105]

The capsules that these two Nazis bit down on used the fast method by producing fumes that they then inhaled.

While backtracking with Weltzin, as Axmann described it, he "came across the bodies of Martin Bormann and Dr. Stumpfegger, lying very close together. I leaned over and could see the moonlight playing on their faces. There was no visible sign that they had been shot or struck by shellfire. At first, they looked like men who were unconscious or asleep. But they were not breathing. I assumed then, and I am sure today, that both had taken poison.[106] Weltzin and I did not linger to take pulses. We were in danger and hardly interested in historical moments. We continued eastward. The dawn did not break until about a half hour later, after we had arrived in Berlin-Wedding."[107]

Axmann's account of Bormann's demise was controversial for many years. His adjutant Gerd Weltzin was not available to confirm it because he died while being held by the Russians. So all that existed regarding this version of events was the word of one high-ranking Nazi that another high-ranking Nazi was dead.[108]

However, much later analysis showed that Axmann had told the truth. Their bodies were eventually found in 1972,[109] and, in 2011, DNA testing confirmed Bormann's identity.[110]

Bormann's death left Dönitz as the only one alive of the three people that Hitler had named as the heads of what remained of the Third Reich.

While Axmann had successfully traversed across the front line, he still had to make his way out of Berlin and Russian controlled territory, a dangerous mission with Russian troops combing the area. He hoped to make it to Flensburg, in the north of Germany, to join Dönitz's government there. If he couldn't get to Flensburg, Axmann wanted at least to find a safe place to hide.

TWO

JOINING THE CIC

Today a CIC agent may find himself posing as anything from a deserter to a diplomat, from a clerk to a colonel. One day he may lounge in a smart London bar; the following week he may be assaulting an enemy invasion beach, utterly G.I. He may be interviewing a beggar or a general, a duchess or a prostitute; he may be wearing a dinner jacket or torn trousers.

THE AMERICAN MAGAZINE[1]

As Axmann and his fellow refugees from the Berlin government center were scrambling for a path to safety, his eventual nemesis was still in the States. Second Lieutenant Jack Dayton Hunter had completed his training for the Counter Intelligence Corps ("CIC") and was awaiting his transfer to Germany.

The CIC recruited Hunter in part because he spoke fluent German and knew German World War I military history. As Hunter later put it, "There was a screaming need for American officers with knowledge of German."[2]

He was especially attractive to the CIC because while he spoke German, he was neither German nor of German descent. Instead, he was Scottish.[3]

A history of the CIC explained that "the problem of obtaining men fluent in French, German, Italian, Japanese, and other foreign languages was made more difficult because of War Department policy which directed that no persons of close foreign background would be assigned to or retained in the Counter Intelligence Corps. Many naturalized Americans, in and out of the Army, were fluent in several languages, but the [CIC] was unable to use this source of language personnel because of this strict policy."[4]

Of course, there were exceptions to this policy (including those who had fled the Nazis), and it was dropped entirely after victory in Europe, but at the time the CIC recruited Hunter, they were happy to find that he had learned German for reasons that had nothing to do with familial ties.[5]

Hunter traced back his interest in Germany to a film he saw at the impressionable age of six. His father, Whitney, an engineer, was busy at his job at the American Radiator Company. His mother, Irene, instead of paying for a babysitter she could not afford, took him with her to see *Wings* (a 1927 silent film about fighter pilots in World War I). The first movie to win the Academy Award for Best Picture, *Wings* captured young Hunter's imagination and inspired a lifelong love of World War I aviation. "I saw those airplanes and was blown away," Hunter later said.[6] He dreamed of becoming a pilot himself someday.

As a boy, Hunter read everything he could about the Great War (as it was then commonly called) and the fights that took place in the skies over Europe. His favorite ace was the German Manfred von Richthofen (aka the "Red Baron"). He had the most kills of all pilots in World War I (eighty) and achieved lasting fame after death as, among other things, the pilot frequently shown shooting down Snoopy in the *Peanuts* comic strip.

Hunter wanted to read the Red Baron's autobiography. In fifth grade, a classmate lent him the original German version of it. Hunter was so desperate to read it that he checked out a teach-yourself-German book from the local library.[7]

Hunter went on to study German for all four years he was at Ridley Park High School in Pennsylvania, until his graduation in 1939. Another four years of German followed at Penn State, where he graduated with a journalism degree in 1943. In spite of not having the patience to finish music lessons, Hunter taught himself to play the piano so well that he used this talent to work his way through college.

While at Penn State, he'd joined the U.S. Army via the Advanced Reserve Officers' Training Corps ("ROTC") there. He had a joke about volunteering for the army that he later used in one of his novels: "I figured the best way to outwit my draft board was to join the Army. They couldn't touch me there, by golly."[8] But as he later explained, "We were patriots, everybody wanted to join back then."[9]

On May 26, 1942, he was activated as a corporal in the infantry, but he was allowed to finish his education. When he graduated college in 1943, the army sent Hunter to the U.S. Army Officer Candidate School ("OCS") for Infantry at Fort Benning, Georgia. There they would train him to become an officer.

However there was one key fact about Hunter of which the army was unaware. He had concealed from them that he was color-blind.

He'd been born with this deficiency. His grandfather on his mother's side was color-blind, and while his mother was not color-blind, she passed it on to her sons Jack and Bob.[10]

Hunter hadn't thought of it as a serious problem that should keep him out of military service. Instead, for him, it was more like someone lying about his age in order to join the army. He wanted to do his part for his country and didn't want to be kept out of military service because of not being able to tell the difference between red and green.

There was a standardized test given to check for vision problems. He first had to take it while in the ROTC and again in OCS.[11] The test was not set up to catch people who willfully cheated. The same exact test was given every time so it was easy for someone to prepare beforehand. Hunter memorized the answers to the test so that he could pretend not to be color-blind. Even though he could not see the correct answers, he pretended that he did.

What Hunter did not know though was that the military had a very good reason for conducting a test to detect color-blindness. One reason it was an extremely serious issue was that ground troops used combinations of different colors of flares to communicate with airplanes while maintaining radio silence. The inability to tell a green flare from a red flare meant that Hunter could not read these messages.

It was during a field combat exercise that Hunter came to understand that he had made a major mistake by lying on his color-blindness test. Hunter was in charge of a group of his fellow trainees during an exercise when he had to respond to a signal sent via a flare. A green flare meant to attack; a red flare to retreat. He turned to the sergeant who accompanied them and asked, "Sergeant, did you see that flare?" The answer was yes. "What color was it?" The sergeant said green. "Then let's attack."[12] With this trick, Hunter was able to complete the exercise without exposing his hidden disability.

This close call did make him think though. As he later recalled, "I couldn't read the color of flares, and realized I was going to get someone killed."[13] He had managed to get through the exercise without anyone noticing that he had no idea what color flare had been sent up, but he turned himself in midway through his training at Fort Benning. He admitted that he'd lied and was ready to accept the consequences of his actions. The army gave him the color-blindness test again, and this time Hunter answered according to what he actually saw, not what he'd memorized. He failed the test.

Now that the military knew about Hunter's color-blindness, they were not going to complete his training to become an infantry combat commander. As fate would have it, this setback may have saved his life. Many of the guys he trained with died during the D-Day invasion at

Omaha Beach.[14] Survivor's guilt plagued him for the rest of his life, as part of him felt as if he should have been fighting his way up the beach with his friends in the infantry.

The army sent him to the Army Air Corps Administrative OCS in San Antonio, Texas. Back then, the Air Force did not exist as a separate service branch, but was part of the army (the Army Air Corps). On August 5, 1944, he became a second lieutenant and was given an officer's serial number: O-545169. The War Department granted him a waiver for his color-blindness, "for appointment for limited service only," although he was still considered "fit for overseas duty."[15]

He was not in the Army Air Corps to fulfill his childhood dream of becoming a pilot. Even though he already had flight experience, having taken lessons on a biplane when he was a teenager, the military had other plans for him. They were not going to let someone color-blind serve as a pilot.

Instead, they gave him a job as the public relations officer for the Kearney Army Airfield near Kearney, Nebraska. At the time, it was used primarily as a processing station for B-17s and B-29s.

He lived there with his wife. He had married his college sweetheart, Shirley "Tommy" Thompson, in October 1944, which was before he'd received his officer's commission.

Fortunately, Hunter escaped this desk job purgatory three months later when he was sent to the War Department Military Intelligence Training Center ("MITC") at Camp Ritchie, Maryland, in late March 1945.

When he entered Camp Ritchie, Hunter was twenty-three. He was born on June 4, 1921, in Hamilton, Ohio, which meant he was eight years younger than Artur Axmann.

At Camp Ritchie, Hunter trained to become a CIC agent. His teachers there included former German military personnel who taught him how to pass for a German military man, among other skills. The teacher from his documents interpretation class referred to this process as training him to be a "Dick von Tracy"—an American spy who could work in German territory.[16]

There was a lot for Hunter to learn before he was ready to go to Germany. He wrote of his training that "I study Wehrmacht order of battle, Nazi paramilitary organization; I learn to espy military significance in captured trivia, from matchbook covers to booze tabs. I learn how to pick locks, open safes, make surreptitious entries, the opening and re-sealing of mail. I learn infiltration techniques, how to kill with my hands."[17]

His fellow future CIC agents were an impressive group. As a former CIC agent wrote in 1946, "The CIC received the cream of the army. Every man in it was an expert on some phase of intelligence work. He might be a skilled linguist, an attorney with experience in ferreting the truth out of a maze of conflicting evidence, a traveler with years of residence in Europe, a missionary who understood the natives and customs of some particular district, an expert on anything from ballistics to zoology, a financial expert who could winnow spies from a mass of bank statements, or a man who was an extraordinarily gifted fellow with a snub-nosed pistol."[18]

An article in *Reader's Digest* gave examples of the lengths the CIC went to recruit agents with a wide variety of skills. "The [counter intelligence] corps included at various times a forestry expert, a dance-band leader, a Syrian rug dealer, a poet. One difficult investigation required a man with 13 qualifications, among them that he be a Negro and an Elk and speak French. [The] CIC produced him."[19]

According to a U.S. Army history of the CIC during World War II, it helped in recruiting such talented personnel that "the lure of the word 'intelligence' and the prospect of working in civilian clothes was tempting bait."[20]

At Camp Ritchie, Jack Hunter was assigned to Company C of the

First Military Intelligence Training Battalion on April 11. Here, he met Werner Michel, a German who had fled his native country to avoid persecution as a Jew. As Michel recalled, "We soon became good friends and I remember his astonishing irreverence and his diabolical sense of humor."[21]

They had a highly irregular schedule at Camp Ritchie, as Michel explained, owing to "the MITC commander's evident idiosyncrasy concerning the length of the training week during the course. He apparently believed that if students studied seven instead of the normal six days, the course would be more effective. Reputedly naming his system after himself (COL. Banfill), we were scheduled to study and train for seven days. The eighth day . . . was off. This meant that we might be off one week on a Sunday; the next week on Tuesday and so on. These days off were jocularly referred to as Ban Day. As I recall, Jack, as often was the case, made some irreverent and ribald comments about this convoluted arrangement."[22]

Besides speaking German and being familiar with German military history, his appearance also made Hunter a desirable recruit for the CIC. With his deep blue eyes, exceedingly fair skin, and blond hair, he could pass for German.

Moreover, he had the sort of face that inspired trust and yet did not stick out in a crowd. Everything about him was nonthreatening, from his height (five-foot-five), to his rounded nose, to his short, straight hair parted near the middle of his high forehead. He weighed only 135 pounds. The overall impression he gave made him seem harmless— more like a momma's boy than a hardened counterintelligence agent.

A final reason that Hunter made a good recruit for the CIC was his journalism training in college. The CIC liked to recruit those with professional training in journalism (among other fields) as this meant that Hunter knew how to investigate a story. These skills could be used to investigate a case.

In recruiting, the CIC worked to obtain a wide variety of talented future agents. A January 1945 article in *The American Magazine* explained, "Such drastic selection produced men of astonishing talent, experience, and education. Almost all hold college degrees, and at one time, in the London office alone, there were 8 Ph.D.'s. The composite experiences of one 15-man group were typically startling: Among them, they had raced cars in Italy, played hockey for Harvard, newspapered in Paris, investigated credit ratings in New Jersey, taught English in France, fought legal cases for the Government, studied science in Germany, learned naval aviation, taken scientific photographs in Alaska, investigated the Bund, taught political science, prospected for Gold."[23]

With the rise of the Axis threat and the United States entry into World War II, the need for counterintelligence agents had exploded. The CIC's roots were in the Corps of Intelligence Police, which had been founded in 1917. After World War I ended, it had shrunk in size until it had less than two dozen men. In 1942, it became the Counter Intelligence Corps.

Members of the CIC during World War II who went on to later fame include J. D. Salinger (the author of *Catcher in the Rye*, who, like Hunter, served in Germany after the war) and the future secretary of state under President Nixon, Henry Kissinger.

The CIC had a number of important duties; its mission was "to contribute to the operations of the Army Establishment through the detection of treason, sedition, subversive activity, and disaffection, and the detection, prevention, or neutralization of espionage and sabotage within or directed against the Army Establishment and the areas of its jurisdiction."[24]

During the Second World War, CIC agents conducted background checks for security clearances and hunted enemy intelligence agents. They also helped guard top-secret work like the Manhattan Project. In

Europe and the Pacific, CIC agents accompanied American troops to analyze documents as they were intercepted, interrogate prisoners, make contact with resistance forces, and debrief civilians. These agents also taught American troops how to secure locations, locate and gather sensitive enemy documents, and avoid booby traps while doing so.

As for what counterintelligence itself means, a former CIC agent, Ib Melchior, explained it this way: "Military Intelligence is the gathering of information about the enemy—his plans, his strength, his operations—evaluating it, and disseminating it. Counterintelligence is preventing the enemy from gathering such information about you and from carrying out clandestine operations against you."[25]

Another former CIC agent, John Schwarzwalder, gave a similar definition of this kind of work: "Counter Intelligence is the art of catching spies. It is also the science of denying the enemy the information he has to have and the monotonous routine work involved in making military installations secure against the enemy's attempts at sabotage."[26]

While doing this work, Hunter and his colleagues had to be discreet because much of what they did was classified. As the *New York Herald Tribune* reported in 1947, "The CIC has more adventure stories buried in its secret files than a month's output of blood and thunder comic books. Unfortunately for the reading public, these bona fide cloak and dagger stories are not for publication."[27]

Once in occupied Germany, a CIC agent had virtually unlimited powers. The restraints that the FBI had in the United States, such as needing to get a warrant before arresting someone, bugging someone's phone, or searching someone's house, did not apply. Prisoners did not even have the right of habeas corpus. In other words, they had no right to go before a court to have their imprisonment reviewed.

While suspects being interrogated in the United States had a constitutional right to speak to an attorney, those questioned by the CIC in Germany had no such right. One CIC agent wrote that when he detained two seventeen-year-old Hitler Youths, "they wanted to see a lawyer before they talked since they had heard that such was the American custom. They were disabused of this concept."[28]

Hunter, like other army personnel, could even commandeer a German's private residence and use it for his own purposes.

In the United States, the Third Amendment forbids the government from forcing people to quarter soldiers during peacetime, or in time of war, unless it's done "in a manner to be prescribed by law."[29] In occupied Germany, not only did soldiers stay in civilians' houses without their permission, but also they often kicked out the lawful occupants entirely. The CIC often arrived first in a town and would take the best property for themselves, upsetting higher-ranking army officers who felt entitled to such housing.

A tongue-in-cheek flyer, handed out to some returning army personnel, purported to cover the subject of "Indoctrination for Return to U.S." and included this clause: "In traveling in the U.S., particularly in a strange city, it is often necessary to spend the night. Hotels are provided for this purpose. . . . The present practice of entering the nearest house, throwing the occupants into the yard and taking over the premises will cease."[30]

Now that the war was swiftly coming to an end in Europe, the CIC's focus there shifted from fighting the Nazis to locating high-ranking Nazis and war criminals, as well as ensuring that there was not a Nazi insurgency during the coming occupation. As part of this task, Hunter had been taught how dangerous HJ could be. A classified counterintelligence document from 1944 explained that "the Hitler Youth is not a Boy Scout or Girl Guide organisation. It is in no respect comparable to any organisation for young people known to the Western World. It is a compulsory Nazi formation, which has consciously sought to breed hate, treachery and cruelty into the mind and soul of every German child. It is, in the true sense of the word, 'education for death.' Under no circumstances should the Hitler Youth be taken lightly or be considered a negligible factor from an operational or occupation point of view."[31]

This handbook on the HJ gave examples including the following: "A thirteen year old boy manned a machine gun against advancing Allied tanks on the Rhineland frontier, while his mates passed the ammunition. An execution squad composed of 14–16 year olds shot Polish civilian hostages. A monument was erected to a boy still living, commemorating the fact that he denounced his father 'loyally to the Führer': (the father was executed for treason)."[32]

At the same time as the war in Europe was coming to a close, a race began between the Western Powers and the Soviets for the resources of Nazi Germany. These included technical documents and devices as well as scientists themselves. Of especial import were atomic and rocket technologies. The Nazis had been behind the United States in atomic research, but way ahead of it in developing rockets. The Soviets, with whom America had been allied in fighting the Nazis, were quickly becoming competitors, and would eventually become enemies.

THREE

DEATH THROES OF THE THIRD REICH

When an opponent declares, "I will not come over to your side, and you will not get me on your side," I calmly say, "Your child belongs to me already. . . . You will pass on. Your descendants however now stand in the new camp. In a short time they will know nothing else but this new community."

ADOLF HITLER[1]

Early in the morning of Wednesday, May 2, 1945, Axmann and his adjunct Weltzin were still stuck in Soviet-occupied Berlin. They had started out their escape with around a thousand of their National Socialist comrades; now it was only the two of them. After taking a quick look at Bormann's and Dr. Stumpfegger's dead bodies on Invalidenstrasse, they left these corpses behind. They didn't have time to waste on the dead, as they still needed to escape from Berlin.

On Invalidenstrasse, near the Sandkrug Bridge,[2] Axmann buried the one gun he had left.[3] He'd already given away one pistol to a BDM girl who was left behind at the Reich Chancellery. He now hid one of the most famous guns in the world, the pistol Hitler used to kill himself.

If he were caught with a gun, it would astronomically increase his chances of being detained or even executed by the Soviets. And a single pistol would not provide much protection in the case of a fire-fight. As much sentimental value as it held, it had to go.

He never retrieved the gun from its burial spot by this bridge over the Berlin-Spandau Canal. When the Berlin Wall went up, this location became a tightly controlled border crossing between East and West Berlin.

Next, Axmann and Weltzin walked northwest along the Heidestrasse toward Berlin's Wedding district.[4] After finding some cover on Heidestrasse, Axmann ditched the leather coat that he'd been wearing up to now. After his run-in with the Russians, who had mistaken him for a low-ranking member of the *Volkssturm*, it occurred to him that he'd been very lucky. His high-quality leather jacket looked like something an officer would wear.

In fact, he'd received it as a gift from an SS general (Josef "Sepp" Dietri).[5] Axmann needed civilian clothes as soon as possible, but for now he attempted to appear like a lowly soldier. He had taken off his jacket, his medals, and his insignia. With just a plain uniform, he hoped to resemble a *Volkssturm* soldier. However, it would be even better to look like a civilian. With his missing right forearm, he could look like someone who had been discharged from the military after he was wounded.

It was around five in the morning by now and no longer safe to be on the streets. The cover that nighttime, even a moonlit and fire-filled one, offered was quickly fading with the sun emerging to cast an eerie glow on the ruined city. They found an uninhabited structure in which to hide out and rest for a bit.[6]

Despite the daylight, however, they decided that it wasn't safe to stay where they were. Their best bet was to continue on their journey. After resting for only a short time, they headed out again on foot. Axmann now wore a gray coat and blue sailor cap that he had received after asking Germans walking by for civilian clothes.

As they made their way through the city, they could hear Russians handing out food to German civilians, but managed to avoid them.[7] Axmann was trying to get back to Wedding, but the bridge they wanted to use to cross the Berlin-Spandau Ship Canal had been destroyed. They stumbled upon a sort of makeshift ferry though that Germans were using to cross this canal. Axmann and Weltzin rode it across the water to Wedding.[8]

From those buildings that remained standing, white sheets and towels indicating surrender hung from windows. A short while before, roving court-martial teams on the streets of Berlin would have found these to be a capital offense. Any sign of surrender or desertion could result in a quick shot to the head or being hung from the nearest pole. It used to be that all males living in a house with a white flag were to be shot, in accordance with the "Flag Decree" of *Reichsführer-SS* Heinrich Himmler. Now white flags were the norm.

Meanwhile, in another part of Berlin and unbeknownst to Axmann, at around 5 A.M., General Weidling (who had been in charge of Berlin's defense) walked escorted across Russian lines to Soviet General Chuikov's command post. There he wrote a surrender letter, which began:

"On the 30th April the Führer, to whom we had all sworn an oath of allegiance, forsook us by committing suicide. Faithful to the Führer, you German soldiers were prepared to continue the battle for Berlin even though your ammunition was running out and the general situation made further resistance senseless."[9]

This surrender of all forces defending Berlin was to take effect by 1 P.M., although sporadic fighting continued until about 5 P.M. that day.[10] Like Axmann, many of those who could changed into civilian clothes and hid evidence of their military service.

Russian soldiers were particularly eager to find high-ranking

Nazis, anyone who might have knowledge about Hitler's last days, and members of the SS (regardless of rank). At the time, the Russians did not know that the SS could be recognized by the tattoo of their "blood-group on the inside of their left arm."[11]

One SS member later wrote, "It was done as a medical insurance for a quick and life-saving blood-transfusion on the battlefield. However, after the war, it proved to be a stigma for tens of thousands. It was known as 'the mark of Cain.' . . . It cost them, in many cases, no less than their lives."[12]

When the fighting stopped late that afternoon, the shooting of guns in battle was replaced by the shooting of guns in celebration. Vasily Grossman, a Soviet reporter who was in Berlin that day, wrote that "this overcast, cold and rainy day is undoubtedly the day of Germany's collapse in the smoke, among the blazing ruins, among hundreds of corpses littering the streets."[13]

The triumphant Russian soldiers had a keen sense of irony, many of them gathered to celebrate in the shadow of the Berlin Victory Column (Siegessäule). This giant column with a bronze, winged statue on top of Victoria, the Roman goddess of victory, commemorated German war victories. Here, Grossman observed that "The tanks are so covered in flowers and red banners that you can hardly see them. Gun barrels have flowers in them like trees in spring. Everyone is dancing, singing, laughing. Hundreds of coloured signal flares are fired into the air. Everyone salutes the victory with bursts from sub-machine guns, rifles and pistols."[14]

Elsewhere in Germany, the fighting continued even though news had spread of Hitler's death. Around 10 P.M. on Tuesday, May 1, German radio announced Hitler's death as follows: "Our Fuehrer, Adolf Hitler, fighting to the last breath against Bolshevism, fell for Germany this afternoon in his operational headquarters in the Reich Chancellery. On April 30, the Fuehrer appointed Grand Admiral Donitz his successor. The Grand Admiral and successor of the Fuehrer now speaks to the German people."[15] German radio lied about when Hitler had died (it had been the day before) and how he had died (by committing suicide).[16]

On Wednesday, May 2, the *Stars and Stripes* (the newspaper of the U.S. Armed Forces) announced in huge letters taking up half the front page: HITLER DEAD.[17] On the back page, it ran a photo of Hitler and Mussolini, with the darkly comic headline HITLER JOINS HIS PAL.[18]

With Hitler's death, Grand Admiral Karl Dönitz became the president of the Third Reich in accordance with Hitler's political testament. He ruled over what became known as the Flensburg government. Dönitz's provisional government ruled from that city in the far north of Germany, just below the Danish border.

When Axmann had been in the early stages of his breakout from the bunker, the head of the SS, Heinrich Himmler, showed up in Dönitz's office in Flensburg.

As Dönitz remembered it, "At about midnight he arrived, accompanied by six armed SS officers, and was received by my aide-de-camp. . . . I offered Himmler a chair and I myself sat down behind my writing desk, upon which lay, hidden by some papers, a pistol with the safety catch off. I had never done anything of this sort in my life before, but I did not know what the outcome of this meeting might be. I handed Himmler the telegram containing my appointment. 'Please read this,' I said. I watched him closely. As he read, an expression of astonishment, indeed, of consternation spread over his face. All hope seemed to collapse within him. He went very pale. Finally he stood up and bowed. 'Allow me,' he said, 'to become the second man in your state.' I replied that that was out of the question and that there was no way in which I could make any use of his services. Thus advised, he left me at about one o'clock in the morning. The showdown had taken place without force, and I felt relieved."[19]

Himmler had been responsible for the systematic murder of six million Jews as well as millions of others (gypsies, Communists, homosexuals, the disabled, and many more). He had personally inspected his handiwork, visiting concentration camps to see the results of his orders, and was considered by the Allies to be a major war criminal. Dönitz wanted nothing to do with him.

Back in early April, before the Battle of Berlin, Axmann had already put into motion his plans for after the fall of the Third Reich.[20] He had planned to personally gather together the leaders of the Hitler Youth under his command. But Hitler threw a monkey wrench into his carefully laid plans when he unexpectedly ordered Axmann to remain in Berlin to command his HJ boys fighting there. Even though he followed orders and stayed in Berlin with his Führer, Axmann still commanded certain HJ leaders to gather in Bad Tölz.

Those leaders of the BDM who were with Axmann in Berlin wanted to stay there, but as things looked increasingly hopeless in late April, he ordered them to go to their meeting place in Bad Tölz. The only one to remain behind was the BDM's Reich physician, Dr. Gertrud Huhn, as they desperately needed her help with caring for the wounded.[21]

Bad Tölz is in the south of Germany, in an area known as Upper Bavaria (which is part of the German state of Bavaria). The use of "Upper" and "Lower" for regions of Bavaria can be confusing, since the modifier refers to the elevation and not north/south direction. Bad Tölz, for example, is over two thousand feet above sea level, and other parts of Upper Bavaria are much higher.

Bavaria, which includes Munich, is the largest and southernmost of the German states. The Nazi party had been popular in this region—in fact, it started in Munich—and it was here that Hitler famously gave his first political speech at one of their meetings in a beer hall.[22]

Bad Tölz is a picturesque medieval town famous for its natural springs baths and breathtaking Alpine views. The Isar River runs through the town, and historically it had been used to transport lumber and salt. Natural hot springs were discovered there in the nineteenth century. In a brilliant public relations move, the town changed its name from Tölz to Bad Tölz in 1899, "Bad" meaning "Spa" in German.[23] The town's hot springs contain high levels of iodine, which were promoted as helping people to relax while improving their health at the same time. There was also a medieval old town and an impressive Gothic church, Stadtpfarrkirche, built in 1466.

Munich, a Nazi stronghold, was about an hour's drive directly north of Bad Tölz, and the Austrian border was nearby to the south.

Axmann had not ordered the leaders of HJ to gather in Bad Tölz to take in its baths and wander its cobblestoned main street though. While tourists went there to go skiing in the winter or hiking in the summer, its mountain location was perfect for hiding out and preparing a resistance to the Allied occupation.

In accordance with Axmann's plans, by April 28, around 150 adult leaders of the HJ had arrived in Bad Tölz.[24] While the HJ was comprised of youths, adults held the higher positions.

With Axmann still in Berlin, Brigadier General (*Hauptbannführer*) Hans Franke was in charge of these gathering HJ leaders. Franke had worked under Axmann in the Reich Youth Leadership National Office.

In Bad Tölz, the Hitler Youth gathered at the Highlands Camp of the Hitler Youth (*Hochland Lager der Hitler Jugend*), an impressive structure which could hold up to five thousand people. From here, Franke sent out his men "on reconnaissance in the mountains of Tyrol and Salzburg to find retreats and hideouts for depots. They were to report on their return to Bad Tölz the number of places they had found, their accessibility, whether they could be observed from ground and air, the availability of food and water, the number of persons that could be accommodated, and their opinions as to how freely and how far operations could be conducted from these bases. After the receipt of these reports supplies and clothing were divided according to the estimates and sent to the several sites."[25]

Franke endeavored to coordinate his HJ leaders with other Nazi resistance activities. And herein lies the story of *Werwolf* (German for werewolf). A CIC agent wrote that "the origin of the Werewolf, the Nazi radios screamed, was found in the myths of antiquity where wolves who were half human devoured their enemies and saved the righteous from numerous perils."[26]

Besides the reference to the mythical werewolf, which transforms from an ordinary man into a ferocious wolf, the name refers to a well-known book. *Der Wehrwolf* by Hermann Löns came out in 1910 and "by the end of World War II, the novel had become one of the most widely read books in Germany."[27] It was about German peasants engaged in brutal guerrilla warfare during the Thirty Years War. The title was a play on words, combining *Wehr* for "defense" with wolf in a way that also resembles "werewolf." And so this organized resistance was often referred to as *Wehrwolf*, including in various CIC reports. The spellings were often used interchangeably, with some documents using *Werwolf* while others used *Wehrwolf*.

The head of the SS (*Reichsführer-SS*) Heinrich Himmler had developed Operation Werwolf. As he envisioned it, this would involve specially trained commandos operating behind enemy lines in occupied areas of Germany to commit acts of sabotage and attacks on both Allied forces and any Germans who cooperated with them.

However, adequate preparations were not made for continuing operations in the event that Germany lost the war. As British historian H. R. Trevor-Roper wrote: "The Werewolves were never intended to operate after defeat; since the mention, or suggestion, of defeat was forbidden, that was out of the question. They were intended as a paramilitary formation, an auxiliary arm, to fight behind the Allied lines as diversionary forces, and thereby to assist the German armies. Thus their activity was parallel to that of the regular armies, not in succession to it."[28]

Himmler appointed SS Senior Group Leader (*Obergruppenführer*) Hans-Adolf Prützmann as the head of Operation Werwolf.[29]

On March 20, Prützmann used a captured U.S. plane to parachute six Werwolves into American-occupied territory in the far west of Germany, near the town of Aachen. Five months before, Aachen had been the first German city captured. On March 25, these SS-trained commandos ambushed the Allied-appointed mayor, Dr. Franz Oppenhoff, outside his home. They shot him in the head after yelling, "*Heil Hitler.*" This group included Eric Morhenschweiss, a sixteen-year-old HJ member, and Ilse Hirsch, a BDM sergeant (*Hauptgruppenführerin*). This assassination was the most prominent action taken in the Werwolf name.

Prützmann had some resources in place—he had coordinated with Axmann for selected HJ members to be trained in sabotage and other related skills. However, the term "Werwolf" came to be known for much more than the limited organization that Prützmann had put together.

Joseph Goebbels saw the propaganda value in Werwolf, and so, instead of using it as a top-secret name for Prützmann's commando-style activities, toward the end he broadcast it publicly in an effort to galvanize the German populace and scare the Allies.

On April 1, Goebbels's *Radio Werwolf* began broadcasting with its message that "we will fight on even if we suffer military defeat."[30] It went on to claim "the werewolves will make collaboration with the Allies impossible and finally drive them out of all German territories."[31] Radio Werwolf declared, "Hatred is our prayer and revenge is our war cry."[32]

Goebbels's radio program was independent of Prützmann and his organization.[33] *Radio Werwolf* spread the idea that the Allies needed to watch out for die-hard Nazis who would threaten them in occupied territory even after the war was over.

John Schwarzwalder, a CIC agent who listened to these broadcasts at the time, worried about Werwolf. He later wrote, "All this information we had heard over the German Radio many times and the prospect disturbed us considerably.... A well-administered partisan movement is no joke to any army as the Germans had found out in many countries. If the Werewolf was ready, able, and willing to do its work it looked as though Allied occupation of Germany was going to be a difficult and dangerous task. And until we actually got into Germany there was no real way to find out how seriously to take the matter. It might well be another one of . . . Goebbels's red herrings but we could not afford to take that chance."[34]

And so, as Agent Schwarzwalder explained, "Among the first things that required the immediate attention of every Counter-Intelligence Corps unit as it entered Germany was the organization known as the Werewolf. . . . Nazi radio programs had been plugging the organization as intensively as ever the American radio had plugged toothpaste but whether or not it was sold to the German people was not known to us. And we had to find out."[35]

When Dönitz became president of Germany, following Hitler's death, he ordered all Werwolf operations against the Western Allies to end operations.[36] Flensburg radio broadcast an order issued by Dönitz stating that "by virtue of the truce which has been put into effect I ask all German men and women to abstain from any illegal fighting in 'Werewolf' or any other organisations in the enemy-occupied western territories, because such activity can only be detrimental to our people."[37]

Dönitz's later orders of a cease-fire for all German operations (as part of Germany's unconditional surrender) were comprehensive. They also included any activities being done in the name of Werwolf.

Prützmann was in Flensburg, where he followed Dönitz's orders to stop Werwolf activities. He had been acting as Himmler's liaison officer with the Flensburg government, but it was a meaningless position as Dönitz wanted nothing to do with Himmler.[38] Prützmann later committed suicide while in Allied custody after Germany's surrender.

In late April, Hans Franke sent fifteen of the HJ Axmann had put him in charge of to Gilching, a small town just west of Munich.[39] At the time, Gilching was "to be the Wehrwolf Hqs for Southern Germany. Along with this group, one female wireless operator went to Gilching to learn the new [radio] code and return to Bad Tolz, so constant wireless contact could be maintained between Wehrwolf Headquarters and HJ Hqs, regardless of their change of location. The staff of the HJ Message center at Bad Tolz consisted of one Feldwebel [Sergeant] of the Marines, and two BDM operators. The dispersal camps in the mountains were not equipped with ... sending apparatus of any kind because the Allies overran the country before planning could be completed."[40]

When they came back to Bad Tölz, the group informed Franke that this Werwolf headquarters would soon move from Gilching to the small town of Bergen, southwest of the Bavarian freshwater lake Chiemsee (also known as the Bavarian Sea).

On April 29, Franke moved the Hitler Youth headquarters from Bad Tölz to Bruck, a small town in Austria by Zell am See. Others remained behind to run things in Bad Tölz though. Bruck is where the overall Hitler Youth headquarters remained once the occupying forces moved in. Other HJ headquarters were established in secret throughout Germany, at locations such as Frankfurt, Passau, Weimar, Nuremberg, Erfurt, and Bremen.

Axmann had another plan in motion in Bad Tölz in April, in

combination with this gathering of Hitler Youth leaders. In early April, Axmann had given HJ *Oberbannführer* (Major) Willi Heidemann instructions to take with him Hitler Youth money and build a transportation business near Bad Tölz. Reichsmarks still had some value after the surrender of Germany, otherwise the country would have fallen even deeper into economic ruin. It was not until the summer of 1948 that the old currency was replaced. Heidemann wisely spent some of his funds before Germany fell, stockpiling what he could in anticipation of not only the currency dramatically going down in value, but of certain goods becoming scarce.

Heidemann looked like an older, confident businessman and exuded a sense of gravitas. He had very thin dark hair that he combed over in an attempt to conceal his balding. His hawkish, arched eyebrows were the most noticeable feature on his face, which started off wide and narrowed toward the bottom.

Willi Heidemann's mission was to create a transportation company so that after the occupation of Germany and Austria, Axmann's minions could move around to stay in contact with one another, gather information on the occupation forces, provide employment to their followers, and build up funds to further their National Socialist political goals. As the CIC later determined, "Heidemann's economic capabilities which made him Referent for Economics of the HJ for all Germany, make him the logical person to organize large business concerns to conceal future realization of National Socialistic doctrines."[41]

Heidemann had been in charge of financial matters for the HJ, and now he would put that expertise to use building this transportation concern. Before leaving Berlin, Heidemann needed to gather the funds to do this. In addition to the Hitler Youth money given to him by Axmann, Heidemann had access to funds from the National Youth Welfare Bureau (*Deutsches Jugend Förderungs Werke*), which he'd previously run.[42]

Heidemann visited Deutsche Bank and tried to empty the National Youth Welfare Bureau's account. He asked "one of the bank officials if they would withdraw these funds since it was evident at that time that everything was lost anyway."[43] Fortunately for Heidemann, the bank official was a DJFW director and agreed to give him all the cash the bank had left—a total of 408,000 reichsmarks. Eleven million reichsmarks remained in the account.

In Bad Tölz, another refugee from Berlin joined him, Max Lebens—"the SS Unterfuehrer [noncommissioned officer] of the Berlin Wehrwolf, [who] was charged with establishing a reception center for all refugee Wehrwolf personnel arriving in Bad Tolz from Berlin. LEBENS directed Wehrwolf activities in Berlin and Brandenburg."[44]

To build this transportation company, Heidemann used the corporate shell of Christian Tessmann & Sons.[45] Tessmann had been founded in Lübeck, which is in the north of Germany, on the Baltic Sea. It was an ideal location for a transportation firm as Lübeck was the biggest port on the German side of the Baltic. On the night of a full moon in March 1942, the British Air Force had rained destruction on Lübeck. The bombing and resulting fires destroyed Tessmann's facilities there.

The company then relocated its headquarters to Dresden, Germany. But the American and British bombings of February 1945 again destroyed Tessmann's warehouse and trucks. All that remained after the bombings and resulting firestorm in Dresden was the corporation itself.

Max Lebens's father-in-law (Mr. Tessmann) had donated the corporation for the use of HJ. Heidemann used HJ-related funds to add 154,000 reichsmarks to the firm's books as its operating capital.[46]

In mid-April, Heidemann, accompanied by Dr. Wandel (Tessmann's new business manager) and Lebens, traveled from Bad Tölz to the nearby hamlet of Wackersberg. Heidemann was officially in charge of Christian Tessmann & Sons, while Dr. Wandel ran the day-to-day operations of this business as the assistant manager.

In Wackersberg, they obtained premises for their new business by kicking out the *Kinderlandverschickung* ("KLV") from their rented space in the Haus Zeppelin building. The KLV ("sending of children to the land")[47] evacuated children from the cities to the countryside, where they would be safer from enemy bombings. By the end of the war, the KLV had placed more than 2.8 million children into private homes, farms, inns, hotels, and special camps.[48] Because the Hitler Youth was in charge of the KLV program, Heidemann could order them to leave their rented accommodations in Wackersberg.

Heidemann arranged with Miss Mayer, Haus Zeppelin's owner, to pay 2,000 reichsmarks a month to rent the place for their offices. She could live in the unused portion of the house, although visitors to the firm would be housed there as well.

On April 20, while Hitler celebrated his birthday and awarded twenty of Axmann's HJ boys the Iron Cross in Berlin, Christian Tessmann & Sons officially opened for business in Wackersberg. It had only four vehicles in that office at the time; one of them used to belong to the HJ in Berlin and the other three they had taken from the German Army.

On the evening of April 30, a snowstorm saved Bad Tölz from a bombing run by more than two dozen American planes.[49] The next day, the town was spared the ravages of heavy fighting because the commander of the nearby *Waffen* SS military academy ordered the bulk of his men into the mountains rather than mounting a defense.[50]

But in the midst of this relative calm, there was still some isolated resistance to the conquering of Bad Tölz. This fighting took place as Axmann was breaking out of the bunker area in Berlin.

Sixteen-year-old Gregor Dorfmeister, a member of Hitler Youth in the *Volkssturm*, found himself facing the American enemy during the night of May 1. A truck had dropped him and seven other HJ boys to protect a bridge outside of town. As he recounted to a German newspaper in 2005, "If by noon the next day nothing had happened, we would have gone home."[51] They hunkered down in water-filled trenches, guarding the bridge, while rain poured down on them. Suddenly, a few tanks started coming up the road. "We were terrified, especially because we could not see the enemy, but only heard them."[52]

Dorfmeister and his fellow boy soldiers shot *Panzerfaust* at these tanks. An eerie silence filled the air, until the hatch of one of the tanks opened up, and an American soldier exited his vehicle and fell to the ground. There was literally smoke coming off his body. Dorfmeister explained that seeing this injured man was "terrible. . . . That was the moment when I became a pacifist."[53] His change of heart after this experience didn't mean the battle stopped, though.

"Seconds later, all hell broke loose. . . . They hunted us like rabbits. When we arrived in the forest, there were only three of us."[54] He had started in a group of eight Hitler Youth, but they had lost five boys since attacking the tanks.

All Dorfmeister wanted to do was go back home. However, on the walk back into town, they ran into German military police who had a very different idea of what he should be doing. He and his remaining comrades were ordered to defend another bridge, this one in the town itself. Their position had only sandbags to protect it and a single machine gun with which they could attack the Americans crossing this bridge.

Once the military policemen left, Dorfmeister suggested to his comrades that they all leave this bridge over the Isar River. Despite his urging, the other two wanted to stay and fight. It remains a mystery to him why the other boys stayed while he left, but he said that it might have been because he had a family to go home to in Bad Tölz, while the others did not.

The next day, he came back to the bridge, dressed as a civilian, and found his friends' bodies there. It was a powerful moment that was burned into his memory forever. While an American soldier stood nearby, an old German woman spit upon his friend's bodies. In this interview, he commented, "I cannot understand to this day. We were just kids. We were used by the Nazis as cannon fodder."[55]

He turned his tale into a bestselling novel that he wrote under the pen name Manfred Gregor. A German newspaper that interviewed him wrote, "His version of the horror he experienced is in his literary novel *Die Brücke* [*The Bridge*]: seven guys defend a strategically unimportant bridge. Only one survives.... In reality, there were two bridges, one about 20 kilometers away from Bad Tölz in the forest and the Isar Bridge in downtown Bad Tölz. The bridge in the forest Dorfmeister has never seen again. 'I do not want to even go there. What I experienced there is too horrible.'"[56]

He wrote this novel because he "wanted to make clear why we had been so stupid."[57] It was adapted into an award-winning film of the same name in 1959.

By the time the sun rose on May 2, the U.S. Army controlled Bad Tölz.[58]

Before conquering Bad Tölz, the American soldiers experienced an evil that stood in sharp contrast to the postcard-perfect beauty of this health spa town. Just north of Munich, they came across Dachau, Germany's first concentration camp.[59]

One of these American soldiers wrote: "The 29th of April was a cold, wet and morbid day. This part of Germany was dotted with concentration camps, and road signs contained the names Dachau and Hurlach [a Dachau satellite camp]. The roadsides were littered with bodies, dead and living, of the miserable inmates that had flooded out of the concentration camps as their SS guards fled before American armored columns. Many of us saw Hurlach, but our minds could not comprehend the sights, sounds and stenches we found there. Even minds conditioned and fatigued by months of combat could not evaluate or accept this gruesome sight. We regarded the emaciated political prisoners, wearing the familiar zebra striped suits and peculiar knit caps, with mottled emotions of pity, anger, repulsiveness and awe."[60]

That same day, before entering Dachau, another American soldier was tasked with going after snipers outside of the camp. "We did find some snipers—one we did away with that was firing away from a house nearby. After we silenced him, we went up to see who it was. He was eleven or twelve years old, one of the Hitler youth, who were actually worse than the SS. They were just so brainwashed. . . . We ran into a lot of those kids in their short pants."[61]

The American soldiers found "outside of the camp, adjacent to the camp, there were actually forty boxcars of bodies.[62] . . . The prisoners were just walking skeletons, and they just dropped where they were and died. There were piles of bodies, of bodies that had been gassed and readied for the ovens. Some of them still lived because those boxcars were brought to Dachau to burn those bodies. It was a total mess. And the smell was not a farm; it was Dachau that we had smelled miles before we got there. And yet, people in the village who were right next to the camps said they didn't know what was going on. People in Munich, which was actually only nine miles from Dachau, didn't know what was going on. Now if you want to believe that, the Brooklyn Bridge is still for sale."[63]

Some of the soldiers forced the captured HJ to look at the boxcars of dead bodies. A photograph from April 30, 1945, shows this moment with the boys peering into one of these boxcars full of dead bodies and U.S. soldiers standing in a semicircle behind them.

While the U.S. military did not yet know the details of the HJ activity in Bad Tölz, there had been rumors circulating of the Bavarian Alps serving as a mountain retreat for the Nazis. The concept was one of a national redoubt—a defensive position where an invaded nation could gather its remaining forces.

The Nazi leadership had always had a special connection to the Bavarian Alps. Berchtesgaden, a village in southern Germany very close to the Austrian border, was where the Nazi elite went for holidays. The party controlled Obersalzberg, an area a couple miles away from this village. Obersalzberg was fortified, a place exclusively for the Nazi elite, where Hitler had his Bavarian home (the Berghof) and his Eagle's Nest (Kehlsteinhaus) mountaintop chalet.

As an example of this concern that the Nazis would hole up in the Alps, *Time* magazine contained the following in its February 12, 1945, issue: "What of the top Nazis who cannot hide? With a compact army of young SS and Hitler Youth fanatics, they will retreat, behind a loyal rearguard cover of Volksgrenadiere and Volksstürmer, to the Alpine massif which reaches from southern Bavaria across western Austria to northern Italy. There immense stores of food and munitions are being laid down in prepared fortifications. If the retreat is a success, such an army might hold out for years."[64]

This fear was still present toward the end of the war. A war analyst for the Associated Press wrote in early April 1945: "Faced with the certainty that time and the allied tide won't wait even for the Fuehrer of the super race, Herr Hitler will have to move fast if he is to carry out to the full his desperate scheme of holing-up in the Bavarian Alps with picked Nazi troops for a final stand against the invaders."[65]

In Germany, this concept of using the Alps as a national redoubt was called the Alpine Fortress (*Alpenfestung*). While Goebbels used the idea of the Alpine Fortress for propaganda and misinformation purposes, the Nazi regime did not make this a reality. They did succeed in spreading the fear that they would do this, while they failed to make adequate plans for the fall of Berlin.

In the end, Hitler was not willing to leave Berlin; he chose to die there instead. For the most part, what was left of the German military after the Soviets captured Berlin tried to make their way to the Americans in the west.

U.S. Army General Omar Bradley wrote in his memoirs, military intelligence "had tipped us off to a fantastic enemy plot for the withdrawal of troops into the Austrian Alps where weapons, stores, and even aircraft plants were reported cached for a last-ditch holdout. There the enemy would presumably attempt to keep alive the Nazi myth until the Allies grew tired of occupying the Reich—or until they fell out among themselves. . . . Not until after the campaign ended were we to learn that this Redoubt existed largely in the imaginations of a few fanatic Nazis. It grew into so exaggerated a scheme that I am astonished we could have believed it as innocently as we did. But while it persisted, this legend of the Redoubt was too ominous a threat to ignore and in consequence it shaped our tactical thinking during the closing weeks of the war."[66]

FOUR

ZERO HOUR

To walk through the ruined cities of Germany is to feel an actual doubt about the continuity of civilization.

GEORGE ORWELL[1]

From Berlin to Flensburg in northern Germany, where what was left of the Nazi government was based, was too far for Axmann to try to flee through occupied territory. Besides, the smart move was to hide out and wait for the war to end, as it was clear that all of Germany was soon to be conquered.

He'd arrived in the Wedding district of Berlin with his adjunct, Weltzin, during the daylight hours of May 2. There were already German civilians wearing red armbands (to indicate they were working with the Soviets), who looked at them suspiciously, but did nothing.[2]

Axmann and Weltzin needed a friend to take them in, but the problem was that any of their friends from high up in the Nazi government would likely soon be arrested and have their apartments searched by the Russians. They couldn't go to their own apartments or to relatives' places either, as those were also likely to be searched.

Axmann remembered that a friend of his mother's lived nearby. He went to see if she was home, while Weltzin waited in a doorway down the street.[3] There was no answer at her door, so Axmann tried a neighbor he knew, who was shocked to see him but let him into her apartment anyway. The last few days in the bunker combined with their overnight escape had left Axmann exhausted. He fell asleep while sitting at her kitchen table, the warmth from the room sending him off to rest despite all his worries.

His hostess woke him up, telling him that he had to go as the Russians were nearby. He thanked her and was about to leave when he overheard German voices from the hallway saying, "Axmann is in our building. If the Russians find out, they will kill us. We prefer to deliver him to them."[4]

Someone must have seen him entering the building. He could just run, but his chances of escape were slim if someone decided to tell the Russians that he had been there. Axmann opened the apartment door, and instead of fleeing, he approached his host's neighbors and said to them, "I grew up among you and I have fulfilled my duty."[5] This persuaded them. They decided to let him go and keep his visit there a secret. The head of the building association led him to the back exit and wished him well.[6]

Before leaving, Axmann asked this man about his adjutant, and was told that the Russians had just captured him. Once outside, Axmann looked all around for Weltzin just in case, but he was gone. He never saw him again and later heard that he had died while being held by the Soviets.[7] This left Axmann the only living witness to the fact that Martin Bormann, one of the most powerful of the Nazi elite, was dead.

He walked past Soviet tanks and civilians with red armbands, who were checking the papers of anyone that they found suspicious. Instead of trying to hide and risk standing out, Axmann blended in with the crowds on the main shopping promenade of Seestrasse. A German walked up to him and asked if he was Axmann. He'd heard on a Russian radio station that Axmann had died in Berlin. Axmann explained away the resemblance by claiming to be his brother. This was a bit ridiculous as it was unlikely his brother would have the same kind of injury and prosthetic as him. Whether this man believed Axmann's absurd lie or not, he did not turn him in.

This close call, the disintegration of the Third Reich, and the capture of his aide left Axmann in a confused state as to his next move. His world had fallen apart—he'd seen his beloved leader's dead body and witnessed the collapse of the government that he had dedicated his life to. He was physically and emotionally exhausted, leaving him unable to think clearly about what to do. Should he try to find a friend who could hide him in Berlin, find a hiding place on his own, or try to flee the city? And if he did flee the city, then which way should he go and how would he pass any checkpoints?

He walked to the cemetery in the hopes that there he could collect his thoughts and come up with a plan. He decided that turning himself in to the Allies someday might work, but not until things calmed down. And he wasn't going to turn himself in to the Soviets. He knew how his fellow Nazis who'd been captured by them earlier in the war had suffered.

The new Nazi government was in the north, and he got along well with its president, Karl Dönitz. However, without money or identification, getting there would be next to impossible.[8] While he'd started the flight from the bunker with bags of money from the HJ, he'd lost it before he'd crossed the Weidendammer Bridge. Instead of carrying the reichsmarks himself, he'd given them to his messenger Lehmann, who carried one bag and gave the other to an HJ district leader.[9] When Axmann had handed over the two heavy briefcases just before the breakout began, he told Lehmann it was more than half a million reichsmarks.[10]

Unfortunately for Axmann, Lehmann was hit by shrapnel and knocked out before crossing the Weidendammer, and so Axmann lost the money during the confusion of trying to get across this heavily guarded bridge.[11]

While at the cemetery, Axmann met an older man and they decided to travel together. Axmann told him that his name was Erich Siewert and that he was a former soldier who was now a businessman. It was the name of his dead cousin. He was filled with nostalgia when, while walking through the city, they passed a handball court where he used to play with this cousin.

They walked west through the ruined city, trying to avoid the Soviets and their civilian auxiliaries. Even though the old man didn't know who Axmann really was, and his own papers were in order, the smart thing for most Germans at that point was to try to avoid the new authorities, regardless of whether he had something to hide.

At one point, a column of German prisoners of war approached. Aware that there was nothing to be done for the POWs, Axmann and the old man hid out and watched them pass by. They were now in the westernmost borough of Berlin—Spandau.[12] At the locality of Haselhorst, they had to go through a Soviet checkpoint in order to exit Berlin.[13] While Axmann had no papers at all, his companion somehow had all of his in order.

Axmann asked him to pretend that he carried both of their papers. At the checkpoint, Axmann used his prosthetic as a prop to suggest that he couldn't carry his papers and so his companion had them. His companion had so many documents that their bluff was accepted as true. If someone at the checkpoint had carefully looked at the papers and noticed they were only for one person, they both would have been in trouble.

They ran into another checkpoint in a town just to the west of Berlin called Falkensee. They timed their approach to arrive at the same time as a bunch of people arrived from the other direction. Once again, they managed to get through. They continued on foot, with the sound of occasional gunshots in the distance breaking the silence. A good night's rest at a ransacked dwelling made all the difference. Axmann felt much better as they headed north the next day.

They talked to other Germans on the road and heard of Soviets looting and raping. For food and water, they were reduced to begging. Sometimes people gave them nothing; sometimes they gave a bit of food and water. Very rarely, a farmer gave them milk, which was a long remembered treat during this time of hardship.

Among the refuse they found scattered about in towns were papers related to the HJ with Axmann's mass-produced signature on them. People had tossed out their HJ-related certificates en masse. They formed a standard part of the postwar street trash in the way that fast-food wrappers now plague the sides of America's highways.

In one town, a drunken Russian soldier ordered them to come with him to talk to an officer. When he left them alone in an unlocked room while he went to look for the officer, they fled. No one chased them. All they had to do was walk out the door and hurry away. After this lucky escape, they continued on their way slowly moving north.

While Axmann hid from the Russians, the Flensburg government ruled what little remained of the Third Reich out of this small north German town. President Dönitz understood that his government only controlled an ever-shrinking bit of territory and that the war was lost. His goal though was to slow down the diplomatic process to enable as many German forces as possible to surrender to the Americans and the British, rather than be captured by the Russians.

The supreme commander of the Allied Forces, General Dwight D. Eisenhower would not allow Dönitz's representatives to stall and forced them to surrender promptly. Dönitz wanted to surrender only his forces fighting the Western Allies, in order to allow his men fighting the Russians to continue to fight and flee until they reached American or British lines. However, Eisenhower put a stop to this by threatening that if an unconditional surrender was not signed, then he would close his lines to Germans, forcing them to either surrender to the Russians or fight to the death.

Very early in the morning on May 7, Dönitz's representatives signed Germany's unconditional surrender to take effect late on the evening of May 8.[14] The United States and the United Kingdom celebrated Victory in Europe Day (V-E Day) on May 8, while the Soviets celebrated it on May 9.[15] Although some isolated German forces continued to fight, and the fighting against Japan continued in the Pacific, the war in Europe was now officially over.

The Allies celebrated in style. In Piccadilly Circus, London, "servicemen with British girls jitterbugged, sang and cheered."[16] In New York City, "wild street celebrations were whitened by snowstorms of paper cascading from buildings in Times Square, Wall Street and Rockefeller Center. Ships on the rivers let go with their sirens . . . workers swarmed out of their shops, singing and dancing, drinking whisky out of bottles, wading in their own weird confetti."[17]

The Soviets waited until June 24, 1945, to have a victory parade in Moscow. The head of the Soviet Zone in Germany, General Georgy Zhukov, dramatically led this parade while mounted on a white horse. In what one spectator considered the highlight of the parade, two hundred soldiers cast captured German military banners and standards onto the wet and muddy ground in front of Lenin's mausoleum in Red Square.[18]

On the morning of May 8, U.S. President Harry Truman's sixty-first birthday, he announced Germany's surrender in a radio broadcast. Truman had become president when his predecessor, Franklin D. Roosevelt, died on April 12, 1945.

In this speech, President Truman reminded the American listening public that "our rejoicing is sobered and subdued by a supreme consciousness of the terrible price we have paid to rid the world of Hitler and his evil band. Let us not forget, my fellow Americans, the sorrow and the heartache which today abide in the homes of so many of our neighbors—neighbors whose most priceless possession has been rendered as a sacrifice to redeem our liberty."[19]

For many Germans, the unconditional surrender of the Third Reich came to be known as the zero hour (*die Stunde null*).[20] Germany was in ruins—like something out of a post-apocalyptic nightmare. Most of its once great cities had been reduced to collections of rubble. And under some of this rubble lay bloated corpses—decaying and emitting a miasma of noxious odors into the urban environment. It's impossible to calculate exactly how much rubble there was. One estimate has 1.4 billion cubic feet worth of rubble in Germany.[21] After zero hour, came "the Time After the War" (*Nachkriegszeit*).

By the time the U.S. Army occupied Bavaria, as the CIC later documented, the Tessmann transportation concern was "already established and operating, and it was fairly easy to secure permits and passes for their vehicles and drivers and continue the enlarging of their operations."[22] For example, "the firm had been given sole charge of the buying and selling of vegetables for [the rural district of Tölz], because they were in a position to carry this through, due to the equipment the firm had."[23]

The American occupation authorities and local CIC office did not know that there was anything seditious about Tessmann and its transportation business. German industry, transportation, and infrastructure had been demolished by the war. A fully intact, functioning transportation company ready to do business with the Allies was a godsend to the occupation officials in charge of making sure that civilians had access to food and coal.

And so the local American Military Government officials, based in Bad Tölz, contracted with Tessmann for their civilian trucking needs and gave them official travel passes, which allowed Tessmann's drivers to travel with their trucks for both government contracted business and their own private business deals. Without such passes, they would not have been able to get far before hitting a checkpoint. One needed to have permission to travel in those days, especially with a vehicle.

In May 1945, Jack Hunter was still stateside. As his friend and fellow Camp Ritchie graduate Werner Michel put it, "With anticipation we looked forward to put into practice what we had learned during this excellent and very professional course. However, the war ended and victory had been achieved even without our assistance."[24]

Of course, the war in the Pacific was still being fought, but Hunter and Michel had trained for dealing with Germans. So even with "Victory in Europe" accomplished, that is where the army would soon send them.

Although the war in Europe had ended, the CIC still had work to do. A burgeoning black market had emerged. People were hungry and wanted more than they could legally obtain using their ration books. Through his work with the CIC, Jack Hunter would become an expert on the workings of the black market. It was a shadowy world, not just of hungry Germans trying to trade heirlooms for food, but also of spies and counteragents trying to get information and military materials.

If you had the money or the cigarettes, virtually anything was for sale. For example, wanted Nazis could purchase false documents providing them with a new identity or clearing them of any wrongdoing. Meanwhile, army personnel profited tremendously from selling items on the black market. For example, an American soldier could turn fifty cents' worth of cigarettes (ten packs) from the base store into about $100 on the black market.[25]

The Allies faced the overwhelming task of identifying who among the Germans and Austrians could be trusted in positions of power and who should be arrested. CIC agents helped to screen millions of people as part of this process. In American-controlled territory, all Germans over eighteen were required to fill out a lengthy questionnaire called a *Fragebogen* as part of the denazification process. It had 131 questions, which ranged from the expected (name, place of birth, present address) to the self-incriminating ("Have you ever been a member of the NSDAP? Yes, No, Dates")[26].

The NSDAP was the Nazi Party. The date that one joined was important because the true believers joined early, when being a Nazi could hinder one's career prospects. Once the Nazis gained power in 1933, joining the party helped one to get ahead in society.

Some of the questions were absurd, such as asking whom one voted for even though voting had been anonymous, so there was no possible way to check someone's answer.

The CIC had access to Nazi Party records and other documents from the Third Reich that could be used to check the veracity of many of the form's questions. The fact that such records still existed would make Germans think twice about lying on these forms. If all the records had been destroyed, there would have been little to stop them from doing so.

Across the top of the first page, the form carried the stern warning that "Omissions or false or incomplete statements will result in prosecution as violations of military ordinances."[27]

CIC agents followed behind the American troops and quickly set up offices in occupied towns and cities. While many of the CIC's activities took place in the murky cloak-and-dagger world of secrecy, these offices were open to the public and even had the CIC sign posted outside them. Many Germans referred to the CIC as the "American Gestapo"—a name that, while not accurate, was sometimes helpful in intimidating Germans into cooperating. In contrast, Americans often called CIC agents "G-Men in Khaki" as though they were FBI agents in military uniforms.[28]

When setting up in a new town, CIC agents screened the local elite to remove any Nazis and replace them with Germans who were relatively free of Nazi ties. Germans also were required to surrender cameras and firearms (with some exceptions). Agents conducted countless interviews looking to find automatic arrestees hiding out among locals and travelers alike. Those who were traveling through a town needed to obtain a travel pass, which meant that they had to stop by the CIC office. Other times Germans were caught by American soldiers and forced into the screening process.

Agents came to learn what was suspicious when interviewing Germans. For example, if someone's papers were all perfectly in order, then that could be a sign they had fake papers. Few people had everything in order given the chaos of the war. Eventually, CIC agents learned to check for the SS blood-type tattoos or signs (a burn or scar) that they had been removed.

Given that he was a cabinet-level officer, Axmann fell into the automatic arrestee category. Also, the United Nations War Crimes Commission, in their seventh list of war criminals, named him as a wanted man.[29]

An example of how an astute CIC agent could quickly spot something suspicious during a screening interview is found in the story of a man who walked into a CIC office in the Bavarian town of Viechtach.[30] He claimed to be a war correspondent for a newspaper in Sweden. He had a thoroughly prepared story, but ran into trouble when he wrote out (in print lettering) the name of the paper he worked for. He said the name properly, but the agent wanted to see how he wrote the name. This man wrote down "Swenska Dagbladet." At this, the agent laughed uncontrollably.

The CIC liked to recruit agents with language skills, and this man had the bad luck to run into an agent who was familiar with Swedish. The correct name had a "v" in it, not a "w"—this sound is spelled differently in Swedish and German. Moreover, it was (and remains to this day) one of Sweden's biggest newspapers; for someone familiar with Sweden, let alone someone who supposedly wrote for it, not to know how to spell this name was a dead giveaway he was lying. Once caught, the man admitted to being a Nazi spy.

While working, CIC agents wore civilian clothes or a Class "A" officer's uniform without rank on it. Instead, they simply wore a set of brass "U.S." insignia—one each on the left and right side of their collar, above the lapel. Such collar tabs were used outside the CIC to indicate that the wearer was an officer, but CIC agents wore them regardless of whether they were officers or enlisted men. These tabs were useful as they often created the impression that the wearers were officers, even if they weren't, and as one former CIC agent explained, this "was very effective in letting agents do their job."[31]

However, Werner Michel (Hunter's friend from Camp Ritchie) clarified that while agents wore only these tabs, "support and administrative personnel as well as [commanders] wore uniforms with the appropriate rank insignia."[32]

Agents also carried with them their CIC credentials and a gold badge inscribed with "War Department Military Intelligence." Owing to secrecy requirements, agents only showed their credentials when absolutely necessary; the badge was supposed to be a backup to be used only in cases when people had trouble reading one's credentials or needed additional proof that one really was a CIC agent.

An amazing power, almost akin to a superpower in the rank-based military, was for CIC agents to refuse to answer questions about their rank and to even give orders to army personnel who would normally outrank them. For example, as a second lieutenant, Jack Hunter held an entry-level commissioned army officer rank, yet once he became a CIC agent, he could give orders to a superior officer without that person knowing what rank he held. To put it bluntly, this is not the way the military normally works. It goes against one of the most fundamental military rules—that orders flow downward from those higher in rank to those lower in rank. It was an upside-down world where a second lieutenant, or even an enlisted agent, could command someone who not only outranked him but vastly outranked him.

As CIC Agent Ib Melchior explained it: "Because our duties were such that we might easily find ourselves in a situation requiring the immediate and unquestioned assistance of available troops, we were empowered to request such assistance—if need be, *order* [italics in original] it—from any officer up to and including a full colonel. Only general officers were entitled to know our true rank. To all others our standard reply to the inevitable question, 'What *is* your rank?' was simply a firm, "'My rank is confidential, but at this moment I am not outranked!'"[33] CIC agents were authorized to say this even when they would otherwise have been outranked.

FIVE

THE INFORMANT

If Hitler invaded Hell I would make at least a favourable reference to the Devil in the House of Commons.

WINSTON CHURCHILL[1]

After the signing of the final surrender agreement, the Allies proceeded to ignore the Flensburg government run by Karl Dönitz in the north of Germany. A military correspondent for *The Times* of London wrote in May that "the so-called Dönitz regime really consisted of Dönitz, Schwerin von Krosigk [the leading minister of the Flensburg government], and a microphone, with the third-named the most important."[2]

As former minister of armaments and war production Albert Speer remarked on the Flensburg government's continued existence after their surrender, "Our government was not only impotent; the victors did not deign to notice it."[3] He commented at the time "that the tragedy was turning into a tragicomedy."[4]

On May 23, Allied Supreme Headquarters notified the Flensburg government that they were officially disbanded and arrested its leaders, including its president, Dönitz. While Dönitz had removed the bust of Hitler from his office and ordered his government to stop using the Nazi salute,[5] such efforts were not enough to keep him in power.

They had continued to use the Nazi flag though. As Albert Speer later wrote, "If anything proved that the Doenitz government, try though it might, was not a new beginning, it was the persistence of this flag. As a matter of fact, at the beginning of our days in Flensburg, Doenitz and I had agreed that the flag must remain. We could not pretend to represent anything new, I thought. Flensburg was only the last stage of the Third Reich, nothing more."[6]

That night, *Reichsführer-SS* Heinrich Himmler committed suicide in the town of Lüneburg, in northern Germany. The British had captured him the afternoon before in nearby Bremervörde when he had tried to make his way through a British checkpoint on a bridge. He had papers identifying him as a Sergeant Heinrich Hitzinger. With an eye patch and his mustache shaved off, Himmler no longer looked like the proud man who had ruled over the SS and overseen the systematic murder of millions of innocent people.

The soldiers who arrested him did not know that they had captured the former *Reichsführer-SS*; they had detained him because they found him and his paperwork to be suspicious. When the British later learned that they had Himmler in custody, they had a doctor search him for cyanide. During this examination, Himmler bit down on the poison he'd hidden in his mouth.[7] Like Eva Braun Hitler, Martin Bormann, and Dr. Ludwig Stumpfegger before him, Himmler died of cyanide poisoning.

On June 5, the Allies officially took over governmental control of Germany when they signed the "Declaration Regarding the Defeat of Germany and the Assumption of Supreme Authority by Allied Powers."[8] It set forth a number of "requirements arising from the complete defeat and unconditional surrender of Germany with which

Germany must comply."[9] Of most interest to the likes of former high-ranking Nazis like Axmann, Article 11(a) declared that "the principal Nazi leaders as specified by the Allied Representatives, and all persons from time to time named or designated by rank, office or employment by the Allied Representatives as being suspected of having committed, ordered or abetted war crimes or analogous offences, will be apprehended and surrendered to the Allied Representatives."

The day before, on June 4, Jack Hunter had turned twenty-four. On June 14, Hunter and his friend Werner Michel shipped out on the RMS *Queen Elizabeth*. At the time, she was the largest passenger liner in the world. During World War II, she served as a troopship—for this voyage, carrying troops from the United States to Great Britain. Despite weighing more than eighty thousand gross tons, she moved fast enough to be safely used to carry troops across a hostile ocean—up to twenty-nine knots in good weather.[10] She could carry more than fourteen thousand passengers.[11]

One soldier recalled what it was like before boarding her. "We pulled up alongside this great big wall. Well, that wasn't a wall. That was the *Queen Elizabeth*. You couldn't see the top of it, it was so big."[12] During its transformation from a luxury passenger liner to a troopship, she had been painted in what was known as "war-time gray" to make it harder for German U-Boats and other enemy vessels to spot her at sea.

They arrived in Greenock, Scotland, on June 20. That same day, the *Queen Elizabeth*'s sister ship, the *Queen Mary*, arrived in New York City with the first load of American troops returning home after V-E Day.[13] Hunter and his fellow arriving soldiers were there to replace the Americans heading home or to the Pacific Front.

Even though Hunter, Michel, and the other American soldiers who were deployed to Europe post–V-E Day arrived after the war had been won in the European Theater, they would still be considered World

War II vets. And this was not because the war was still ongoing in the Pacific Theater against Japan. The United States did not declare the official end of hostilities until Truman signed Presidential Proclamation 2714 on December 31, 1946. As far as the United States is concerned, all military personnel who served between December 7, 1941, (the attack on Pearl Harbor) and December 31, 1946, are World War II veterans.

Once they arrived in Scotland, Hunter and Michel "traveled by train and truck to a camp in the south of England identified to us as Hursley Park. For the probably five days or so we spent there in wretched Quonset huts and were issued 'C' ration cans three times daily consisting of only beans . . . [we] had been advised to converse in German to maintain our proficiency. The digestion of all these beans after two days in the huts in close proximity to one another . . . created an almost unbearable odor.[14]

"We cursed the Army and the quartermaster major who commanded the Hursley Park camp. We speculated that 'C' rations containing more digestible selections had probably been sold on the black market. Still the cans of beans continued to be issued to us by German POWs who manned what we mocked as the 'chow line.' As I remember one day as we mightily tried to eat yet another dreaded can of beans, one of the German POWs, a sergeant (Unteroffizier), approached, clicked his heels, then in an apparent Berlin dialect asked politely if he could ask a question.

"Lt. Fritz (Fred) Niebergall . . . immediately took charge and replied in the affirmative to the sergeant's question. The latter then asked whether we were Germans or Americans. Niebergall, never at a loss, asked the POW what his opinion was. The Unteroffizier responded without hesitation that he was certain that we must be Germans. Niebergall nodded.

"The Unteroffizier then asked, 'if you are Germans, then how did

you become American Army officers?' Without missing a beat Niebergall explained that all of us had been in the Afrika Korps of the Wehrmacht but had been captured in Tunisia in 1943. He embellished the
fable by adding that the Americans had been so impressed with 'our
bearing and discipline that they immediately offered us commissions
in the American army.'[15]

"The German NCO thanked Niebergall, saluted, and returned to
his kitchen detail. Shortly before our departure from Hursley Park, we
learned that the German POWs had submitted a request to the camp
commander applying for commissions in the U.S. Army. Just before
we embarked on the ship taking us across the channel, we found out
that the despicable commander of Hursley Park camp had reportedly
directed an investigation into the unfounded rumor that German
POWs had applied for Army commissions. We were elated to have gotten even for the indignities of the bean episode."[16]

As Michel recalls, from this camp, he and Hunter "shipped out to
Le Havre [in France] and thence to a camp identified as HQ, Military
Intelligence Service (MIS) Rear, near Paris. From there we traveled by
train through the devastated countryside to Germany."[17] On this trip,
they rode "through bombed towns and destroyed villages. The roads
were littered with German tanks, trucks, and artillery pieces."[18]

"Our destination was HQ, MIS (Forward) then located at Bad
Schwalbach, a German spa [town] in the vicinity of Wiesbaden. We
were housed in confiscated German hotels. Members of the staff there
told us that we would be interviewed shortly and based on our backgrounds and experience would be assigned as replacements for intelligence personnel returning to the US.[19]

"Jack was assigned to G2, USFET (US Forces European Theatre),
located in General Eisenhower's headquarters in the former IG Farben
Building in Frankfurt. It was the right place for him. He was a writer,
and as most of us knew, he had a staccato wit, and could think on his

feet. As he told me, he expected to be on the CI (counterintelligence) staff in the G2 shop."[20] G-2, USFET, was the military intelligence section of the USFET.

General Dwight D. Eisenhower had been the supreme commander of the Allied Forces that fought in Europe during World War II. Now that he had beaten the Nazis, his job changed from being the head of a massive military invasion to running the American part of the occupation. As the military governor of the American Zone of Occupation in Germany, he based his government in the Farben Building in Frankfurt.

The largest office building in Europe at the time, it had belonged to the IG Farben Company.[21] IG Farben had been a huge conglomerate of German chemical companies.

Eisenhower took over the building, which survived the war intact and relatively undamaged. Kicking out the company based there was a non-issue. They had been an integral part of the Nazi war machine and even committed war crimes.

In one of the subsequent Nuremberg Trials (the IG Farben trial), a U. S. military court convicted many of the company's directors for war crimes and crimes against humanity.[22] In 2001, a plaque was installed in front of the Farben Building's main entrance proclaiming that: "This building was . . . the headquarters of IG Farben. Between 1933 and 1945, as one of the very largest chemical concerns in the world, the company increasingly put its scientific knowledge and production technologies into the service of war preparations and the National Socialist regime of terror. From 1942 to 1945, IG Farben, together with the SS, maintained the concentration camp at Buna-Monowitz next to the IG Farben factory at Auschwitz. Of the tens of thousand prisoners made to work for the company there, most were murdered. In the Nazi extermination camps many hundreds of thousands of people, mostly Jews, were killed by Zyklon B gas, which was sold by an IG Farben company."[23]

In this building where businessmen and chemists had once toiled, Hunter reported to work for the military government. The army assigned Hunter to the Operations Section of G-2, to run the German desk. The head of G-2 (the senior intelligence officer) was forty-eight-year-old Brigadier General Edwin Sibert.

In Hunter's words, his "administrative boss in [the] CIC (the guy who saw that I got my orders and pay and whatnot) was an over-the-hill lieutenant-colonel."[24] While he did not get along with this boss, this was not a huge problem as Hunter was not micromanaged. Instead, he had a great deal of freedom to determine what counterintelligence matters to pursue.

Jack Hunter was in the heart of the bureaucracy that ran the U.S. military. While he was just a low-ranking cog in this machine, he managed to keep a healthy perspective on his role in the occupation of Germany. His no-nonsense and, at times, contrarian approach did not always fit in well with those officers who were trying to rise up the ranks as quickly as they could. Making jokes and staying focused on the task at hand, though, helped him keep his sanity while working in the IG Farben Building.

As chief of the German desk, Hunter sat on the building's third floor along with other desks monitoring counterintelligence from countries all over Europe. These included ostensible allies such as France and the Soviet Union.

Given the high ranks typically stationed at Eisenhower's headquarters, Hunter at first wondered why he had been given such an important job as an inexperienced, lowly second lieutenant. Much later in life, he wrote that "in a way I was in the right job, because I have an insatiable curiosity, and it was hugely interesting to read through the sheaves of field agents' reports, the dossiers on fugitive war crimes suspects, the interrogations of captured Nazi functionaries, and the piles of minutiae that materialized in my in-box every morning. Nobody told me what to do with any of this stuff, and I finally realized that they'd given the German Desk to a second-looie [second lieutenant] klutz because the Germans were now out of the war and posed no real threat to anybody, least of all the drunken, wenching GIs awaiting redeployment to the Pacific Theater of Operations (or in many miraculous cases) assignment to bases in the Continental USA.[25]

"But something else occurred to me as I read through those piles. Real live American agents were sending in those reports. Faceless men and women were out there in the shattered German boonies, still believing it important to tell Eisenhower what was going on in Scheisshaus am Rhine [Shithouse on the Rhine River] or where former SS Gruppenfuhrer Wiener von Schnitzel [Group Leader Breaded Cutlet] was hiding."[26]

There was more to his job than just combing through reports. He also went into the field to investigate things himself. While doing so, he had his share of nerve-wracking experiences.

As his younger brother, Bob Hunter, tells the story, Jack was once "supposed to meet one of his agents" at a bar while "dressed as a civilian," but "he got there early" and had to use the bathroom.[27] He let the bartender know that he was going to use the facilities in case anyone asked for him.

So now Jack Hunter was in the bathroom all by himself. As Bob recounts, "This guy walks in and stands next to him even though there were plenty of empty urinals, he grabbed Jack and shoved his face into the urinal. Jack was so surprised he wasn't able to fight back, he thought he was not long for this world when the guy who was meeting him came in and rescued him."[28] And so he was almost beaten to death in a bathroom.

As Jack told his brother Bob when explaining how this assailant had come to target him, "this guy . . . recognized Jack coming out of the IG Farben building in an American uniform once so he recognized him as an agent and was going to do him in. Jack thought this guy was going to kill him."[29] He was lucky to just have his "head shampooed in a nightclub urinal" as Jack Hunter once wrote.[30]

In mid-May, Artur Axmann stopped in the small village of Lansen.[31] He was still with the older man he had met in a Berlin cemetery. They had traveled on foot through the back parts of Germany.

Lansen is in the northeast German region of Mecklenburg, which was occupied by the Soviets. This was farm and grazing country—its flat landscape stood in sharp contrast to the jagged mountains of southern Germany where Heidemann and the other HJ leaders had gathered on Axmann's orders.

Axmann, who had recently been at the center of German power, reporting to Hitler himself in the bunker, was now reduced to depending on strangers for food and water. At a farm in Lansen, a woman there gave them milk instead of water; this had only happened one time before during their travels. Milk was a rare and precious gift for these penniless travelers.

After talking with him for a bit, this woman unexpectedly invited Axmann to stay on her farm. His traveling companion planned to continue on his journey because his sister lived nearby. Once again, Axmann's war injury had proven useful. The woman believed that the Russians might soon detain her husband, but that Axmann would be allowed to stay on the farm because of his handicap. She wanted a man there to help her protect her daughters and take care of the farm.

It seemed like a good idea to lay low for a while as the Russians already believed him dead and he had no papers, so Axmann said yes. Even though he felt like he could trust the people he was staying with, he decided to keep his real identity a secret and let them believe him to be his dead cousin Erich Siewert.

While Axmann was hiding out, a former SS officer (and HJ leader) turned himself in to the Public Safety Office of the American Military Government ("MG") in Munich. This man, named Siegfried Kulas, was wearing civilian clothes, but he had been in the military. He'd recently fled Berlin with his family to avoid capture by the Soviets.

Munich CIC Agent Staff Sergeant Timothy Matthew Reis later wrote, "It was after V-E Day in Munich—and our detachment was swamped with work. Automatic arrests were being ferreted out in large numbers daily, interrogated and shipped on to detention quarters according to their importance. Germans were denouncing each other to CIC and MG, producing long-winded documents listing the crime or political beliefs their victims were supposed to have committed or believed in. Every lead was followed by the CIC agents but with the immensity of the load staring us in the face, we sometimes had to cut short the interrogation when it seemed evident it was of minor importance. In addition to interrogations and screening, I was the liaison from our detachment to the Munich Military Government detachment. . . . I checked with the Public Safety Office daily to see if his force had picked up anyone that we should screen and return these individuals to our headquarters for processing."[32]

Reis took custody of Kulas on May 25, bringing him to the CIC office in Munich for questioning. There "his interrogation was handled with the same routine as many of the others and he was returned to the temporary quarters we had for prisoners. He asked to be returned to speak on a matter of great importance. This was an old gimmick to us but we usually accommodated the request, and, in this instance, it seemed to prove worthwhile. [Kulas] said he wished to be of some help in our work, because, as he put it: 'We believed in an ideology, fought for it and lost, and I am sick unto death of further suffering.' I thanked him for his statement and asked him what he had in mind. He asked me if I had heard of WEHRWOLF. This surprised me but I said I had. [Kulas] then began his revelation of a planned movement that was to commence operations on the day of Germany's surrender.[33]

"He said the inception of this plan or movement had its beginning with PETER KLOS, an officer high in the Hitler Jugend, in 1944 on the West Front. He conceived the idea that should the enemy be successful in invading Germany, certain picked units overrun by the enemy forces, should begin underground operations against the enemy in various ways. The plan was bucked on to the High Command and Himmler approved it finally. Organization proceeded slowly, partly because the conceit of the German High Command refused to admit an invasion possibility, and, partly because the Plan's author was not of a high enough rank to push it faster, and it was lost in the shuffle. With the advent of 1945, the Plan was finally revived by the Hitler Jugend Staff at Berlin and roughly sketched organizationally in the final weeks there."[34]

While the plan's author was of high rank in the HJ organization, his rank was low compared to those in the German High Command.

Kulas went on to claim that he knew where the HJ and BDM leaders were hiding out in Bavaria. Moreover, given his having served in the adult leadership of the HJ, he was already familiar with many of them.

Reis worked on this case with another agent in his office named Werner D. Nordheim, who interrogated Kulas further. Nordheim had been born in Germany and knew the country, the language, and the culture well. Eventually, another German-born agent, Tech Sergeant George Hochschild, would come to replace Nordheim as Reis's partner in this case. Jack Hunter later wrote that Agent Hochschild had a "dark, thoughtful face."[35] Unlike Hunter and Reis, who were blondes, Hochschild had black, thick hair.

Agent Hochschild's version of how Kulas came to be in their office at the start of the case appears to differ from Reis's telling. This could just reflect the passage of time, as Reis wrote down his recollections in 1979 and Hochschild related them to the author in 2010. The events in question happened back in 1945.

The way Agent Hochschild remembered it, "Siegfried (or Karl [Kulas's ultimate codename]) walked into our office and he talked to the man in charge who was an officer who had nothing to do with casework and he looked around, and I happened to be in the office and he said 'you want to talk to this guy?' So, I said, 'fine.' So, I took him to a room and we sat down. And he started talking a long story. I said, 'Well why don't you go home and write it up and then come back. Let me read what you wrote and then we can discuss it.' He agreed with that and he left. It was about ten days later, he came back, and he had written in a [composition] book a long story in handwriting. I had a hard time to read it, but I took it into where I usually do my work and I finally read the whole story, what he told me. And then I made an appointment, I said, 'Come back in 3 or 4 days and we'll talk [about] what to do next.' And that's how it started."[36]

Regardless of exactly how it started, CIC Agent Reis was a key agent in this case, primarily handling developments in Bavaria with Agent Nordheim. Jack Hunter eventually became the case officer in charge. For now, though, Reis reported to his CO. Hunter described Reis as having a "squarish, Central-European face" and a "way of looking at the world with a kind of wry disbelief."[37]

Once Reis came to believe Kulas and agreed to work with him, Reis sent him to Bad Tölz to infiltrate Tessmann & Sons. The agent in charge of his office, George Mosely, approved this. It was a bit of a risk as Kulas could have taken off for good. The fact that he'd volunteered the information about Tessmann and Werwolf suggested that he wasn't a flight risk. Of course, it could have been an elaborate ploy to get a car, gasoline, and the necessary passes to travel from Munich to Bad Tölz. In such a case, though, Kulas would have been certain that the CIC would start actively hunting for him, so they considered it highly unlikely that he would try such a risky move.

Kulas was a handsome man, in a cold way. He kept his slicked back dark hair parted on the left. His pale complexion was clean-shaven. The overall impression he gave off was of a businessman who was involved in the darker side of things. His suits hung a bit loose over his slender frame.

Reis gave Kulas a cover job with the Military Government as a "surveyor of used civilian automobile part stocks" to enable him to travel freely from his home in Munich to Bad Tölz and to make him attractive to those running Tessmann.[38] His ability to obtain used car parts would be indispensable to a trucking concern operating during the hard times following the war. Materials of all kinds were tightly rationed, and the black market could be very expensive and dangerous to navigate. So this would be like dangling candy in front of a hungry baby.

The CIC agents knew that Kulas fell into the automatic arrestee category, given his activities with the SS. They did not promise him anything other than that they could keep him out of jail while he was working with them and that they would put in a good word for him afterward based on his performance as a penetration agent. They could hide him from their fellow allies (including Americans) who were hunting for war criminals, but they would only do this as long as this operation lasted. He would still have to face the music someday for what he had done during the war.

The Americans might give him a pass based on his cooperation with the CIC, but to what extent the other Allies would take that into consideration was unknown. Plus, the Germans themselves would be in charge of their country someday. There was no way to predict how they would handle things once they took over. But for now, working with the CIC kept Kulas out of jail.

The CIC first gave him the codename "INFANT," which they changed later to "KARL." The biography they put together and included in a report had his date of birth as October 13, 1914, in Berlin. His last address was in the Berlin district of Reinickendorf, where he had lived since 1936. For his military service, they listed that he was a member of the *Wehrmacht* (army) from 1935 to 1936; in December 1937, he joined the *Kripo* (police); in 1939, he was appointed a *Kriminal Kommissar* (criminal detective); and on Hitler's birthday (April 20) in 1944, he became an SS *Hauptsturmführer* (captain).

He had worked investigating alleged homosexuals and youth culture adherents the Nazis had deemed subversive. Kulas pursued criminal actions against many of these suspected homosexuals as part of the Berlin police, and later did similar investigations for the Hitler Youth.[39] Those found to be homosexual were sent off to concentration camps.[40]

Kulas had a background in the Hitler Youth Leadership since 1932, and he continued to be active in the organization until the end of the war.[41] He held a position as a *Bannführer* (colonel) in the HJ. His involvement in the HJ and the SS meant that the HJ leadership in Bavaria would trust him as one of their own.

He had joined the HJ in 1930; five years later he joined the Nazi Party (NSDAP # 3 255 473), and in 1939, the SS (SS # 344 707). Now that the Nazis had lost the war, his activities under them as part of the SS meant that he was in serious danger of arrest and punishment.

As the saying goes, though, "conspiracies hatched in hell are not witnessed by angels."[42] And Kulas was no angel. While the CIC agents knew he had been in the SS, they do not appear to have known that their new informant had been a member of one of the mobile killing squads in German-occupied Eastern Europe. He was with the *Einsatzkommandos* 1b (which was part of *Einsatzgruppe* A) during the summer of 1941. In August 1941, he was shot in his right knee and so left the *Einsatzgruppe*.

The *Einsatzgruppen* were groups which followed the Nazi advance eastward to eliminate Jews, gypsies, the insane, and Soviet political officers. The International Military Tribunal ("IMT") in 1946 held them "responsible for the murder of two million defenseless human beings."[43] At a trial of prominent figures from the *Einsatzgruppen*, the IMT pointed out that "no human mind can grasp the enormity of two million deaths because life, the supreme essence of consciousness and being, does not lend itself to material or even spiritual appraisement. It is so beyond finite comprehension that only its destruction offers an infinitesimal suggestion of its worth. The loss of any one person can only begin to be measured in the realization of his survivors that he is gone forever. The extermination, therefore, of two million human beings cannot be felt. Two million is but a figure."[44]

This case was known as the *Einsatzgruppen* Case, and the court explained that "when the German Armies, without any declaration of war, crossed the Polish frontier and smashed into Russia, there moved with and behind them a unique organization known as the Einsatzgruppen. As an instrument of terror in the museum of horror, it would be difficult to find an entry to surpass the Einsatzgruppen in its blood-freezing potentialities. No writer of murder fiction, no dramatist steeped in macabre lore, can ever expect to conjure up from his imagination a plot which will shock sensibilities as much as will the stark drama of these sinister bands."[45]

"Under the guise of insuring the political security of the conquered territories, both in the occupational and rear areas of the Wehrmacht, the Einsatzgruppen were to liquidate ruthlessly all opposition to National Socialism—not only the opposition of the present, but that of the past and future as well. Whole categories of people were to be killed without truce, without investigation, without pity, tears, or remorse. Women were to be slain with the men, and the children also were to be executed because, otherwise, they would grow up to oppose National Socialism and might even nurture a desire to avenge themselves on the slayers of their parents. . . . One of the principal categories was 'Jews.'"[46]

In the killing of women and children, "the Einsatzgruppen leaders encountered a difficulty they had not anticipated. Many of the enlisted men were husbands and fathers, and they winced as they pulled their triggers on those helpless creatures who reminded them of their own wives and offspring at home. In this emotional disturbance they often aimed badly and it was necessary for the [Einsatzkommando] leaders to go about with a revolver or carbine, firing into the moaning and writhing forms. This was hard on the executioners . . . and to relieve their emotional sensitivity, gas vans were sent to the rescue. These strange vehicles carried spurious windows and curtains and otherwise externally resembled family trailers. Women and children were lured into them with the announcement that they were to be resettled and that they would meet their husbands and fathers in the new place. Once inside the truck, the doors automatically and hermetically closed, the driver stepped on the accelerator, and monoxide gas from the engine streamed in. By the time the van reached its destination . . . the occupants were dead. And here they joined their husbands and fathers who had been killed by rifles and carbines in the hands of the Einsatzkommandos."[47]

On July 16, 1941, then SS *Obersturmführer* (First Lieutenant) Kulas was in Rezekne, Latvia, as part of *Einsatzgruppe* A, when local Latvian police executed at least sixty unarmed Jewish civilians in the woods. Kulas later maintained that he was there solely as an observer and defended himself as having no responsibility for this massacre.[48]

Kulas must have been worried than his involvement with *Einsatzgruppe* A and his presence at this execution could cause him trouble in the future. He may have been present or even involved in others that he was never tried for; at the time he could not know if any such atrocities would come back to haunt him. There was no way to know if there were survivors out there or other people willing to testify who could place him at the scene of any of the crimes committed by *Einsatzgruppe* A while he was a part of it.

He knew that his status as a former SS *Hauptsturmführer* alone could be a problem. While he could have fled and taken his chances at avoiding being caught, he decided instead to use what he had heard about the growing organization in Bavaria to try to protect himself.

While he was in Bad Tölz, Kulas's cover story worked perfectly. The HJ leaders he met with there trusted him, given his involvement with the HJ and his wartime service with the SS. They thought him a committed Nazi who was in a position to help them. Kulas hung around their operations and learned about the activities of these men since Axmann had sent them to Bavaria (before the end of the war).

Business was booming, as there was a tremendous demand for civilian transportation of all sorts of goods given how Germany now lay in ruins. A working business that could transport food would help keep the population from starving to death. And while it was summer, large amounts of coal to keep people from freezing would be needed when winter came.

According to an Associated Press story on June 2, 1945, "Munich is a hungry, dispirited city. Potatoes are scarce. The daily bread allowance is a little more than five ounces a person. Cabbage and lettuce have run short. The beer is thin and a new restriction will cut further into the brewery output. All these are mainstays of Germany's meatless diet."[49] Later in the article, the writer observed that "There are complaints that while the population used to be sure of getting its bread ration under the Nazis, today the bread often is gone before the end of the line gets into the bakery shop."[50]

On June 10, Kulas said good-bye to his new comrades in the Tess-mann concern, telling them he would be back in a couple of weeks. They invited him to join "as a permanent member of the organization" upon his return.[51] He used his MG pass to travel from Bad Tölz to nearby Munich. Once in Munich, he met with his CIC handlers for extensive debriefing on everything that he'd learned.

The CIC considered using what they'd discovered to make arrests and shut down Tessmann, but decided instead to pursue this matter further in order to gain "a true picture of HJ potentialities and any real-istic plan for its destruction."[52] The fear was that they didn't know enough about this group and that if they shut down Tessmann, while it would hurt this conspiracy of HJ leaders, it might not put an end to it.

And so, Kulas would go back to Bad Tölz to join the Tessmann group.

SIX

OPERATION NURSERY

Every good spy needs a cover. Be a journalist, they said.
You're good with words.

PAUL SOAMES IN THE MOVIE *SHANGHAI*[1]

The CIC reports on what would eventually be called Operation Nursery began on June 11, 1945. These first memorandums were designated secret, the second-highest level of protection. As such, they were above confidential and below top secret. In order to read them, one would need to possess a clearance of secret or higher and have a need to know the information in these reports as part of one's official duties. So, for example, even if someone had top-secret clearance, if his job was to monitor Japanese activities in the Philippines, he would not have a need to know about potential German resistance to the Allied occupation.

The first memo had the subject line of "Undercover activities of HITLER-JUGEND and WEHRWOLF In Southern Germany."[2] As Kulas had come to the CIC with talk about a Werwolf organization, that was what the CIC agents investigating the activities of the HJ in the Alps focused on. They knew that the initial setup of the Tessmann operation and the activities of the HJ leaders in the mountains of southern Germany and nearby Austria had their origins in Werwolf activities.

What they didn't know was what the current plans of the HJ leadership were, how many people were in this organization, what its resources were, or who was ultimately in charge of it. They knew that Axmann had ordered his followers to Bavaria, but knew nothing of what had become of him since he was last seen with Hitler in Berlin. The Soviets had pronounced him dead on a radio broadcast, but no body had been found.

While some Nazi organizations had neglected to properly destroy their records, one CIC agent working in occupied Germany later explained that "the Hitler Jugend made no such elementary mistakes for which, as a younger and less professional organization, they might have been excused more readily. Their headquarters was completely gutted not only of records but even of blank correspondence paper. This applied as well to each of the little sectional clubrooms. There were no membership lists, no financial statements, nothing at all. Even their bank accounts had been withdrawn and the bank officials had been forced to burn all records."[3]

This meant more work for the CIC to put together what the Hitler Youth National Office had been up to toward the end of the war. They had old intelligence about the organization and its leadership, but the current records had gone up in smoke.

It took time for CIC agents to debrief Kulas after he left Bad Tölz on June 10. He'd been down there for two days, and, fortunately for Agent Reis, he'd come back to the CIC office in Munich, instead of going on the run.

The Seventh Army had captured Munich at the end of April and still occupied it. As such, the CIC office there was run by the 307th CIC Detachment, which was a part of the Seventh Army.

A change in the disposition of American forces almost caused Reis and Nordheim to have to transfer this case to the Third Army CIC. The Third Army, under Patton, would take control of Munich while Reis, Nordheim, and the rest of their office (as part of the Seventh Army) would have to relocate to Augsburg, which was about an hour drive northwest of Munich. With this move, normally Reis would have handed over any active cases he had in the area to the incoming CIC agents.

As he later recalled, "I was reluctant to comply with this order because many of us in Seventh Army CIC knew that the agents in Third Army CIC were not given the same latitude and encouragement to 'operate' as we were, and any successful CIC work requires a tremendous amount of flexibility and skirting of military decorum."[4]

After some bureaucratic wrangling between the Third Army G-2, Reis's detachment commander Lieutenant Colonel Alvie MacDuff, and a Captain Timm of the SCIC (Special Counter Intelligence Corps) in Munich, the Seventh Army was able to keep this case.

Reis had to come up with a plan for how to handle this investigation and get approval for going forward with Kulas as a penetration agent instead of just rolling up what they knew of the Tessmann operation so far. If they wanted to get their questions answered and capture everyone involved in this conspiracy, they would need to keep investigating Tessmann.

Reis took everything he'd learned from Kulas about the Tessmann operation to date and "held a conference with Agent Mosely and other fellow agents, and discussed the various aspects of the events so far. The consensus was that our tail was either being pulled very cleverly, or we were coming on to something very important. We decided to play along with [Kulas] for a couple of weeks and see what transpired. We had a lot to gain and not much to lose. As one can readily see, we were hesitating somewhat because the information looked too good to be true. One must remember that Bad Tolz was the then headquarters of Lucky Rear, [the administrative headquarters of][5] General George Patton's Third Army, and it seemed highly inconceivable that anyone would have the audacity to begin such operations right under the nose of such a rugged personality, and almost under his patronage, so to speak, because the local MG unit was under Third Army's direction and it was this unit that had equipped this transportation firm with passes allowing them to travel anywhere within a 100 km. radius for the purpose of collecting foodstuffs. This circumvented, by legal means, the tough roadblocks Third Army was fond of bragging about and permitted a serious breach of security by German Nationals many of whom were automatic arrests."[6]

The Third Army roadblocks mentioned by Reis were otherwise so thorough that Reis himself was picked up by them and detained during this operation when driving from Munich to Bad Tölz. Reis should have had a badge, but he'd never been issued one. So far, he had gotten by with just an index card saying he was in the CIC, signed by his detachment commander.

This process went so far as his being "arraigned before the Provost Marshal at Lucky Rear"[7] before he was able to prove he was not a German spy, but an American CIC agent. Meanwhile, HJ leaders were passing through these same checkpoints by showing genuine travel passes issued by the local MG.

General George S. Patton, Jr., was perhaps the most famous American general of World War II, not just for leading the Third Army, but also for his often crude straight-talk.

In one speech to his troops, Patton proclaimed, "We'll win this war, but we'll win it only by fighting and by showing the Germans that we've got more guts than they have; or ever will have. We're not going to just shoot the sons-of-bitches, we're going to rip out their living Goddamned guts and use them to grease the treads of our tanks. We're going to murder those lousy Hun cocksuckers by the bushel-fucking-basket. War is a bloody, killing business. You've got to spill their blood, or they will spill yours. Rip them up the belly. Shoot them in the guts. When shells are hitting all around you and you wipe the dirt off your face and realize that instead of dirt it's the blood and guts of what once was your best friend beside you, you'll know what to do!"[8]

Patton also told his men that day, "There is one great thing that you men will all be able to say after this war is over and you are home once again. You may be thankful that twenty years from now when you are sitting by the fireplace with your grandson on your knee and he asks you what you did in the great World War II, you *won't* have to cough, shift him to the other knee and say, 'Well, your Granddaddy shoveled shit in Louisiana.' No, Sir, you can look him straight in the eye and say, 'Son, your Granddaddy rode with the Great Third Army and a Son-of-a-Goddamned-Bitch named Georgie Patton!'"[9]

The idea that the German resistance would center itself in the same town that Patton used as a base was hard for the CIC to swallow. Of course, when Axmann decided on Upper Bavaria as a retreat for HJ and BDM leaders, he would not have known who would be running the Military Government there. In fact, Patton himself had hoped to be transferred from running the Military Government for Bavaria to continue fighting in the ongoing war against Japan. Running an occupation force did not hold the same appeal to him as active combat.

While the Tessmann organization could have relocated when they found out Patton was in charge of this area, they were already well entrenched by then.

Although they were not entirely convinced that Kulas was telling them the truth, CIC Agents Nordheim and Reis proposed on June 25 to once again get an MG pass for their informant and send him down to Bad Tölz.[10] This time he would try to join the Tessmann concern to learn more about their operations, aims, and leadership.

Agent Mosely approved of their plan, and so on June 26, Reis and Nordheim headed toward Bad Tölz. Meanwhile, in San Francisco, delegates from fifty countries signed the United Nations Charter. For Reis and Nordheim, though, it was just another day of work as part of the American occupation of Germany.

They set Kulas up with passes and a vehicle permit for the areas occupied by the Americans in Munich and Bad Tölz. Kulas also had the use of a car, and the CIC paid him a salary for his full-time services as an informant. Reis also gave Kulas "proper instructions and identification in the event he was picked up by other CIC units."[11]

They had him continue with the cover story he'd already used. As Reis explained in a memo at the time, "his passes simply stated that he was employed by the Military Government to gather vehicles and auto parts, and that he had an operation area of 200 kms. from BAD TOLZ. To make certain that no German civilian working in Military Government would report who obtained [Kulas's] passes, no record was made of the permits and passes."[12]

That day, Reis and Nordheim drove ten kilometers to the west of Bad Tölz to a prearranged meeting spot. At 8 P.M., they met Kulas in person to give him the final go-ahead to try to join Tessmann. One of the first things that they wanted him to do was to check to see if high-ranking HJ leaders were still in charge of this trucking concern. Before taking off, the CIC agents told Kulas to meet with them the next night at a specific side road where no one would see them.

While Kulas worked on joining Tessmann, Reis and Nordheim stayed in Bad Tölz. Upon arriving, they first contacted Special Agent[13] Lawless, who was in charge of the CIC in Bad Tölz, to let him know they would be operating in his territory.

It was a small town and they needed a cover story to explain their presence there. Reis and Nordheim decided on the cover of being reporters with a focus on politics.[14]

Journalism was an especially useful cover for the CIC agents as not only did it explain what they were doing in Bavaria, but also it enabled them to interview people without raising undue suspicion.

If they ran into trouble and needed backup, the U.S. Army had forces in Bad Tölz in addition to the local CIC office. They were based where the *Waffen* SS had run their elite officer candidate school in this historic spa town. Called the *SS-Junkerschule Bad Tölz*, it trained the officers of the *Waffen* SS amid the majestic natural splendor of the Bavarian Alps.

The school made use of prisoners from Dachau for forced labor; they were kept in a subcamp in Bad Tölz itself. The Third Reich had put a great deal of money into building a premier facility—it included such amenities as a heated pool, sauna, and football stadium. Near the end of the war, the staff and students had formed a military group to fight the American soldiers. This group surrendered on May 8, 1945. The Americans took over this facility (known as Flint Kaserne) for themselves and stayed there long after the occupation was over.

At 7 P.M. on June 27, seven kilometers to the west of Bad Tölz, on a side road by the woods, the agents and their informant met again. The agents learned that the HJ had taken over Haus Zeppelin in Wackersberg two months before. While Kulas was able to hang around and pick up some useful intelligence, he had hit a wall in his attempt to get a job with Tessmann.

The head of the company, Heidemann, was not in town. Dr. Wandel, who said he was second in charge (the assistant manager) and the head of the local office, told Kulas that he couldn't hire him at this time. Kulas would have to wait to meet with Heidemann himself if he wanted a job with Tessmann.

Kulas did learn more about the firm though. Dr. Wandel told him the history of Tessmann, how it had been destroyed by the bombing of Dresden and later came to belong to the HJ leadership. By the time the

American forces came to Bavaria, Tessmann was ready to work with them. It had drivers, laborers, and working vehicles. As such, getting passes and permits from the Military Government had been easy. Tessmann now had a monopoly on the lucrative trade of vegetables in the area, among other contracts.

The next day, Kulas went back to Tessmann with the task of learning more about anyone new who had arrived at the firm while he had been in Munich. At 8 P.M., he again met with his CIC handlers, at a new location well outside of Bad Tölz. Kulas reported that HJ leaders had tried and failed to open two more offices of Tessmann—in Bremen and Weimar. His next task was to find out what the personnel at Tessmann thought of the occupation and what their long-range plans might be.

After having met at deserted locations outside of Bad Tölz where it was unlikely that anyone would see them together, the CIC agents came up with a way to meet with Kulas at their residence in Bad Tölz. They lived in a boardinghouse at Annastrasse 2, which was owned by a Mr. Muller, who knew them not as CIC agents, but as journalists.[15]

Agent Reis later described what living in this Upper Bavarian town was like: "While we were in Bad Tolz we were like fish out of water because we were in Third Army territory and the troops were still dressed in combat boots, head liners (some with steel helmet) and carried their weapons while we were in Class A uniform, overseas cap and oxfords and lived in a Pension."[16]

Kulas stopped by Annastrasse 2 and pretended not to know Reis or Nordheim. His stated purpose in coming there was to ask if anyone had certain spare auto parts he was looking to purchase. The owner then introduced him to the agents. Next, the agents said that while they did not have any parts to sell, their own vehicle could use some work. Now that they had business together that would satisfy anyone's suspicions, the three of them moved to Reis and Nordheim's rooms, ostensibly to discuss getting the car fixed.

Kulas felt that Dr. Wandel and the others had come to trust him. The attitudes of those at Tessmann toward the occupation forces were exactly what one might expect—they were against it, but much preferred the American and British Zones to the French and Soviet. Kulas also learned that "HEIDEMANN is the sole power in the firm of TESSMANN AND SONS, and is a man of very strong will with which he influences the thoughts of his co-workers. These co-workers of HEIDEMANN's are mostly all former members of the REICHSLEITUNG [national leadership] of HITLER JUGEND in BERLIN, and still very much in favor of rebuilding Germany along Nazi Doctrine Principles. When the Allies allow the German people the privilege of voting for a government system, HEIDEMANN wants to be in a position to be able to carry out certain ideas adopted by the INNER CIRCLE or the WEHRWOLF committee."[17] These ideas consisted of various tenets of National Socialism.

In the end of June, Kulas met the new dispatcher at Tessmann's Bad Tölz office—Kurt Pommerening.[18] When reporting to his handlers about Pommerening, Kulas explained that the dispatcher had never been part of the Nazi Party or any of its affiliates. Agents Nordheim and Reis realized that Pommerening might make a good informant.

His low position in the firm meant that he was unlikely to be part of the conspiracy of the HJ leaders running Tessmann. The fact that he was a recent addition also suggested that he could be someone who just thought he had a job at a trucking concern, not a large-scale Nazi conspiracy. He had arrived in Bad Tölz after the war (on May 13), as his fiancée lived there. His first day of work with Tessmann had been on June 25.

A second informant was useful both "to be prepared for the . . . future expansion of the firm and to insure a source of information."[19] It made sense to find someone who was already part of the firm rather than try to recruit an outsider, set him up with a cover, and then hope that he could entice someone at Tessmann into hiring him.

In order to vet Pommerening as a potential informant, Nordheim and Reis approached him directly on the evening of July 2, using their cover as journalists. They claimed that they'd heard of his life story and wanted to write about it. In this way, they were able to question him extensively about his life without arousing his suspicions.

Pommerening "created a good impression on these agents, because of his hatred of Nazism, his frankness and his political outlook."[20] While it was easy to claim to two American journalists that he hated Nazism now that Germany was occupied, Pommerening seemed sincere and his background was compelling.

Born in Berlin on June 21, 1917, Kurt Pommerening had a degree in engineering from the technical high school of Berlin. He had served in the German Army, but been discharged because of his Jewish ancestry—he had a Jewish parent (as the CIC put it, "he was half-Jew").[21] He'd worked as an engineer but had troubles, again because of his heritage. Eventually, the Nazi regime took away his freedom and made him work as a forced laborer in a salt mine in west-central Germany from October 1944 to April 1945, when American troops finally freed him.

Nordheim and Reis felt like they'd found their man, but they decided to wait a few days before approaching him about becoming an informant. It was not surprising to find that Tessmann had hired someone of Jewish descent. Such hires would help to conceal the fact that this organization was run by Nazis.

On July 4, while American servicemen were celebrating their first American Independence Day in conquered Germany, the CIC anointed Kulas with his new codename of Karl.[22] It was not a day off for Nordheim and Reis though; they spent this holiday following two suspects about a half hour west of Bad Tölz to the town of Habach. Among other things, Habach had a vehicle depot used by the German

Army. Not only had Tessmann used German Army vehicles to start their operations, but they were using this depot to get parts.

When Siegfried Kulas returned to Bad Tölz on June 26 (on the trip discussed above), Willi Heidemann was away on important business for Tessmann & Sons. He was in the Ruhr trying to get coal supplies to deliver to Bavaria and Austria. While there, he was also working on expanding Tessmann's reach to include using ships to transport materials from the Ruhr to Bavaria.

It was important for him to get new contracts, new bases of operations, and new means of transportation as quickly as possible. Although Tessmann had been the first on the ground in Bavaria and so had been ready to transport goods from day one of the occupation, as time passed, other transportation firms had set up operations elsewhere. In order for the reach of his operation to grow, Heidemann needed to secure access to key goods before his competitors did.

The Ruhr area in northwest Germany contained large amounts of coal and was controlled by the British. Another major coal area, the Saar region, was controlled by the French, who Heidemann feared would have more of a grudge against the Germans than the British or Americans, as their country had suffered greatly from German occupation.

Coal (along with food) was key to survival in postwar Germany and Austria. It was used to heat buildings, and without it, people would freeze to death in the coming winter. There was already a huge black market in luxury goods such as alcohol and cigarettes, but food and coal were basic items that even with severe rationing would be hard to procure.

If he could secure a steady supply of coal, not only would Tessmann be able to provide an invaluable service to the Military Government in the areas where it operated, but he would also enable the expansion of the firm's territory and the accumulation of profits for their cause.

In making this trip, Heidemann had been able to get passes through the American Zone from the current economic minister for Bavaria. He then used his own resources to get through the British Zone. This trip was a success—Heidemann received a contract for forty thousand tons of coal to bring to Bavaria and thirty thousand tons for Austria.[23] He created a new company to handle this transaction—the Rhino-Bavaria Coal Company.

While Heidemann was away, HJ *Hauptbannführer* Dweblow, who had been the head of finance for the HJ, and HJ *Bannführer* Kowalksy, who had worked for him, failed to open an office in Bremen as the local transportation companies blocked them from operating there. In Weimar, HJ *Obersbannführer* Suess ran into problems because a group of survivors from the nearby concentration camp of Buchenwald had set up operations there.

Not only were these survivors already up and running, but the occupation forces there preferred to deal with victims of the Nazi regime rather than Tessmann's operatives. Even though the Military Government in Weimar didn't know that unrepentant Nazis ran Tessmann, they still could not compete there given the Military Government's sympathies for those who had survived the brutalities of Buchenwald.

It was in his position on the German desk that Hunter came across the reports being filed by CIC Special Agent Timothy Reis about the HJ activity around Bad Tölz. These reports intrigued him, and he checked them out with other sources of intelligence. None of the other desks knew anything useful, so Hunter started asking questions beyond the third floor of the Farben Building. He went to lunch with the British liaison officer and got nothing.[24] Trying to pull files on some of the names mentioned also went nowhere.

Having hit a dead end, Hunter drove to the nearby city of Heidelberg to see if the Office of Strategic Services ("OSS") knew anything. The OSS was a predecessor to the CIA. Hunter was surprised to learn that the OSS had been made aware of this operation early on through its X-2 branch, which handled counter espionage. The OSS though had declined an active role in this operation, leaving it to the CIC. However, the relevant documents about this had not crossed Hunter's desk, as they should have.

Around this time, Hunter's job changed as part of a larger reorganization. He was now a CIC special agent assigned to the 970 CIC Detachment, USFET, though he still worked in the Farben Building. In his new role, he had the privilege of just wearing a plain uniform with brass U.S. insignia when not undercover. Hunter was happy about this change as it meant "no more prim looks from condescending jerks."[25] He remained the case officer for Operation Nursery.

The CIC issued Hunter credentials (No. 6296) and a badge (No. C-5076).[26] When in uniform, he carried them in his pockets. While undercover, he hid them in the lining of his overcoat so he had them in case of an emergency, but hopefully, they would not be found if he were casually frisked or his pockets turned out.[27]

In Frankfurt, Hunter lived in a large apartment on Vom-Rath-Strasse.[28] While much of the city had been bombed back to the Stone Age, the area near the IG Farben Building had fared better. Hunter was even able to walk to work, as his apartment was just a fifteen-minute stroll from his office.

Meanwhile, in the northern German village of Lansen, Artur Axmann, the onetime head of the Hitler Youth, now lived on a simple farm.

Using the name of Erich Siewert, he lived in Soviet-controlled territory with a family of farmers—a woman, her husband, and their three daughters. Their daughters varied in age from fourteen to twenty years old.

Although the daughters had all been in the BDM, they did not recognize Axmann.[29]

Even though he only had one arm, he was able to perform his central function on the farm. His job was to sit in the barn and gaze out a small window that overlooked the main road into town. When he saw anyone coming toward the farm, he sounded an alarm. The girls then scurried to their hiding places within the hay stacked in this barn.

The family worried that Soviet soldiers would rape the girls, maybe also killing them or taking them away. This family was not being paranoid; such sexual violence against women was endemic in Soviet occupied Germany.[30]

And so Axmann sat in the barn, looking out a window. He had gone from commanding nine million German youths, to a bunch of armed boys in Berlin while at Hitler's side, to now sitting watch in a barn to protect three girls.[31]

SEVEN

THE FIRST ARRESTS

The problems of victory are more agreeable than those of
defeat, but they are no less difficult.

WINSTON CHURCHILL[1]

Now that the war was over and the Allied occupation firmly in place,
Heidemann wanted to move his trucking operation from an unimportant backwater in the American Zone (the Bavarian Alps) to the center
of American power—Frankfurt. General Eisenhower himself was
there as head of the American Military Government, in the massive IG
Farben Building.

Axmann had sent his leadership to Upper Bavaria because it was to
be part of the National Redoubt from which the Nazis would continue
the fight if Berlin fell. And the Werwolf operation there could fight
even if all of Germany fell. But now that Germany was occupied, and
Heidemann and his followers were working with the Americans and
British to deliver goods, Heidemann wanted to keep the office in Bad
Tölz while transferring the group's leadership to the heart of the American occupation.

This brazen attempt to hide a postwar Nazi operation as a mere trucking concern achieved some significant initial success. They did business with the Military Government, and it provided them with the travel passes and other permissions they required to conduct their commercial and political enterprises.

Heidemann hoped to be able to move Tessmann's HQ to Frankfurt once he concluded his negotiations for coal in the Ruhr. Dr. Wandel, as the assistant manager, would go with him. While awaiting Heidemann's return, Dr. Wandel confessed to Kulas that "he was becoming worried over having so many high ranking former officials of the REICHSLEITUNG [national leadership] of the HJ, hiding in the HAUS ZEPPELIN in WACKERSBURG."[2]

HJ leaders kept streaming into Upper Bavaria—many of them had been unable to come earlier owing to the chaos at the war's end and the difficulty of traveling once Germany was occupied. Few Germans had access to working automobiles, the gas needed to run them, or the Military Government papers authorizing them to travel by any means, let alone with a vehicle. Former leaders of the HJ would generally have to travel on foot, along with the hordes of displaced persons and others clogging the roads.

As the HJ and BDM leadership arrived into the Bad Tölz area, it became increasingly important to expand the business and move people to offices elsewhere. If the Allies, through the CIC, were to get word that a large group of former HJ leaders were congregating in one place, they would certainly investigate.

Dr. Wandel had no idea that his concerns were moot, as the CIC already knew all about those HJ leaders who were in Bavaria. Ironically, he was revealing his fears to the very person who had already made them come true by telling the CIC everything he knew about the operation.

Max Lebens, who toward the end of the war had been in charge of setting things up in Bad Tölz for arriving Werwolves, now returned to

Bad Tölz. His father-in-law had donated the Tessmann company corporate shell to the HJ. Lebens had been busy setting up and running the local office for Tessmann in Bruck by Zell am See in the nearby Austrian Alps. He'd had a close call on his trip to Wackersberg, when the American Military Police (MPs) arrested him for speeding. He'd spent eight days locked up without anyone questioning him about his Nazi past. Despite his desire to meet with Heidemann, Lebens had to rush back to Austria before his travel permit for Germany expired.

Siegfried Kulas had heard that Tessmann was opening an office in Munich. *Bannführer* Moser, who had worked in the KLV, had been tasked with setting up a branch office at Trogerstrasse 15 in central Munich.

On June 30, the CIC sent Kulas to Munich to find out more about what, if anything, was happening there. They would meet him there the next day. There had been a lot of talk at Tessmann about expanding quickly and setting up new offices, but it was not clear as of yet which plans would actually come to fruition. For example, when Lebens had visited Tessmann's headquarters, he'd mentioned the possibility of opening up a new office in Lübeck—a major port city in the north of Germany. Before Lübeck had been heavily bombed during the war, the prior incarnation of Tessmann had been based there.

Whether Lebens would be successful or find himself unable to compete with existing transportation companies, only time would tell.

In Munich, Kulas found that an office for Tessmann's transportation business had been set up with a small staff, but that since it lacked any vehicles, it was not yet a going concern. With nothing more to do in Munich, Kulas went back to Bad Tölz to await Heidemann's return.

When in Munich, Reis and Nordheim stayed in a private residence they had requisitioned near the local CIC office. The shift in control of Munich from the Seventh Army to the Third Army, which had initially threatened to pull this case from them, ended up giving them a great deal of freedom. Reis still turned in weekly reports, but he and Nordheim were able to work on this case full-time without having to put in face time at their office. They could stop by the local CIC office in Munich to enjoy the free food, but were otherwise on their own. They only had to visit Seventh Army territory every few weeks to get their mail and check in. This was the only case to which they were assigned.

On July 5, CIC agents Nordheim and Reis recruited Pommerening as their second informant. They gave him the codename of "Paul" and revealed to him that the people he was working for had been high-ranking members of the HJ adult leadership. He "was very much surprised and agreed to these Agents' request that he cooperate with them by supplying all available information on the daily happenings and operations of the firm, and that he follow their future orders. PAUL was told to report to these agents at Anna Str 2 every day in the evening, or in the event of something important, as soon as possible. The instructions given him were to report the arrival and departure of any new people in TESSMANN and SONS firm, and to make copies of any correspondence passing through his department or available to him without revealing his purpose as to the disposition of such papers. PAUL was further told not to endanger his person and under no circumstances make himself suspicious by an unexpected display of knowledge concerning TESSMANN and SONS."[3]

Unlike Kulas, Pommerening had nothing in his past that would be considered criminal now that Germany had lost the war. Nor did he ask for money or a car. He helped because he genuinely hated the Nazis and was upset to discover that he'd been working for them.

The next morning, July 6, Pommerening met his handlers and gave them copies of letters that he'd found at Tessmann. These letters included mention of an office in Augsburg and of three new offices in the works: Regensburg, Nuremberg, and Wurzburg.

Kulas finally arranged to meet with Heidemann, and an unexpected opportunity arose. Heidemann's car had broken down, and he asked Kulas to drive him and his companions on a five-day trip to Austria. Kulas's penetration of the firm continued with Dr. Wandel asking him to move into their residential facilities at Haus Zeppelin.

Meanwhile, Pommerening continued to gather intelligence on Tessmann. He was not hobnobbing with the firm's leadership like Kulas, but he had access to routine documents and correspondence that Kulas did not have.[4]

When CIC Agents Nordheim and Reis tried to meet with Kulas in Zell am See, at 8 P.M. near the town post office, they saw him talking with Heidemann and a buyer for Tessmann. The agents watched discreetly for half an hour, until Kulas walked by them and "whispered that he would return to the same place at 2200 hours."[5] When they came back at the appointed time, they all stayed in their respective vehicles. They weren't taking any chances on being spotted together in town. Instead, Kulas drove a mile or so outside of town while his handlers followed him to this secluded spot.

As Reis later described them, "Our meetings with [Kulas] varied from village taverns to a manure pile behind a farmer's barn with an occasional meeting in our quarters at the Pension. It was like having a good hunting dog on an invisible leash and following him around from one interesting scent to another."[6]

At this debriefing, Kulas told his handlers about the meetings Heidemann had in Austria regarding Tessmann and the distribution of coal. He informed them that Max Lebens had to give up Tessmann's operations in Austria and leave there, as he was one of many Germans being expelled from the country. The company was turned over to Austrians, with Heidemann still controlling the business as the primary stockholder (he had 500,000 reichsmarks invested in the company). They changed the name in Austria to Klug and Company.

Reis was surprised to learn that Tessmann had a penetration agent of its own working in the Third Army's Military Government office. As Reis recalled, "During his visits to Bad Tolz [Kulas] came to know that the local MG office had a girl secretary, a former BDM member who . . . was able to influence the officer in charge of the MG unit, to issue permits to their transportation firm to travel to Frankfurt on the Main over 400 kms. away. This was fantastic! All Germans were under strict curfew not to travel over 30 kms. from their residence and only with passes. Their arms had been confiscated, they were not allowed to operate vehicles, had to stand in ration lines, not allowed to fraternize with their conquerors and to cease all political activity—but in Bad Tolz a favored few were furnished passes, supplies, gasoline and allowed a line of communication denied other civilians. [Kulas] also reported that he had seen several young teenagers, 14 to 16 year olds, at the transportation firm on his visits and he thought that they were being used as couriers. This was something we had overlooked but very logical to the structure of the HJ organization and an arm that could very well be used quite effectively on roadblocks, because of the sympathetic nature of our GI's."[7]

This underground group of former HJ leaders often used BDM girls as couriers, in addition to HJ boys, as they were unlikely to arouse suspicion. Also, they used BDM personnel to infiltrate MG offices. The local Bad Tölz MG office was not the only one with a BDM plant to help this burgeoning HJ-based conspiracy. Reis eventually found out that these plants were more widespread than he had initially suspected.

Later in life, Reis reflected on this stage of his investigation, writing that "this once small organization . . . seemed to be springing up everywhere and infiltrating MG and other units of our military by placing attractive young women in secretarial and other sensitive positions. FRAGEBOGEN which are questionnaires required to be filled out by the civilian population for screening purposes were some of the 'sensitive' areas that these young women would be of great help to their fellow HJ members."[8] Through their administrative positions, these women could, among other things, interfere with the *Fragebogen* process if it threatened any of their comrades, such as HJ leaders.

Reis went on to say that "Some officers in MG were later embarrassed by our disclosures on breaches of security"[9] when these young women were exposed as part of this operation.

On July 9, while still in Austria, Kulas ran into the head of the BDM, Dr. Jutta Rüdiger. He'd heard rumors before that she was in Austria. The CIC, in the person of Agent Reis, very much wanted to locate her.

As Agent Reis later put it, "The whereabouts of Jutta Rudiger and her staff were now our goal for two reasons: (1) If it became known that she had survived [the fall of Berlin] she could become a rallying point for other members of the BDM and possibly form a nucleus for an organization with similar aims to the original one; (2) If we were able to work [out] a plan that would enable us to remove her from the scene without creating too much of a ripple in our operation and, through interrogation extract pertinent information now, it could mean saving time and effort and eliminate a major threat to MG's prime objective— the re-indoctrination of the German masses from National Socialism to a democratic form of government."[10]

When Kulas saw Rüdiger, she was with her counterpart for adult women—*Reichsfrauenführerin* (Reich Women's Leader) Gertrud Scholz-Klink. Scholz-Klink had been head of the women's wing of the Nazi Party, but she had no control over the BDM or Dr. Rüdiger, who instead reported to Axmann. Also with them was *Bannführerin* Karola Hedwig Böhmer (who had been a personnel officer in the Reich Youth Leadership in Berlin).[11]

Dr. Rüdiger was a psychologist who specialized in treating young people (pediatrics). In November 1937, at the age of twenty-seven, she had taken over control of the BDM. Her predecessor, Trude Mohr, had just resigned, in accordance with Nazi Party policy, when she married.

As head of the BDM (*Reichsreferentin des BDM* or Reichs Deputy of the BDM), Rüdiger reported directly to *Reichsjugendführer* Baldur von Schirach and later to his replacement, Artur Axmann. Although the BDM and the Nazis in general had a policy of not using women to fight in the war, at the end there were BDM girls who did directly fight the enemy along with their HJ peers.

Rüdiger credibly maintained that she had nothing to do with this, and that such actions were taken by the girls themselves during the confusion of the end of the war. Also, one BDM leader, Ilse Hirsch, took part in the Werwolf operation that assassinated Aachen mayor Franz Oppenhoff, but that operation was not run by Dr. Rüdiger.

While Martin Bormann had expressed a strong interest in having women fight, both Axmann and Rüdiger were against this. Rüdiger later said, "Only at the very end did I allow the girls to be trained in pistol shooting, in order to defend themselves if they were in dire need or even to kill themselves."[12]

What she did sanction though was the use of BDM girls to assist at antiaircraft artillery batteries, starting in 1943. This resulted in casualties because such groupings of antiaircraft guns were of course targets for Allied planes. BDM girls also served in supporting roles during the end of the war, which could be quite dangerous, such as helping wounded soldiers. Serving in any capacity toward the end was perilous. One such example was Berlin BDM leader Gisela Hermann, who was seriously injured after exiting Axmann's final command post near the Reich Chancellery.

Unlike Artur Axmann and Gisela Hermann, Dr. Jutta Rüdiger had not stayed in Berlin until the bitter end. She took a train on April 13,

1945, from Berlin, arriving in the Bad Tölz area a week later to meet up with other HJ and BDM leaders.[13]

As she later recounted, "from the Reichsjugendführer [Axmann], we were given the instruction that all the leaders of the Reich Youth Leadership should be sent home to their parents, but not the section chiefs who should be sent to the south into [the Highlands Camp] of the HJ near the area of Bad Tölz."[14] According to Rüdiger, when Axmann gave these orders, he "had promised to follow us into the camp" but "he remained in Berlin, after the Führer had decided not to leave the capital."[15]

From Bad Tölz, she went to the KLV camp in Zell am See on April 30, and later made her way to Austria, where Kulas eventually found her.

Kulas only spoke with Rüdiger briefly that day, but he learned that she was hiding out on a nearby farm. Heidemann told Kulas that he felt "responsible, in a sense, for all former High HJ personalities, and that he wouldn't rest easy until women like JUTTA RUEDIGER and other high ranking BDM people were safely out of his territory, because of the danger of arrest and possible disclosure of facts pertaining to the present activities and future goal of HJ."[16]

Reis and Nordheim were in a bind—they wanted to capture Rüdiger, as she could tell them more about the current HJ conspiracy, and she had been a high-ranking Nazi, but they didn't want to compromise Kulas. And they didn't have much time to come up with a way to capture her without raising Heidemann's suspicions that Kulas had something to do with it. She was going to move soon and hide out far away from Tessmann's operations, so they knew that they might never find her again.

The first part of his handlers' plan was for Kulas to visit Rüdiger at her hiding place on an Austrian farm and volunteer to drive her to her next location. This took advantage of the fact that he had a car, gasoline, and travel passes for himself and his vehicle. Of course, he had all of this thanks to his CIC handlers. It made him appear as a godsend to those who needed to travel in occupied Germany and Austria.

Kulas was supposed to try to find out where Rüdiger was traveling, so even if something went wrong while he was driving her or she got a ride with someone else, the CIC would know where she was going. However, the key was for Kulas to make the offer casually, because if he appeared too eager to give her a ride, it could raise Rüdiger's suspicions. While a wanted woman hiding out in occupied territory might not look a gift horse in the mouth, there still was the danger that Rüdiger could realize that even someone who had served with the SS and the HJ could have his reasons for turning her in.

When Kulas made contact with Rüdiger at her hiding place outside of Bruck, Austria, he was in luck. She'd previously made plans to get out of the country, but they had just fallen through. She would be stuck where she was unless she could come up with a new way out. And so Kulas had what his handlers called "the perfect opening" to offer her a ride.[17]

With this stroke of good fortune (for Kulas that is, not so much for Dr. Rüdiger), they were in business. Rüdiger would ride with him on the afternoon of July 13.

Moreover, Rüdiger clearly trusted him, as she not only agreed to the ride, but also told him in advance of her travel plans. The smart move would have been for her not to trust anyone more than she needed to, even an SS war veteran. She could have waited until they were under way to tell him her final destination.

On the morning of July 12, Kulas told his handlers what the plans were for the next day's travels. Given this information, Reis and Nordheim decided to allow the trip to play out and apprehend Rüdiger, and any companions she brought with her, once they arrived at their destination. They theorized that this would minimize the chance that anyone would suspect Kulas of having something to do with Rüdiger's capture.

On July 13, Kulas met his handlers in the nearby town of Zell am See an hour before his scheduled departure. Everything was a go, he reported, with a new passenger, BDM *Bannführerin* Melita Maschmann, added to his little group for a total of four female Nazis.

Maschmann had been a press officer in the Reich Youth Leadership in Berlin. She joined her fellow BDM officers after she had "chanced to hear where they were living. They wanted to avoid being arrested by the Austrian Resistance, and as I had some experience of crossing frontiers illegally, they asked me to take them to Reichenhall. Just as we were ready to start, a former employee of the Personnel Department of the Reich Youth Leadership suddenly appeared and offered to drive us to Reichenhall in his car. I did not even know him by sight, but my colleagues had worked with him."[18]

The man who offered to drive them was, of course, Kulas. After meeting with CIC Agents Reis and Nordheim, Kulas drove to Bruck to meet up with Rüdiger, *Bannführerin* Karola Böhmer, *Bannführerin* Melita Maschmann, and a BDM leader named Gerda Dinglinger.[19]

They squeezed into Kulas's car and left Bruck, driving east, then heading north via Wefen and Hallein toward Salzburg. Salzburg is a major Austrian city close to the German border for Upper Bavaria.

None of these passengers noticed they were being followed. Because Reis and Nordheim knew where Kulas was heading, they could hang back and follow from a distance without worrying about losing him.

Outside of Salzburg, Austria, their first destination was an intersection of three different major highways. This intersection lay near the border with Germany. The Americans had a checkpoint in operation along the road into Germany where they inspected people's papers.

According to the CIC report filed by Agent Reis, Kulas dropped off his passengers before the checkpoint and then proceeded to drive up to it on his own.[20] His papers were in order—the CIC had made sure of that. Meanwhile, in this version of events, Rüdiger and her three comrades hiked through the surrounding woods.

The CIC report for July 12, 1945, stated that "where the three auto-bahns meet . . . RUEDIGER would get out and walk through the woods to avoid the border control post because she didn't think her pass papers were in order enough to let her through. After passing the border, RUEDIGER would meet [Kulas] about one kilometer in Germany, and continue the journey."[21]

Seven years before, in March 1938, Germany had annexed Austria. The border between them was not fortified—there was no fence or other barrier for Rüdiger to have to slip past. The long, mountainous border through the thick forests of the Bavarian Alps was all but impossible to police. All the BDM women had to do was walk about a kilometer into Germany, and then meet back up with Kulas.

Unlike Axmann, who was then hiding out with no papers at all, these BDM leaders did have some documents. Walter Bergemann, Tessmann's legal adviser and an *Oberbannführer* (major) in the HJ, had earlier furnished three of the women with ID documents known as *Kennkarten*.[22] They also had on them half a year's pay each, provided by Heidemann. As she had just arrived, Maschmann had not received any documents from Bergemann. Instead, she had papers that she had forged herself. During the time since Germany lost the war, Maschmann had gained the ability to "forge every kind of American pass on a typewriter."[23] She also had a legitimate certificate from the local police in Zell am See.

Melita Maschmann's recollection of this border crossing appears to differ from what is in the CIC report. Decades later, she wrote, "Getting past the sentry at the frontier, a negro soldier, was so easy that looking back, I realize that we should have guessed he was expecting us."[24] She didn't mention any walk through the woods, despite what was in the CIC report. Nor did Jutta Rüdiger's account in her memoir of this trip.[25]

Regardless of how they crossed the border, once they were in Germany, Kulas drove the women to their final destination—the town of Bad Reichenhall. Like Bad Tölz, this was a small Upper Bavarian spa and vacation village. Bad Reichenhall, though, was even closer to the border—from the center of town to the Austrian border was about a mile.[26]

Rüdiger's sister-in-law was at the hospital there. Kulas did not know what their travel plans were after they visited this hospital.

However, Kulas did know that Heidemann had relayed to Rüdiger that he wanted her to relocate to the British Zone. Heidemann was afraid that she was too high-profile, and that if the Americans found her, she might inadvertently lead them to him and the rest of the Tessmann operation. Heidemann also wanted to hold on to the funds he had accumulated. He worried that she might lay claim to some of them, given her position directly below Axmann. As such, he wanted her to have nothing to do with his ongoing buildup of Tessmann.

Now was the time for the CIC to capture Rüdiger, while she was in American controlled territory and they knew exactly where she was. Picking up these unarmed women would be easy. Reis did not expect them to resist. The tricky part was to do so without implicating Kulas. They didn't want anyone back at Tessmann to suspect his treachery.

Agents Reiss and Nordheim figured out a way to make these first arrests in Operation Nursery without Kulas being there. In the hospital, Reis arranged to pretend to have someone happen to recognize Rüdiger and so arrest her and her companions. Rüdiger was high-profile enough that this was plausible—many young German women and girls, at least, would recognize their former leader.

Reis later described this operation: "We carried off the chance encounter in the hospital and the ensuing automatic arrest and loaded them bag and baggage in our jeep and headed for Munich arriving late in the night. After a little rest we transferred them to a larger vehicle to the Seventh Army Detention Center for interrogation. It had taken us just 36 hours of continuous travel to pull off this snatch—taking one of the bigger HJ personalities out of circulation and apparently without causing much commotion in our operation of the case."[27]

Once arrested, Maschmann wrote, "We were taken into Munich in a jeep the same night. On the way I tore up my forged passes with tiny movements of my hands, so that our guard did not notice, and scattered them to the night winds."[28] The CIC did not discover this and so had no idea that she had possessed forged papers. The only document they found on her was her certificate from the Austrian police.

Despite the precautions taken by the CIC, those captured did suspect that Kulas had betrayed them. "The 'helpful' comrade had deliberately driven us into a trap," Maschmann later wrote. "At least that is how we interpreted what happened."[29] However, these BDM officers had no way to get word back to their comrades in the HJ leadership about their suspicions regarding Siegfried Kulas.

Although they tried to deny their true identities, all four captives quickly cracked and admitted the truth.

Kulas had dropped off his passengers and left the hospital before they were arrested. Now that they had been picked up, he anxiously kept an ear out for any word about their capture. This was the first action that he had taken that could result in his Nazi comrades suspecting him of being a rat. Until now, the only risk he had taken was in meeting with the CIC; this time the CIC had actually done something based on the intelligence provided to them.

If the HJ leaders at Tessmann figured out that Kulas was working with the Americans, they would likely kill him as a traitor. While the

CIC would then try to quickly arrest everyone they knew about and shut down Tessmann, it might take them some time to determine that their operation was blown. So not only would the operation then end before they found out who else was involved in this Nazi conspiracy, but those hidden in the shadows would be able to go to ground. The CIC did not know where the Tessmann funds were being stored (beyond what was in the company's accounts), so these HJ leaders might be able to take the money and disappear into the chaos of postwar Germany.

When the news of the BDM arrests reached Tessmann headquarters two or three weeks later, no one suspected Kulas at all. In fact, Heidemann assumed that Rüdiger was caught because she had been careless and he was relieved that she was out of the picture. He didn't think she knew enough about his current operations to be a danger, or that if she did, she wouldn't say anything. He had no idea that she had talked, and everything she'd said validated what Kulas had been reporting to the CIC.[30]

One night, while with Siegfried Kulas and various HJ leaders, Willi Heidemann proclaimed that "when Hitler died, Frederick the Great died a second time."[31] Frederick the Great had been the King of Prussia in the eighteenth century, and he was a popular German historical figure. Hitler admired him greatly and famously had a portrait of Frederick the Great with him in the bunker.

When asked which of the three Western occupation forces (American, British, or French) he found the easiest to work with, Heidemann said they were all sons of bitches, "but that the English were the most polite and smoothest of the three."[32]

While in Austria, Heidemann met up with Max Lebens. There they had a nasty fight over money. When Lebens had been in jail for speeding, someone had taken 100,000 reichsmarks from his bags. He thought it had to be someone from Tessmann, but instead of trying to figure out who exactly took the money, he told Heidemann to pay up. This was a lot of money. Heidemann felt there was no reason for him to hand it over, as he didn't know anything about this incident and he'd had nothing to do with it.

Heidemann said to Kulas, "I have worked very hard in the past three months, but if I am to be blackmailed by one of our own men, I'll give up the whole idea."[33] He went on to say, "I was ordered to invest the money of HJ for future use, and if the things I was ordered to do are not possible, I will give up!"[34] Although Heidemann did not use his name in this talk with Kulas, Axmann had given him this order.

The U.S. Army in Europe had been part of Supreme Headquarters, Allied Expeditionary Force ("SHAEF"). In the middle of July, SHAEF ceased to exist. Now that the war in Europe was over, there was no longer any need for this joint command of American, British, Canadian, and French forces. American forces in Europe were now organized as United States Forces, European Theater ("USFET").[35] General Eisenhower had been in charge of SHAEF, and he was now in charge of USFET.

However, life in the Farben Building was the same for Hunter under either name. He still worked in Frankfurt much of the time.

As his brother later told the story, one summer day in Frankfurt, Jack Hunter was driving around in a Mercedes while wearing civilian clothes. He pulled up to a stop by a traffic cop, and while waiting to be waved through, a jeep full of army nurses pulled next to him. The driver asked him in bad German which way it was to the IG Farben Building. He mustered his best Brooklyn accent to give directions in English, and the nurse who was driving was still sitting there with this look on her face like she didn't know what had happened to her.[36]

He enjoyed being a bit of a goofball. In a postcard he sent to his wife that summer, he wrote about being in Germany: "Lots of Germans—many, many Germans. They speak German too. . . ."[37] On the face side of the postcard was the Hotel Nassauer Hof, which was in use as a rest facility for CIC personnel.

What he didn't know at the time was that he had just become the father of twin daughters. On July 23, 1945, his wife gave birth, but it took time for the news to reach him.

Meanwhile, Artur Axmann spent June and July of 1945 continuing to hide out in northern Germany.

If he could be useful to the occupying powers, then he could turn himself in and hope that they would cut some kind of deal with him. For example, the OSS recruited German scientists and technical personnel who had worked with areas the Third Reich had excelled at, such as rocketry, cryptography, synthetic fuel, and aeronautics.

As part of OSS Operation Paperclip, even scientists who had been Nazis or who had committed war crimes were relocated to the United States. The OSS used various tricks to hide the scientists' troubled pasts because President Truman had ordered them not to recruit Nazis. If Truman's order had been followed though, many valuable scientists would have been left behind for the British, French, or Soviets to recruit.

Another group of Nazis recruited by the Allies had previously spied for Germany. With tensions rising between the United States and the Soviet Union, German intelligence agents who had knowledge of the Soviet Union were in demand. The most prominent of these was General Reinhard Gehlen, who turned himself in to the CIC in late May. Brigadier General Edwin Sibert, Eisenhower's G-2, eventually approved the use of Gehlen and his former associates to continue their work against the Soviet Union. This time they spied for the Americans, instead of the Nazis.

However, Axmann was neither a scientist nor a spy. Turning himself in to one of the occupying powers would accomplish nothing for him, as he was not useful to them.

Some other high-ranking Nazis in this situation tried to escape Europe altogether. One of the best known examples is SS *Obersturmbannführer* (Lieutenant Colonel) Adolf Eichmann, who eventually fled Europe using a fraudulently issued Red Cross travel document with a fake name and escaped to Argentina. Different escape routes for wanted Nazis came into existence in the years after the Third Reich collapsed. They were known as ratlines and often ended in South American countries like Argentina.

However, Axmann had no desire to leave his beloved Germany. His wife Ilse still lived in Berlin with their young son. Although things were over with his wife, they had decided not to go through a divorce in the midst of the chaos of the war turning against Germany. Now that he was in hiding, a divorce was out of the question. His girlfriend, Erna, lived in the German countryside with her family.

He had another reason to stay—his followers were still hard at work building up Tessmann. Although he knew his former underlings in the HJ and BDM had gathered in the Alps (as he was the one who sent them there), trying to contact them now would have been risky and difficult.

He had no money, as the HJ funds he'd tried to take with him out of Berlin had been lost during the breakout. He did own some real estate in Berlin, but he could not claim it since he was in hiding. If things had gone according to plan, though, Heidemann would be busy in Bavaria building up a future for them.

He felt it best to wait until things calmed down a bit in Germany, and he was in a better position to travel safely.

EIGHT

LIFE IN OCCUPIED GERMANY

He alone, who owns the youth, gains the Future!

ADOLF HITLER[1]

In mid-July, the CIC's main informant in this case, Siegfried Kulas, was busy working his way into Tessmann and Sons. He received a contract from Tessmann for a job as an assistant to Walter Bergemann, the firm's legal adviser. HJ *Oberbannführer* Bergemann had previously been in charge of the HJ's Bureau of Legal Administration (*Amt Rechtsverwaltung*). In addition, Bergemann had served with Axmann in the army in 1939.

Kulas's real job with them, though, would be to help with procuring the parts for their vehicles. Ironically, clause three of the contract specified, "Mr. KULAS is ordered not to divulge any business secrets of the Firm TESSMANN & SONS, GmbH."[2] Of course, he already was divulging every secret of theirs he could learn, and would continue to do so after signing the contract. This included even giving a copy of this contract itself, with this clause, to his CIC handlers.

Meanwhile, another CIC informant, Kurt Pommerening, was introduced to the local CIC agents in Bad Tölz so he could continue to turn over any documents or information he uncovered even when Reis and Nordheim were back in Munich.

On July 17, the CIC obtained another informant when Reis and Nordheim questioned the man who had driven Willi Heidemann and Max Lebens from Berlin to Bad Tölz on April 18, 1945. His name was Hans Willand and he was forty-seven years old. HJ in Berlin had ordered him to be ready to use his truck to drive personnel out of the city. He took with him fifteen people, including Heidemann and Lebens. He had known that he was driving Nazis out of Berlin before the city fell, but he kept this information to himself until confronted with it. For him, it was a much-needed job, which continued afterward as a driver for the Tessmann office in Passau, a Lower Bavarian town.

Willand agreed to let the CIC know of anything he learned in the future, in return for being able to keep his truck and trailer, both of which he himself owned.[3] He was afraid they might otherwise confiscate his vehicles because he'd used them to help the Nazis. Although the information he provided about the trip out of Berlin was of interest to the CIC, he did not prove to otherwise have much useful intelligence.

With the Frankfurt office of Tessmann supposed to soon become the company's new headquarters, Reis wanted Kulas to try to get transferred to Frankfurt. Heidemann though was so busy making deals with businessmen and military government authorities that he didn't have time to talk to Kulas about this transfer request.

Kulas talked with Max Lebens on July 21, while driving him to his new accommodations outside of Munich. Lebens was the man who had provided the corporation of Tessmann and Sons to this group, but since the fall of the Third Reich, he had been prone to complaining about the direction the group was taking, among other issues.

Lebens said that his and Heidemann's instructions when they fled

Berlin for Bavaria were to "invest HJ funds in new businesses, and only employ members of the HJ. Through the change of events, LEBENS and HEIDEMANN found out that the plan of only hiring HJ members was not workable, and began hiring in addition to former HJ members, persons who had no connections with any NATIONAL SOCIALIST Organizations."[4]

Lebens went on to explain that once he returned to Lübeck, not only would he open a Tessmann office there, but also he wanted to take in orphans whose parents had been in the ranks of the HJ leadership. He planned to take these children and brainwash them into believing absolutely in Nazi fanaticism.

Meanwhile, Agents Reis and Nordheim traveled to Bad Reichenhall to look at papers confiscated during the arrest of the BDM leaders at the hospital there. Among them, they found the address that Kulas had previously told them was the meeting spot for BDM leaders. Once it was safe to travel freely in Germany, BDM leaders were supposed to meet up at the residence of a Miss Gertrud Hehmel, near the west central German town of Kassel. This find served as additional confirmation that the intel Kulas had given the CIC was good. When they questioned the BDM leaders about this address, they found out it was a made-up name, there was no Gertrud Hehmel, but this was a real meeting place.

In late July, Lebens and Wandel openly expressed that they wanted to get rid of Heidemann. They told Kulas that they believed Heidemann had lost his focus, by going after a wide variety of business opportunities and neglecting to carry out Axmann's orders, as they understood them.

The next day, they changed their minds about trying to simply take over the company in a kind of coup d'état, and instead decided to confront Heidemann and give him a chance to change his ways. They would bring up their original orders and hope that he would conform to what they expected of him. Lebens "told [Kulas] that the orders the RJF [*Reichsjugendführer*] AXMANN had given were:

1. To give a home to the children of the dead HJ FUEHRERS and provide for their education.

2. To provide the WEHRWOLF with all the necessities for operations. (HEIDEMANN, BERGEMANN and LEBENS agreed to drop this point after all Germany was occupied.)

3. To build up a large fund through the medium of a good business, so that former Bannfuehrers and other former members of the RJF would be provided with a means of existence, and so be able to keep an organization for future use."[5]

As far as Heidemann, Bergemann, and Lebens were concerned, Werwolf was dead. To reflect this change, Agent Reis's continuation report dated August 1, had a new subject line. Reis wrote, "In this report the Subject has been changed by these Agents from UNDER-COVER ACTIVITIES OF HITLER JUGEND AND WEHRWOLF IN SOUTHERN GERMANY to read UNDERCOVER ACTIVITIES OF HITLER JUGEND IN SOUTHERN GERMANY, because these Agents have reason to believe that practically all WEHRWOLF intentions and personnel missions have been disintegrated and dissolved by Allied operations in Southern Germany. Therefore, since these reports deal with the activities of former high HJ members, and there has been no evidence of future WEHRWOLF intent to act, it is fitting that the Subject be amended."[6]

Operation Nursery's case officer, Jack Hunter, spent his time going back and forth between his desk job in Frankfurt and his undercover work, mostly centered in Munich. While undercover, Hunter was "Hans Jaeger," whom Hunter described as "a black-market operator who had great connections with the more corrupt members of the American forces."[7] The backstory that Hunter had put together for his undercover persona was that Hans Jaeger was a Lithuanian displaced person who knew how to get black market deals done.

The name was easy for him to remember because it was a literal translation of Jack Hunter into German.[8]

As Jaeger, Hunter acted as a middleman for black market transactions. If Heidemann turned to Kulas for trucking supplies, Jaeger would often be the one to ultimately fulfill these orders, be it tires, gasoline, or some other hard-to-obtain goods. According to Jaeger's cover story, his motivation was not fealty to Nazism, but rather just the money. And so, Heidemann was charged inflated prices for these items.

Hunter didn't get to keep the proceeds of his illicit transactions. The money all had to "go directly and fully accounted to the Confidential Funds reserve at CIC Regional Headquarters."[9]

One day Hunter almost had his cover blown. When he was walking with a former SS member who was now a part of the Tessmann concern, an inebriated American officer came over to him, loudly saying, "What the hell you doing in that crazy get-up, you ole sumbish?"[10] It was an acquaintance from his college days, but Hunter ignored him and played it off to the SS man as a case of mistaken identity induced by too much drink. The reason his buddy from Penn State commented on his clothing was that he was dressed up in a Bavarian outfit of lederhosen (a kind of leather shorts with suspenders) and an Alpine hat (a felt fedora with a braided cord around it and a feather sticking out the side).

Hunter was ready if the opposite scenario ever happened and he ran into a Tessmann operative while wearing his plain American military uniform. He set up his excuse by saying that he had illicitly acquired an American uniform that he sometimes used to get access to American facilities as part of his black market dealings.[11] However, he never had to use this excuse. Usually he was in uniform only when in Frankfurt; while he was undercover in Bavaria and elsewhere he wore civilian clothes.

Later in life, Hunter used his experience as Hans Jaeger when writing his second novel (*The Expendable Spy*). This book featured a fictionalized version of Operation Nursery. Of a trucking concern's need for a black market connection, he wrote, "If he were to keep Kaufmann Kompanie [the novel's version of Tessmann] running he'd need a first-rate black-market specialist who speaks English. He anticipates [sic] trouble operating under American occupation—trouble getting tires, spare parts, that sort of thing—and he wanted a man skilled in black-market operations to head up that activity for him."[12]

Starting in mid-July 1945, while the CIC was working on infiltrating Tessmann and Sons, the fate of occupied Germany and much of Europe was being decided. The leaders of the Soviet Union, the United Kingdom, and the United States convened outside Berlin from July 16 to August 2.[13] They held this conference in a palace in Potsdam, a historic city where the Prussian court used to be. It was here that German President Paul von Hindenburg shook hands with Hitler when he became chancellor in 1933.

Germany had surrendered more than two months beforehand, in early May. Prior to that, from February 4 to 11, 1945, these powers had met at Yalta (a Soviet resort town). Franklin Roosevelt had still been alive then, so he represented the United States, while Churchill and Stalin represented their countries. The main topic of conversation was what would happen, after the war was won, to Germany and the areas it had occupied. Among other things, the leaders decided to divide

Germany into zones of occupation, and Churchill succeeded in getting Stalin to agree to the French having a zone as well.

Germany and Austria were divided among the four Allies, with the capital of Berlin shared among them. While Berlin ultimately was to have four sectors (for the French, Americans, British, and Soviets), the Soviets waited until July to hand over the Western Allies' territory. They used this time to take what they could from the city before they had to withdraw to their zone. This included "almost three tons of Uranium Oxide, a material the Soviets had been short of and enough to give a substantial boost to their [program] to build an atomic device."[14]

As one former OSS counterintelligence officer recalled, "We . . . joked about the division of Germany into zones of occupation: the Russians got the agriculture (Prussia); the British, the industry and coal (the Ruhr); and the Americans, the scenery (Bavaria and the Alps)."[15]

Now that Germany was occupied, a follow-up conference was held to make decisions on remaining issues and various new problems that had developed since the meeting in Yalta. Also, during this time, the United States, the U.K., and China (but not the Soviet Union) issued the Potsdam Declaration calling for Japan's unconditional surrender. This was ten days into the conference, on July 26, 1945.

On August 2, the conference closed with the issuance of the Potsdam Agreement. It's hard to understate the importance of this agreement. It shaped the lives of Germans under the occupation and the fate of those lands conquered by the Soviet Union during the war.

This agreement contained the following language that challenged the plans and viewpoints of the former leaders of the Hitler Youth: "The purposes of the occupation of Germany by which the Control Council shall be guided are . . . to convince the German people that they have suffered a total military defeat and that they cannot escape responsibility for what they have brought upon themselves, since their own ruthless warfare and the fanatical Nazi resistance have destroyed the German economy and made chaos and suffering inevitable . . . [and] to destroy the National Socialist Party and its affiliated and supervised organizations, to dissolve all Nazi institutions, to ensure that they are not revived in any form, and to prevent all Nazi and militarist activity or propaganda."[16]

Other language from this agreement that meant HJ leaders like Axmann were in trouble included "Nazi leaders, influential Nazi supporters and high officials of Nazi organizations and institutions and any other persons dangerous to the occupation or its objectives shall be arrested and interned."[17]

On August 6, 1945, the United States dropped an atomic bomb on Hiroshima, Japan. Atomic research and testing had previously been highly classified, and this marked the first time the public became aware of the awesome power of this bomb.

In the American Occupation Zone that day, General Eisenhower gave a speech on the radio to the German people saying, "The coming months are going to be hard for you. You will just have to be tough— there is no alternative. Every sign indicates a severe shortage of food, fuel, housing and transport. It is therefore up to you to alleviate your hardship by working very strenuously and helping one another. The prospects for this year's harvest look good. But people in the cities will have to go out and work in the countryside. There will be no coal available for heating homes this winter. To meet your basic requirements in the next few months you will have to go into the woods and cut your own firewood. A third priority is the provision of living accommodations. As far as the weather allows, damaged property must be repaired to offer as much protection from the winter as possible. To this end, you will have to collect scrap material over the widest possible area and gather dead wood in the forests. These are your problems."[18]

It would not be easy for the German population to do these things, especially those who were stuck in the bombed out ruins of cities. The elderly, the sick, and the injured would have a hard time making their way to the countryside to try to obtain the supplies they would need. Healthy men were in short supply—those who had not died or been injured in the long years of war were likely being held as prisoners by one of the victorious powers.

Three days later, on August 9, the United States dropped a second atom bomb on Japan, this time on Nagasaki. Finally, on August 15 (August 14 in the United States), Japan agreed to an unconditional surrender. Although it would be another two weeks before Japan officially signed the surrender agreement and Victory over Japan (V-J) Day was officially celebrated in the United States, World War II was effectively over.[19]

As for Germany, reparations were a hot topic among the Allied powers. Germany had wrecked much of Europe and caused untold human and industrial damage. But the memory of how the reparations Germany had to pay after starting (and then losing) World War I led eventually to the rise of Hitler meant that a clause was added to the Potsdam Agreement that "Payment of Reparations should leave enough resources to enable the German people to subsist without external assistance."[20]

An entire section of the Potsdam Agreement dealt with the issue of reparations from Germany.[21] Reparations did not only mean money, they also included industrial resources like factories and natural resources such as timber, as well as services, in the form of forced labor. The labor issue had already been resolved at Yalta—section five of the Yalta Agreement covered reparations. It included the "use of German labor" as an acceptable, in kind, form of reparation.[22]

It was mainly for this reason that the farmer's wife that Axmann was hiding with was worried that the Soviets might detain her husband. He was able-bodied, so they might decide to take him away for use as forced labor. Axmann's war injury—his missing right forearm—made him much more desirable to his hosts. The Soviets were not likely to want an injured man for forced labor, so even if the husband were forced to leave, Axmann would be left behind to help with running the farm and protecting the family.

On August 30, the Allied Control Commission (ACC) for Germany met for the first time and issued the first of many proclamations. The ACC had four members: the commanders of the French, U.K., U.S., and Soviet Zones in Germany. Their decisions had to be unanimous. The agreement on how to run the ACC had already been reached on June 5.[23] But it took almost two months before this group formed and started issuing proclamations, which had the force of law in Germany. Many of the issues that faced the occupying powers had first needed to be sorted out by the countries' leaders at Potsdam.

While world powers were deciding what to do with Germany, Axmann was caught up in the local affairs of the village he was hiding in. A story circulated in Lansen that the Russians were onto the trick of hiding women and girls inside bales of hay. A Russian soldier supposedly had driven a sword into a farmer's haystacks to see if anyone was concealed within them. As this was the hiding place used by the girls on the farm that Axmann lived on, he needed to move them to a safer place. It was no longer enough for him to watch for Russians and then alert the girls to hide inside the hay.

The family he lived with knew someone at the local hospital who had a way to hide the girls. The hospital had been using signs warning of infectious diseases to keep the Russians out of certain hospital rooms. So far, this had worked—the Russians were too afraid to go inside these rooms and search them. The local Germans used these rooms to hide people and goods from the Soviets.

Early one morning, Axmann took the girls with him to the hospital to stay there in these infectious disease rooms. They couldn't stay there forever, but this was a safe place for the time being.

As for Axmann's own safety, he felt secure where he was. It seemed unlikely that anyone would recognize a bearded farmer in the middle of nowhere as the clean-cut man who had served with Hitler in the final days of the Third Reich and once commanded the youth of Germany. For him to hide though was harder than for most, as his missing forearm and attendant use of a distinctive prosthetic hand made him stick out.

He was lucky with who did end up recognizing him. Just as Axmann used to stop by farms asking for food and water, now he was the one travelers asked for this favor. Remembering his own hard days on the road, he would provide for those who stopped by, and talk with them a bit. One of these times, the recipients of his charity were two men traveling together. One of them abruptly changed the topic of their otherwise standard conversation about the current condition of Germany. He said, "But you are Mr. Axmann. I recognize yours as the voice I had often heard on the radio."[24]

Now, for the first time since he had left Berlin, someone had recognized him. Axmann tried to deny his identity, but when this traveler pointed out that he had the same prosthetic device as the former HJ leader, the jig was up. Axmann had no choice but to admit his true identity.

It was Axmann's lucky day, because these men swore they would keep his secret and then confided their own identities to him. They had been in the Estonian *Waffen* SS and so, like Axmann, fell into the automatic arrest category. Axmann helped them out by providing what supplies he could spare. They in turn repaid him many times over with what he needed most—identity papers. They were able to get him a Russian temporary ID as Erich Siewert (the alias he had been using).

The ID by itself was not much to look at, but the reality of postwar Germany was that few people had their papers in order anymore. And those who did might elicit suspicion for being too well documented during this time of chaos.

But Axmann's ID was lacking the stamp it needed to make it official, and this was a major flaw in its ability to convince checkpoints of his new identity. Axmann needed a stamp, but he lacked the contacts to get one. Instead, he ventured to town and examined a stamp, then copied it as best he could. He had limited tools at his disposal, but at least he had some sort of stamp on his ID.

Much later in life, Axmann thought back on this with the realization that "it hardly seems credible that I never needed to present this ID."[25] He tried to avoid situations where he would need to show it. It was not the best form of ID and the stamp on it was a fake. He went around checkpoints whenever possible.

While these Estonian SS who had never before seen him in person did recognize Axmann, a woman who had lived in the same building as his mother did not. During a visit to a nearby property, a woman there brought up that she knew Axmann's mother as one of her neighbors. She even mentioned Axmann's missing forearm, yet didn't recognize that she was talking to him. Axmann chalked this up to how different he now looked.[26]

NINE

UPPER AND LOWER BAVARIAN GROUPS

One leader, one people, signifies one master and millions of slaves. . . . There is no organ of conciliation or mediation interposed between the leader and the people, nothing in fact but the apparatus—in other words, the party—which is the emanation of the leader and the tool of his will to oppress. In this way the first and sole principle of this degraded form of mysticism is born, the Führerprinzip, which restores idolatry and a debased deity to the world of nihilism.

ALBERT CAMUS[1]

On August 10, Willi Heidemann returned to Bavaria after a trip to Austria. He reported that things were going well with the Tessmann office in Salzburg and that their coal had started to arrive there by train.

Max Lebens was still an active part of the business, despite his disagreements with Heidemann. In mid-August, Lebens deposited 50,000 reichsmarks in a bank so he could obtain a letter of credit to use in Lübeck and buy fish. He already had the necessary travel permit.

During a trip to Passau with the CIC informant Siegfried Kulas, Lebens found that much of the food he'd stored there since he'd left Berlin was missing along with some of his clothing. He'd already been stolen from while in jail, and despite his demands for reimbursement, no one had given him anything. Now he'd been robbed again. Lebens was extremely upset, and threatened that "he would blow things sky high if he wasn't reimbursed for his losses."[2] Eventually, he settled with the head of the Passau office for 6,000 RMs.

Kulas had a bit of a close call when a HJ *Hauptbannführer* named Otto Würschinger asked him questions about *Bannführerin* Karola Böhmer, one of the women he had delivered into a CIC trap. The main target had been the head of the BDM, Dr. Jutta Rüdiger, but the other women who had accompanied her were also arrested.

Kulas admitted that he had driven Böhmer and the other BDM women from Austria to Bad Reichenhall, but he claimed to have dropped them off at the hospital and not known what happened to them next. He said that he'd heard they'd had some issues with Americans regarding their passes, but they'd probably gotten through it okay. He did not let on that he'd led them to their capture and that they now languished in U.S. Army custody. However, he had to admit his driving them, as other people knew about it.

It turned out though that Würschinger had more on his mind than what had happened to a BDM leader. He asked to meet with Kulas and the Tessmann leaders to discuss something highly confidential. He wasn't willing to discuss it in their offices in Munich. Instead, he made everyone drive out of town and into the woods so that they would have more privacy.

Würschinger explained that he was working for HJ *Hauptbannführer* Ernst Ferdinand Overbeck to find leaders of the HJ's national office. Overbeck had been the chief of the Organization Office (*Organisationsamt*) for the HJ, although Würschinger had been the last one to head this office.[3] They knew that various HJ leaders had left Berlin for Bavaria before the end of the war. To help him spot HJ leaders, Würschinger brought with him a sixteen-year-old HJ courier, Alex Stratmann.

Würschinger talked about the fall of Berlin and extolled the valiant fighting of the HJ there in the final days. In late April, Axmann had ordered Würschinger to supervise HJ in the fighting, so he was away from the bunker area and not part of the breakout.[4] When Axmann fled Berlin on May 2, he'd paused to think of Würschinger and wondered if he had survived the fighting.[5]

Toward the end of this meeting, Würschinger asked Heidemann for money to fund a series of "small shops throughout Germany which would deal in postal cards, souvenirs, and other small items." Heidemann said no, saying all the money was already invested in their own business concerns.

The meeting ended with Würschinger saying he was going to meet up with other HJ leaders and would be in touch afterward.

It seemed like lots of former HJ were interested in the money that Heidemann controlled. During a trip to Wackersberg, two different HJ leaders asked him for money, and he again made excuses. He said "that all these funds were at present invested in the TESSMANN firm, and that it would not be possible to withdraw any money without upsetting the accounts completely."[6]

Max Lebens's fight with Willi Heidemann over food Lebens had stored away before the fall of the Third Reich was not about his own personal stash to make sure he had enough to eat. Instead, when it became clear that the war was going to end soon, with Germany as the loser, those involved in Tessmann had stored as much food as they could.

By late April, the leaders of the HJ sent by Axmann to Bavaria had gathered and hidden as much nonperishable food as they could "with the foresight that food was scarce and that it would be the best means of exchange for articles that the group at WACKERSBERG might need after the collapse and surrender of Germany. At that time it was not planned to start a food business but only a transportation business, the latter to serve as means of communication between the different hideouts and WACKERSBERG headquarters."[7]

Agent Reis wrote on August 31, 1945, "There is no doubt that the dominating motive for the men who are managing and are connected with the firm of TESSMANN & SONS, is to revive and keep alive the Nationalistic idea among the German people. . . . There is a great possibility that these men were not only ordered to revive the former Nationalistic idea in Germany, but also to try to build up a new German Intelligence Organization."[8]

A key component of the Nazi idea that the former HJ leaders wanted to revive was the Führer principle (the leadership principle). In essence, it meant that under a National Socialist government, the entire state and the party were ruled by a single individual whose orders were not to be questioned. Adolf Hitler had been this singular leader, but now he was dead.

As Baldur von Schirach, Axmann's predecessor as *Reichsjugend-führer*, testified during his trial at Nuremberg, "Of course, the HJ was founded on the Führer principle."[9] He then made the argument however that since he had discussions with underlings before issuing orders, even though they had to obey those orders, the HJ under him differed from other Nazi groups.

Von Schirach claimed that despite following the Führer principle, "the entire form of leadership of youth differed basically from that of other National Socialist organizations. For instance, we had the custom in youth leadership of discussing frankly all questions of interest to us. There were lively debates at our district leader meetings. I myself educated my assistants in a spirit even of contradiction. Of course, once we had debated a measure and I had then given an order or a directive, that ended the debate. The youth leaders—that is the young boy and girl leaders—through years of working together and serving the common purpose, had become a unit of many thousands."[10] These thousands of young leaders had to obey absolutely the orders of their

Reichsjugendführer and then make sure that the HJ and BDM members they commanded followed them as well.

For now, Germany was ruled by the occupying powers. But someday (at least in the West), they would leave and the German people would be able to vote for their own government. If these HJ leaders could gain enough economic and political power by then, it was possible that they'd be able to run their own political party. Then, through the political arena, they could try to gain enough power to seize control as Hitler had done in 1933.

A single leader would then run not only their organization, but also a revived National Socialist Party and state. The plan of this group was for Artur Axmann to become that leader, but until he showed up, others would have to serve in his place. It is not clear if they knew at this point that Axmann was still alive, but they at least knew it was possible.

For now, Heidemann was calling the shots in regards to their business enterprises, at least in part because he controlled the group's money. There were others though who had their own ideas about how to run things. Max Lebens, for one, had already voiced his concerns about Tessmann focusing more on growth, business opportunities, and staying below the occupation authorities' radar than on providing employment to needy former HJ.

Other potential leaders emerged when Würschinger returned from his trip. In the town of Oberstaufen, in southwest Bavaria, his courier tracked down HJ *Hauptbannführer* Gustav Memminger and HJ *Oberbannführer* Simon Winter. They had a meeting to discuss their respective plans and decided to join forces, forming a single group. Würschinger still represented HJ *Hauptbannführer* Overbeck.

Memminger had run the Press and Propaganda Bureau for the HJ[11]—he had been their equivalent of Joseph Goebbels. This experience with propaganda could prove useful for the group's future political ambitions.

Gustav Memminger had a clean-cut look with an at times penetrating, focused gaze. Other than this stare, he had the rather generic appearance of a dark-haired German who could easily blend into any crowd.

Winter had been in charge of agricultural activities for the HJ as head of the Bureau for Agriculture and Land Work (*Amt Bauerntum und Landdienst*) since Axmann appointed him in February 1942.[12] This meant that he ran the program for HJ where boys learned how to farm. Given the food shortages that currently plagued Germany, having access to agricultural resources would be invaluable.

Reis wrote about this Lower Bavarian group, before it was incorporated into Heidemann's Upper Bavarian group, saying that "although the OVERBECK group uses different methods from that of HEIDEMANN's, their future goals are the same. Both groups believe that the present distribution of food and the scarcity of coal will create a great civil unrest this winter. The labor class will be hit the hardest and it is here that willing listeners and spreaders of rumors will be found. If a situation of this kind develops, it will be easy for HEIDEMANN and cohorts to make a comparison between the THIRD REICH and now, and how much better it was then than now, and so gain many people to share their point of view. OVERBECK was in favor of starting a whisper campaign at once but HEIDEMANN persuaded his emissaries to wait a few months more, until the TESSMANN & SONS firm was economically established and then start with the political program."[13]

The Lower Bavarian group, referred to by the CIC as the Overbeck group, had managed to stay under the radar. It was only through their contact with the Tessmann group that the CIC came to learn about them. On August 19, Würschinger arrived in Munich after his meeting with Memminger and Winter. He'd confided in a BDM woman there about his meetings. She in turn talked to Kulas about this.

These two groups, through intermediaries, set up a proper face-to-face meeting between their leaders for early September in Munich. It was there that they could decide how to divide the power and responsibilities of their underground networks.

As Heidemann nurtured Tessmann and Sons, he favored pragmatic policies over dogmatic Nazi ones. He felt that if he just employed HJ leaders, HJ members, and fellow Nazis that the occupying powers would eventually be sure to take notice. So instead, he spread out such true believers into key positions in far-flung geographic locations. By opening new offices elsewhere, not only could he grow the business during this early, tumultuous period full of opportunities, but also he hoped to avoid undue attention from the CIC and other authorities.

He went one step beyond just hiring people who were kept in the dark regarding his plans for the company and the Nazi pasts of those running it. His pragmatism extended toward a cynical hiring of victims of Nazi crimes, such as concentration camp survivors and people like Kurt Pommerening who had Jewish ancestry. It's possible that other Nazis might disapprove of his hiring Jews, but that was something he could bring up at the September meeting with the Overbeck group.

As the CIC noted, hiring survivors of the terrors of the Third Reich made sense as "these people make a good screen against the public finding out HEIDEMANN's real intentions. To reach his goal, HEIDEMANN does not hesitate to take a concentration camp inmate into the firm."[14]

However, as Kurt Pommerening had already demonstrated, a major problem with Heidemann's strategy of working with survivors was that the CIC could recruit them.

There was another reason for incorporating new people into the

Tessmann concern and its various related businesses. Sometimes it was better to have a local person involved, and sometimes the opposite was true, it was better to appear to be a foreign company. It all depended on the individual politics of an area as to which approach would help them get permissions and contracts from the MG.

In mid-August, Heidemann learned that to get new contracts in Bavaria, he needed the company to appear to be Bavarian. He himself was a northern German. He was advised "to find an outsider, a resident of Bavaria, make him a partner in the firm and so get the concession or permit, and also change the firm name at the same time."[15]

He had done something similar recently in Austria. In Salzburg, Heidemann had formed a company called Austrian Fuel & Farm Produce, Inc. (*Östreichische Brennstoff und Landesprodukte, G.m.b.H.*) to handle their business there. He put an Austrian in charge of it, a former Nazi, so that it appeared to be a local company run by a local.

Heidemann decided to use a new business partner, Hans Garms, as his outside man for transforming the Tessmann corporate structure so he could get government contracts in Bavaria. Garms had survived the camps to become a prominent black marketer in occupied Germany.

As Agent Reis later recalled, Kulas "reported that the new man seen around the transportation firm's office was Hans Garms, a former inmate of several concentration camps for several years who was dabbling in various little business deals and quite a few of them in the black market. . . . He lived high—he had exceptional living quarters with antique furnishings, a mistress, and lacked for nothing—booze, valuable jewelry, watches, diamonds, a chauffeur bodyguard, etc. He evidently wanted to make up for time lost in the various camps during the past 7 years."[16]

Garms already had a number of legal and illegal business ventures in Bavaria. Of particular value to Tessmann, he had a permit for the wholesale buying and selling of foodstuffs. This was the main trade, besides coal, that Tessmann wanted to conduct in the area. Given the scarcity of transportation infrastructure and dependable agriculture in war-ravaged Germany and Austria, there was a lot of power and money to be gained by dealing in food and fuel.

A brand-new company, called Garms & Co., G.m.b.H, would replace Tessmann in Bavaria.[17] Paul Mueller (a businessman) and Hans Garms would be part of this company, with Heidemann having ultimate control of it. The CIC decided to recruit Garms as an informant.

Garms was kept in the dark though in regards to the HJ backgrounds of those running Tessmann—without revealing anything of the politics involved, the agents only told him they wanted to monitor Heidemann's business activities. The danger of telling Garms anything more was that he might reveal this knowledge and blow the whole operation.[18]

As they could get his cooperation without having to tell him the full story, given his precarious legal situation as a black market operator and their power as CIC agents, they decided to take the safe course and keep him in the dark for the time being.

In contrast, Kulas knew all about the backgrounds of the Tessmann leaders, but then again he was the one who had told the CIC about them in the first place. The CIC did inform Kurt Pommerening about the politics of the men he was working with at Tessmann, but they trusted him based on a combination of his having suffered under the Nazis and his having an honest job at Tessmann being a simple dispatcher.

Hans Garms, while he had suffered greatly at the hands of the Third Reich, was a criminal. The CIC decided to run him on a need-to-know basis, his cooperation having been secured without telling him the larger context of this operation.[19]

As Hans Jaeger, Jack Hunter often went out on his own to see Tessmann's operations firsthand. His responsibilities included checking on the reach of this organization throughout Germany. As Hunter later wrote, Agent Reis "spearheaded the Bavarian investigation, I handled the nationwide stuff. He did not know everything I knew (he was kept on a need-to-know basis) and we were seen together rarely."[20]

As the case officer for Operation Nursery, Hunter led a dual life—some days he worked in the impressive Farben Building as a U.S. Army officer, while on others he was undercover as a black marketer. To illustrate what his workweek was like, Hunter wrote, "On Mondays and Tuesdays, I could be in Frankfurt, wearing [a] Class-A uniform and giving a flip-chart briefing to my bosses on the current situation in the Nursery affair. . . . On Wednesdays I'd drive the 200-some miles to Munich, where I'd changed into civilian clothes and become Hans Jäger."[21]

As Hunter explained, he "would use these Munich visits to follow up on new leads, or other aspects of Nursery beyond the purview of Reis and Hochschild. I usually avoided contacting those two directly, thus lowering the risk of over-exposure, and I rarely visited CIC headquarters [in Munich]."[22] Instead, Hunter was either at his safe house in Munich or out in the field.

His Munich safe house was a large, three-story property where Hunter could meet up with other agents and spend the night. It was located a few blocks from the Isar River at Flemingstrasse 49. This is the same river that runs through Bad Tölz.

Hunter and Kulas got along well. Earlier on in the investigation, Agent Reis had introduced them. Hunter understood Kulas's motivations—to save his own hide and his belief that those in the Tessmann concern would ultimately get caught anyways. He also claimed to have abandoned his Nazi views.

Besides protecting Kulas from war crimes investigators, Hunter approved financial compensation to him for his help with this operation.

While in Frankfurt, in addition to briefing his superiors on this ongoing operation, Hunter had paperwork to do. While sitting behind his desk in the Farben Building, he carefully read through Reis's reports. He also went through the reports of other agents in Germany, looking for any connections to Operation Nursery. Hunter compiled all the information gathered by field agents and made charts and lists of names of possible figures of interest. He then took that information and ran it by other agencies, such as the British and the OSS, to see what else he could find out. Although far from glamorous, this was a key part of the running of an operation and necessary for identifying everyone that would eventually need to be picked up when the operation came to a close.

Meanwhile, Artur Axmann was hiding out in northern Germany, in the village of Lansen, where the Soviets had appointed Herrmann Bleckmann, the largest landowner in the area, as mayor.[23] When Axmann reported to Mayor Bleckmann as a refugee from Berlin now living on a local farm, he discovered that they hit it off. As the Soviets started to institute changes in agricultural policy, Axmann found himself in the center of these changes.

The Soviets decreed that all cows would be moved to a centralized location to graze, instead of allowing individual farmers to handle their own cows as they saw fit. All these cows needed someone to watch over them, and the mayor gave the job to Axmann. Only having one arm didn't prevent him from being able to supervise this herd.

Although Axmann didn't mind having this job, from what he could see it was a disaster in terms of milk production. The individual farmers still owned their own cows; the state had not confiscated them. But having them all graze together was a logistical nightmare. As part of his new job, Axmann watched as Germans ran around trying to locate their cows and then milk them. But it took a while to do this, so that farmers were not able to get to their cows in a timely fashion.[24] Axmann saw firsthand that this resulted in greatly reduced milk yields, which led him to think that imposing Soviet collective farming techniques on Germans could result in serious problems.

When not working with cows, Axmann continued to stand watch from the barn window on the farm. The girls he protected had returned from hiding out at the hospital.

One day, he saw people driving up to the farm and so gave the alarm for the girls to hide. Axmann then walked to the front gate to greet these visitors. A Russian came out of the car accompanied by two soldiers. He started to interrogate Axmann, asking for his name, his profession, and how come he was there. Axmann stuck to his story that he was Erich Siewert, a merchant from Berlin. The Russian appeared not to believe him and ordered his men to lock Axmann in a second-floor room and stand guard outside it.[25]

This Russian then yelled at Axmann "as though [Axmann] personally was responsible for the misdoings of the Third Reich."[26] Now Axmann was really worried, as this level of animus toward him suggested that this Russian officer might know that he in fact was personally responsible for some of the actions of the Third Reich.

Axmann had not been asked to produce his identity papers, and so he still had ID unshown in his pocket. He was uncertain of how much confidence he had in it, and he seriously considered escaping through the window. He was low enough to the ground that he could have gotten out without hurting himself, but then he would have been a man on the run again. Although he was more afraid than he had been since arriving in Lansen, he listened to his gut instinct and stayed put.

It turned out though that the Russian had no idea that he was confronting a man who had been a high-ranking Nazi and had known Hitler personally.

In the end, the issue was about cattle; the Russian wanted to confiscate the cows belonging to the farm Axmann was staying on. Axmann was set free because the Russian had no idea who he really was. As Axmann later wrote, "the cattle were more important than I was."[27]

His tremendous feeling of relief though was shattered later that afternoon when a messenger showed up with orders to bring him into town. Panic set in once again when the messenger let slip that a high-level member of the Nazi Party was believed to be hiding out somewhere in the area.

As before, Axmann considered fleeing, but instead he accompanied this messenger into town. There, Mayor Bleckmann saved him by saying, "You, Herr Siewert, you've known me for a long time, you can go home."[28] And so Axmann's decision to face these two situations head-on when he thought he might be caught, worked out for the best.

For now he was in the clear—the Russian who had yelled at him just wanted the cattle on his farm, and the mayor himself had vouched for him.

TEN

FACE-TO-FACE

When the showing ended, someone asked about the plot to kill Hitler. The discussion moved to plots in general. I found myself saying to the assembled heads, "All plots tend to move deathward. This is the nature of plots."

DON DELILLO[1]

Early in the summer of 1945, Tessmann & Sons had hoped to open an office in Frankfurt, where the American Military Government was based. Once it became operational, they would turn it into their headquarters.

But they had been facing increasing problems in getting permission from the MG to run a business there.[2] In late August, Tessmann's legal adviser, Walter Bergemann, was still trying to open their Frankfurt office. Bergemann had served a similar role in the national office of the HJ, as head of the HJ's Bureau of Legal Administration.

Besides the permission problem, Tessmann couldn't find office space. With the Americans headquartered here, the city was a popular place for businesses to rent space. Tessmann was reduced to looking outside of the city.

Bergemann wanted to fill the Frankfurt office with those who had a relatively clean past under the Nazi regime. It would be here that the company hoped to be doing business directly with high levels of the American Military Government, so they needed to hide their Nazi associations. Bergemann had already somehow succeeded in getting a letter from a British major named Piers saying that he should be provided with aid in order to conduct his business operations. While the CIC did not know how he managed to get this letter, they did know that he had shown it to American forces in Munich. Because of this letter, Americans soldiers there had furnished him with gasoline at one point. This is just one example of how such connections could be useful to the Tessmann concern.[3]

Having failed to get permission to open an office in the Frankfurt area for the German trucking concern of Tessmann & Sons, Bergemann now pursued a radically new approach. In Austria, they already had two businesses that were made possible by having been formed locally and managed locally, yet they had not been able to do the same in Frankfurt.

The new plan was to ask for permission as an Austrian company doing business between Germany and Austria. They believed it would be easier to get permission to run a business in Frankfurt if it were a foreign company, instead of a German one.

Bergemann had a power of attorney for the firm Willi Heidemann had founded in Bruck, Austria, called Klug and Company. With this, Bergemann could act as the company's representative in Frankfurt and sign legally binding contracts on its behalf. He now worked on obtaining permission from the American Military Government to open an office in Frankfurt for this ostensibly Austrian business. Once they had this office, they could use it for the Tessmann business as well.

While the trucking concern continued to grow, its leaders also worked on building up other businesses. A movie theater in Bremen was planned, as was a textile company based in Frankfurt. In order to build a closer relationship with the Americans in Frankfurt and gather intelligence from them when they drank, Bergemann also wanted to open a bar or restaurant there.[4]

Heidemann had developed a variety of different business concerns since he'd fled Berlin, and the transportation company of Tessmann had been reorganized. In Bavaria, for instance, it was now Garms & Co. He wanted to create a holding company (*Interessengemeinschaft*) in Frankfurt, which would combine all the various business interests he had developed. But first, he needed to set up a base in Frankfurt, so that he could organize all of his interests in the different companies into one entity.

In early September, the CIC changed the level of classification for this operation from secret to top secret.[5] Agent Timothy Reis attributed this change in classification to the successful capture of the head of the BDM, Dr. Jutta Rüdiger, and her female comrades. What they said after their capture matched what the informant Siegfried Kulas had been telling the CIC, which served as evidence that he had been telling the truth.

As Agent Reis later wrote, the "summation of the facts in our case to date revealed that our penetrating agent was playing ball with us and from this time on the Nursery Case was designated TOP SECRET. General Sibert at Frankfurt took over personal direction and we were given unlimited supplies, funds and any other assistance we might ask for."[6] General Edwin Sibert was Eisenhower's G-2, which meant he was in charge of U.S. Army intelligence for the European Theater. He was well above Jack Hunter in the chain of command.

There are different versions of how the codename "Nursery" was chosen. CIC Agent George Hochschild said it was because the CIC and OSS acted like children at the start of the case, tossing it back and forth between them.[7] As he tells the story, "In Munich, at the same time, there was also a detachment of the OSS, which at that time, when the OSS worked outside the U.S., it was called SSS (Strategic Service Section). And they called our office, and I went over there. There were two people there, and they say, it doesn't really fit into their assignments. Why don't you guys take it? And I said, I don't really know, I'm not in charge of the detachment so I'll discuss it with somebody else. And then I went back and it was like a bunch of kids going back and forth and we were looking for a cover name and he said well why don't you call it Nursery, and I said fine, good idea. And that's how the name happened to be."[8]

Jack Hunter, who was the case officer in charge of this operation, had twin girls born on July 23.[9] He only found out about this news almost two months afterward, when a letter slowly made its way from the United States to Europe.[10] He didn't get to see his girls until after this operation was over and he was back in the United States, so for him, the codename conjured up images of them in their nursery with their mother.[11]

Reis's explanation for this codename was that it was derived from the fact that CIC agents were able to be in on the beginning or "infancy of the case and because it concerned itself with young Nazis— HITLER'S JUGEND."[12] Through Kulas informing on his fellow Nazis, the CIC was able to start investigating the Tessmann concern early on in its postwar operations. As such, the Tessmann concern itself was still in its infancy when the CIC infiltrated it.

Not only was the HJ comprised of youths, but also the adult leadership of the HJ national office (which had been based in Berlin) was relatively young given their high level of responsibilities. Artur Axmann himself was only twenty-seven when he became *Reichsjugendführer.* As his predecessor as *Reichsjugendführer,* Baldur von Schirach explained, the HJ followed "the principle of 'youth leading youth.'"[13]

At the end of August, Agent Reis traveled from Munich to Frankfurt to meet up with Kulas there. Reis learned from Kulas that Walter Bergemann was trying without success to find a place to live in Frankfurt with his family. Tessmann had given up on finding office space in Frankfurt itself, and the company was now resigned to opening their headquarters in one of the small villages nearby. To run the new Frankfurt office, Bergemann planned to hire a Dr. von Behrenberg-Gosslar as the manager.

In the Munich CIC office, on the morning of Wednesday, September 5, the Tessmann operation pulled its gutsiest move to date, but the CIC was ready to match their chutzpah.[14]

Into this office walked a representative of the new company that had replaced Tessmann & Sons in Bavaria—Garms & Co.[15] Bravely entering the lion's den was a man who identified himself as Mr. Burckhard of Garms & Co. He requested to speak with the local CIC officer in charge. Instead of the OIC, Agent Werner Nordheim happened to be in the office that day and so he responded to this request. His partner, Agent Reis, was out of the office.

Agent Nordheim told Burckhard that his name was Mr. David. He'd never run into Burckhard during his time in Bad Tölz (where he had been pretending to be a journalist while he spied on the Tessmann office there). So this wouldn't blow his cover as long as he didn't run into this man in the future. It was a calculated move to let Mr. Burckhard know that he was a CIC agent, as it could potentially have jeopardized Operation Nursery if they ran into each other again in the future.

However, Nordheim would be leaving the CIC and shipping back to the United States soon. So there was little danger in his talking to this man.

Mr. Burckhard mentioned Willi Heidemann's name, saying that he was involved in a number of different businesses and wanted to rent

Maria Theresia Strasse 16 in central Munich. It was not normal to go to a CIC office to ask about renting a building, but for this particular building, it made some sense. The CIC had taken control of it, and as Nordheim truthfully explained to Mr. Burckhard, they were fixing it up with the intention of moving their own offices there.

Instead of taking no for an answer, Burckhard used Heidemann's name again, saying that Heidemann "would probably like to meet Mr DAVID [really Agent Nordheim] and explain why he wanted to rent this particular building, and maybe some arrangements could be made. MR DAVID informed MR BURCKHARD that he would be able to meet HEIDEMANN at 1500 hours that afternoon. MR BURCK-HARD told agent NORDHEIM that he regretted to say it, but GARMS & CO, at present had no office, but that HEIDEMANN would meet MR DAVID at the corner of HOMPESCH STR and ISMANINGER [Strasse] at 1500 hours."[16] With this meeting set up, and his business at the CIC concluded, Burckhard left.

When the time came, 3 P.M., Nordheim was at this intersection. He and Heidemann had never met before, so Heidemann would not know Nordheim as the journalist who stayed in Bad Tölz. This was a strange game that Heidemann was playing, but Nordheim could not turn down a chance to meet with a man he had spied on these past months.

Heidemann was not there. Instead, Nordheim was met by two of his flunkies—the man who had entered the CIC office before, Burck-hard, and a man he had never met, Dr. Stahlmann. "STAHLMANN apologized for HEIDEMANN's absence by telling Agent NORDHEIM he was engaged in an important conference and was unable to get away, and that he, STAHLMANN, would be able to tell MR DAVID why they wanted to rent the building at MARIA-THERESIA STR 16. STAHLMANN invited Agent NORDHEIM to accompany him to Hompesch Str 5 where a friend of his lived."[17]

Once in the apartment, Stahlmann "told Agent NORDHEIM that

HEIDEMANN wanted the building for future use as a place where [he] could open a bar for American officers"and for holding business meetings.[18] Stahlmann went on to name-drop an American officer, Captain Goodlow, based in Zell am See, Austria. He claimed that this captain and Heidemann were friends and were pursuing business opportunities in exporting Bavarian art to the United States.

At this point in the conversation, "a Mr THOMAS came into the room and was introduced to Agent NORDHEIM as the manager of NEUFILM, A.G. STAHLMANN talked about how industrious HEIDEMANN is, how many firms he had founded, and that he was now trying to coordinate all of them. STAHLMANN remarked that HEIDEMANN was a Northern German and much more active and ambitious than any Bavarian."[19]

The meeting closed with Stahlmann inquiring if Nordheim would be interested in the import-export business with the United States and if he would like to meet Heidemann himself someday. Nordheim replied "that [the] CIC had nothing to do with the renting of buildings, and in regard to possible business connections between Bavaria and the United States and meeting HEIDEMANN, he would have to think it over and let STAHLMANN know in the next few days."[20]

And so, this strange meeting ended. It was like something out of a spy comedy in that neither party to this business meeting was actually up to what they claimed. Nordheim, using the fake name of Mr. David, had acted as though he had never heard of Heidemann and was interested in considering a possible deal with some enterprising Germans. Instead, he wanted to know why they had come into the CIC in the first place.

Their pretext of wanting to rent the building that the CIC was moving into was absurd. Imagine if today, an Afghani insurgent walked into a Military Intelligence office, pretending to be part of a business concern interested in renting a building MI was renovating for itself.

The reason for these two strange meetings was that Heidemann wanted to find out if the CIC had any interest in detaining him. In a report a few days later, Agent Reis explained, "HEIDEMANN, to check on whether his identity was known to the CIC, sent one of his employees to contact the CIC on an excuse."[21]

Heidemann now believed that he was in the clear as far as the CIC was concerned. The two meetings had been set up to give the CIC time to check Heidemann out. If Heidemann had been a wanted man, Nordheim would presumably have shown up with backup to arrest him at their meeting, instead of having come alone. And he would not have gone by himself into a stranger's apartment. And yet, Nordheim had known exactly why Heidemann had set up the meeting. So he pretended to go along with things, participating in this farce in which he acted as though he believed the other parties' act about renting a building.[22]

Now that Heidemann felt that he had nothing to fear from the CIC, two days later, on September 7, he met with former department heads of the HJ national leadership office.[23] This first postwar face-to-face meeting of this group took place at a residence in Munich.

They met at the home of Hermann Giesler, an architect whom Hitler had optimistically put in charge of rebuilding Munich once the Nazis won the war. Hitler had already appointed him as the general building inspector (*Generalbaudirektor*) for Munich. His brother Paul had been the Nazi Party leader (*Gauleiter*) for Munich, although according to the CIC, Hermann was the power behind this throne. Moreover, Hermann was known to be a "very ardent national socialist."[24]

Gustav Memminger ran the meeting with Simon Winter, Ernst Overbeck, Heinrich Hartmann, and Willi Heidemann in attendance. Another former youth leader was there—BDM *Bannmäddelführerin*

Bärbel Metger who had been the BDM Sports Bureau Officer (*Sports Amts Referentin*). In addition, the CIC thought Otto Würschinger was there as well, but they were not certain.[25]

One of these attendees had only recently come to the CIC's attention. *Hauptbannführer* Heinrich Hartmann had been the head of the Department of Fine Arts in the Cultural Office of the national HJ Leadership (*Leiter der Hauptabteilung bildende Kunst im Kulturamt der RJF*).[26] The CIC had learned two weeks before that Würschinger had met with Hartmann in Munich. Hartmann had turned in his *Fragebogen* questionnaire to the American authorities and been questioned afterward, but for some reason, no one "paid any attention to his former connections."[27]

At this meeting, they decided to form two main groups. One would focus on growing economically, while the other would develop a political party. Only the individual leaders of these two different sections would have any contact with each other. This was because it would be too dangerous to have future meetings like this, with so many high-level HJ leaders present.

Heidemann would run the business section of this group. Gustav Memminger took charge of the political part as he "was the oldest and politically the best versified at this meeting."[28]

Memminger had been in charge of propaganda for the HJ and he had a clever plan for how to form a political party, despite the limitations imposed by the occupying powers. As the CIC found out through Kulas, "The slogan under which their political ideas are to spread is 'SAMMLUNG DER ANSTANDIGEN'[29] (Assembly or get-together of all decent people). The meeting agreed on this slogan for its simplicity and elimination of any objections MG [the Military Government] would have in permitting its existence. At the same time through the wording of this slogan, every German would understand that it is definitely against Communism. MEMMINGER has already taken into consideration that MG would allow only political parties to be founded and operated within a county area, and to circumvent this, he has worked out a plan under which he can send trustworthy men into other counties of Bavaria to form the same party under the same slogan."[30]

From the CIC's viewpoint, "the danger of this misleading slogan is that many decent Germans will join this party without being able to find out in time the true political intentions and attitude of the controlling group."[31]

The Agents' Notes section of the CIC's September 17 continuation report contained a great deal of information on the economic section. After the meeting, Heidemann confided in Kulas the details of what had transpired, and Kulas in turn told the CIC. As Agent Reis wrote in this report, "At the meeting HEIDEMANN was elected to stay on as economic leader. He is trying very hard to found new firms besides the six firms he has already established with capital which formerly belonged to organizations affiliated with the Nazi Party. HEIDE-MANN is, at present, very much interested in obtaining licenses for opening bars in Frankfurt and Munich. The reason behind this is not so much for the profit, but to get good contacts and get on good terms with as many American members of the occupation forces as possible. At present, he has two import and export firms formed and nearly ready to operate. MG permits import and export between the United States and Germany. HEIDEMANN thinks he already has quite a few friends among the Americans, and is in a position to be the first one to bring food and other necessities from the USA to Germany. To enlarge his business contacts, he needs the cooperation of men who know nothing about his past, and to assure these business men that MG has no objection against his person, he mentions that he has been cleared by the CIC. After hearing HEIDEMANN's assurances, outstanding German business men and firms are much interested in affiliating themselves with his firms and so HEIDEMANN is at the present time, one of the most active business men in all lines concerning the supply of necessities for Germany."[32]

The division of the group into political and economic sections, each with its own leader, still left the matter of internal security or enforcement. Therefore, a third entity was formed to control dissent within their own organization. Although they had no idea that their organization was riddled with informants and that the CIC was on to them, they had already experienced a discipline problem in the form of Max Lebens.

Even though Lebens had been the one to supply them with the corporate shell they needed to start operation (Tessmann & Sons), he had caused problems repeatedly with his complaints about theft, his disagreements with Heidemann over the direction they were taking, and his threat to expose them if he was not reimbursed for his losses.

At this meeting, "OVERBECK has taken it upon himself to become the watchdog over this new set up that the Amtschefs [bureau heads] are working on. During this meeting there was a lot of criticism of LEBENS attitude towards HEIDEMANN in the past two months and OVERBECK thought it best if LEBENS would be removed from this earth or as he put it 'umgelegt' (murdered). OVERBECK's eagerness to watch over this set up in this unscrupulous way, reminds one very much of the Feme which existed after the last war. The Feme . . . has always come into existence after Germany has lost a war and some idealist always thought that they could help Germany by getting rid of the men who cooperated with the enemy or went against the promises they had given their former friends. In old times this Feme Court consisted of a president and eleven judges. The men who had to execute the killing were drawn by lots. It is not known to these Agents if OVERBECK is the judge and executioner at the same time or if he has built up an organization which compared with the one mentioned above."[33]

Heidemann had already employed concentration camp survivors and people of Jewish descent in his operations. To make sure that his fellow Nazis would not someday accuse him of having violated their racist beliefs, Heidemann arranged to have this issue decided upon during their group meeting. And so, at this meeting, "members had agreed to use and employ concentration camp inmates and Jews for the present time only as a front for their organizations. The use of these people was not in anyway later on to be held against them, since it was done only to allow them to have a chance to build up the New Germany."[34]

As the CIC only had penetration agents in the economic section, it would be hard for them to obtain information directly from the political group or Overbeck's secret court. Kulas was trusted by the group, so he could try to find things out from Heidemann or anyone else from this meeting who might open up to him. Otherwise, once political groups started to use their slogan of "Assembly of All Decent People" ("*Sammlung Die Anständigen*"), the CIC would at least now be in a position to know what was really meant by it.

While discussing this meeting with Kulas and Bergemann afterward, Heidemann said "that he would rather have only a two percent interest in a firm than a forty or fifty percent interest in one that might blow in the next few months. Therefore HEIDEMANN said he will attempt to make as many good contacts and connections and found as many firms as possible in the next few months and then, after the danger of arrest is more or less over, former members of the RJF [HJ National Leadership] will gradually and unostentatiously be installed in controlled positions of the firms HEIDEMANN and his friends have interests in."[35]

During this time, in the village of Lansen in northern Germany, Axmann's friendship with the local mayor continued to grow stronger.

Mayor Bleckmann had already proven he was a friend by vouching for Axmann in front of the Soviet occupiers.

When Axmann brought up that he was planning on visiting Berlin, Mayor Bleckmann wanted him to find his daughters and bring them back with him. The risks associated with this endeavor were readily apparent. Travel such as this was dangerous enough for a man, but there were even more risks for women.

Furthermore, even though the mayor owned the largest farm in the area, with the Soviets in charge, it was always possible that they could confiscate his land. This would leave him with no means to support his daughters by the time they joined him. Despite discussing these very serious concerns, Mayor Bleckmann still wanted his daughters with him, so Axmann agreed to help.

Axmann also told the farm family with whom he was living about his travel plans. He would head to Berlin and then come back to Lansen to continue hiding there. Although it was in the Soviet Zone, which was probably the worst zone for him to be in if he were caught, so far Axmann had managed to do well there. He was now part of the local community and protected by both the family he lived with and the mayor.

The Soviets, according to their radio announcement in the last days of the fight for Berlin, believed him dead. Also, if there was someone looking for him, there was no connection between his hiding place in Lansen and his life before Germany's collapse. He had ended up there randomly.

Axmann's hosts wanted him to stop by Württemberg in southwestern Germany to let their relatives there know that they had survived the war. At the time, it was not possible for them to send mail from Lansen to Württemberg, so this would be the first time these relatives would have heard word about things in Lansen.

The farm family and Mayor Bleckmann gave Axmann money and

"Youth Serves the Führer: All ten-year-olds into the Hitler Youth." HJ Propaganda Poster, 1940.   AUTHOR'S COLLECTION

Cover of *Der Pimpf* magazine, April 1938.   AUTHOR'S COLLECTION

Artur Axmann, unknown date.

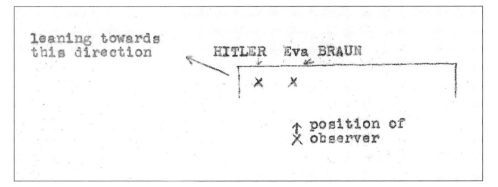

A drawing of Hitler's death in the bunker on April 30, 1945, by Artur Axmann, as part of his interrogation in January 1946.   AUTHOR'S COLLECTION

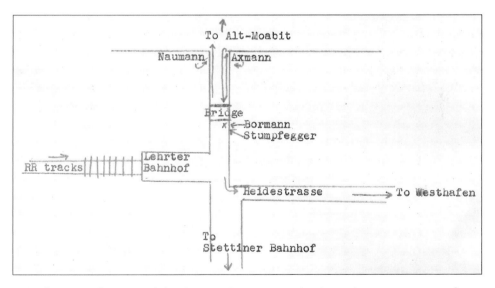

A drawing of Bormann's location on May 2, 1945, by Artur Axmann, as part of his interrogation in January 1946.   AUTHOR'S COLLECTION

Weidendammer Bridge (Berlin). Hermann Rückwardt, 1897.

"Women remove the rubble from the streets of Berlin."

The movie poster for *Wings* (1927).

PARAMOUNT, 1927

Jack Hunter's high school graduation photo. Unknown photographer, 1939.

AUTHOR'S COLLECTION

Jack Hunter upon graduation from OCS. Unknown photographer, 1943.

Jack Hunter in an officer's uniform. Unknown photographer, circa 1945.

HJ confronted by dead at Dachau (Germany).

SIDNEY BLAU, U.S. ARMY, APRIL 30, 1945,
THE NATIONAL ARCHIVES AND RECORDS ADMINISTRATION

"A German girl is overcome as she walks past the exhumed bodies of some of the 800 slave workers murdered by SS guards near Namering, Germany, and laid here so that townspeople may view the work of their Nazi leaders."

CPL. EDWARD BELFER, U.S. ARMY, MAY 17, 1945,
THE NATIONAL ARCHIVES AND RECORDS ADMINISTRATION

The IG Farben Building, Frankfurt, circa 1946.

```
                              SECRET

C             307TH COUNTER INTELLIGENCE CORPS DETACHMENT   •
 O                    HEADQUARTERS SEVENTH ARMY
  P                            APO 758
   Y
                                                  4 July 1945

MEMORANDUM FOR THE OFFICER IN CHARGE:

     SUBJECT:   Undercover Activities of HITLER JUGEND
                and WEHRWOLF in Southern Germany.

     RE    :  Code name for Informant.

     KULAS, Siegfried, informant and contact man for these
Agents in the above-entitled case, will be known under the
name of "KARL."


                                  T. M. REIS
                                  Agent, CIC


                                  W. D. NORDHEIM
                                  Agent, CIC
```

A CIC document giving Kulas his code name, July 4, 1945.

Don Allen (left) and Jack Hunter (right) in Munich Safe House. Unknown photographer, circa 1945. AUTHOR'S COLLECTION

Jack Hunter in uniform,
circa 1946.

Gustav Memminger (left)
and Siegfried Kulas (right).
Unknown photographer,
1945.

From left to right:
Siegfried Kulas, Kulas's
wife, Memminger's wife,
Gustav Memminger,
and Willi Heidemann.
Unknown photographer,
1945.

From left to right:
CIC agents Jack Hunter,
George Hochschild,
and Timothy Reis, in
Hunter's Frankfurt
apartment. Unknown
photographer, circa 1945.

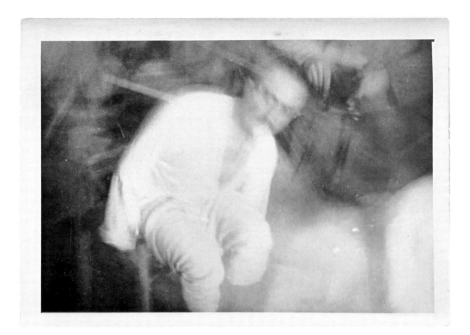

Artur Axmann being arrested by the CIC. Unknown photographer, December 15, 1945.   AUTHOR'S COLLECTION

An arrest made as part of Operation Nursery. Unknown photographer, circa December 1945.   AUTHOR'S COLLECTION

From left to right, seated: bottle of Three-Star Hennesy Coqnac (one of seven consumed that evening); The Prince of Vom Rath Strasse; a German personality whose name cannot be revealed; Capt. Donald M. Allen;
    Standing: Fritz Hauser, German chauffeur and house-breaking expert; Lt. "Tenny" Tenander; Special Agent T.M. Reis; Special Agent Walter Kaufman; and Special Agent Lewis.

A celebration of the completion of Operation Nursery. "The Prince of Vom Rath Strasse" is Jack Hunter. "A German personality whose name cannot be revealed" is Siegfried Kulas. Unknown photographer, circa April 1946.   AUTHOR'S COLLECTION

Still celebrating Operation Nursery. Standing (L to R): "Tenny" Tenander, Timothy Reis, Irving Lewis, and Siegfried Kulas. Sitting (L to R): Jack Hunter, Walter Kaufman, and Donald Allen. Unknown photographer, circa April 1946.
    AUTHOR'S COLLECTION

Jack Hunter (left) receiving the Bronze Star from General Sibert (right). Unknown photographer, 1946. AUTHOR'S COLLECTION

"Axmann . . . giving details in Nuremberg of Hitler's death."

T/4 HEWITT, U.S. ARMY, UNITED STATES
HOLOCAUST MEMORIAL MUSEUM, OCTOBER 16, 1947

food for his trip. He was now making the reverse of his journey out of Berlin, again on foot, while sticking to the backcountry as much as possible. He wanted to avoid inhabited areas with their checkpoints and occupation forces.

In September, Axmann set off from Lansen, where he'd been living since mid-May. This time he was on his own (for the trip to Lansen, he'd had a traveling companion). However, he now had a fake ID, money, and food, whereas before he'd just had the clothes on his back. Moreover, he knew the terrain, having traversed it on his prior journey. Despite all this, there would still be danger for him in leaving the safety of this village to travel through occupied Germany.

ELEVEN

EXPANSION

When Hitler declared war on the United States, he was bet-
ting that German soldiers, raised up in the Nazi Youth, would
always outfight American soldiers, brought up in the Boy
Scouts. He lost that bet. The Boy Scouts had been taught
how to figure their way out of their own problems.

STEPHEN AMBROSE[1]

In September 1945, four months after the fall of the Third Reich, Willi
Heidemann, the man Artur Axmann had sent to Bavaria to organize
the HJ Leadership into a new organization, remained focused on
building up as many business interests as possible, as quickly as he
could.

With Hans Garms, he wanted to create a new company in Munich
called Viktualien Import, G.m.b.H. (Victuals Import), for an import/
export business. In September, he asked Kurt Pommerening to form a
business based in Munich. This one was to be called Bayerische Autodi-
enst, G.m.b.H. (Bavarian Auto Service), with a branch office in Bad Tölz.
As a CIC informant, Pommerening (codenamed Paul) reported this to
Agent Reis and was told to go ahead and try to form this company.

Heidemann claimed "he was cleared (politisch unbedenklich) and
that everyone of his employees would be cleared by CIC. HEIDEMANN,

[Pommerening] told Agents, has no objections to hiring former Party members, but will not take in SS members."[2]

It was too dangerous to hire SS members; they were wanted as automatic arrestees. Many SS members were easy to find once the Allies learned about their blood type tattoo.

Heidemann should have followed this rule early on and not hired Siegfried Kulas. While Kulas's background in the SS made him trustworthy as a fellow Nazi, it also meant that he was a wanted man. It was this fact that likely led him to cut a deal with the CIC in order to save his own hide. This would prove to be Heidemann's undoing.

As the group expanded, when possible, they hired HJ and BDM members. As Reis later explained about this stage in their activities, "The more they expanded, the more HJ members were hired and were provided livelihood and cover. This was part of the Master Plan of the Underground operations [Kulas] had told us about when we first interrogated him just a short while back. Time was important for the HJ people in this phase of their plan—get as many former Hitler Jugend members under cover in reputable endeavor until the hue and the cry of the authorities abated and the country returned to a more stable atmosphere. The opportunity and ability to establish any business firm at this particular time gave the HJ leaders creditability with local governments, a source of employment for their former members, great economic leverage because of their rolling stock and organized branch outlets and communication to reestablish a chain of command with former leaders and members. These leaders were actually the cream of young man and womanhood trained together for years with a built-in discipline that if allowed to reorganize could very easily and seriously disrupt small local MG and German governments. If the Third Reich had survived, many of these HJ men and women would have been the leaders of tomorrow. It was ironic that the only qualified people left after the war with the ability to take over and run the economy and the government were these aforementioned leaders and it also occurred to me that all the other qualified people were not around anymore for various reasons."[3]

These "various reasons" that Agent Reis dryly alluded to included the horrors of the Holocaust. In addition, even "racially pure" Germans who politically opposed the Third Reich had faced death.[4]

When Axmann had started in the HJ in his working-class Berlin neighborhood, there had been an even larger number of youths there involved in the Communist youth groups. But they did not last long. Such organizations had been banned during the Third Reich, and being politically active in any group that opposed the Nazis was a very dangerous business for a young person during that time.

One big question the CIC had about Heidemann's rapid expansion of his group's business interests was: where exactly did the money come from? They knew that these funds had traveled with him from Berlin before the end of the war and had Nazi origins linked to the HJ, but they didn't know the specifics.

On September 10, they found out the source of at least some of this group's funding. Willi Heidemann had taken all the cash he could from a bank account in Berlin while it was still under Nazi control. The account had been for the National Youth Welfare Bureau (*Deutsches Jugend Förderungs Werke*), which he ran, and it theoretically still had 11 million RMS in it. That had been the balance when Heidemann fled Berlin, and no more money had been taken out of the account since then. Presumably the account was frozen.

Heidemann still had some unrealistic hopes of being able to withdraw that money someday. He had only been able to take with him 408,000 RMS. Heidemann told this story to Kulas, who informed the CIC about this money.

Beside the somewhat academic question of the source of Heidemann's money was the more pressing issue of where he was hiding it now. Some (perhaps most) of it was tied up in his various investments, but there was still cash at hand from the last days of the Third Reich.

As Agent Reis documented, Kulas eventually found out during his infiltration of the Bad Tölz Tessmann office "that whenever they needed money for the company one of the partners would leave and in 30 minutes return with fresh money! This seemed to narrow our search for a money cache to the town of Bad Tolz or its environs. We studied the town minutely with regard to areas or buildings the firm was using or associated with and by a process of elimination were led to one building—the Graf Zeppelin Pension. It was and still is perched on a hill west of the Kaserne [where the *Waffen* SS officers used to be trained] overlooking the town. (General Patton's headquarters were in the Kaserne.) It was a three-story building with balconies on each story with an overhanging gable sheltering them. Although we had no hard proof this building was involved we decided to investigate the interior using the old ruse of looking for a 'wanted personality.' We hit the jackpot! On the top outside balcony under a wooden bench we found a cardboard carton filled with newly minted German marks of large denominations. The haul was over a million marks—the smallest denomination was I believe 500 mark notes banded into bundles of 25,000 marks. To cover our finding, we made the appropriate noises to the inhabiters of the Pension and expressing great surprise at uncovering such a cache while looking for the wanted individual. We made wild accusations at those in charge of the Pension demanding explanation why so much money was kept there and generally leading our investigation away from our case.

"We kept our fingers crossed for the next few weeks until [Kulas] reported that the loss of the money was a blow but not unexpected considering the hiding place and the unfortunate search by Americans looking for a 'wanted man.'"[5]

This bit of misdirection had worked, and the CIC had successfully recovered some of the cash possessed by Heidemann. Fortunately for the CIC, no one suspected that Kulas had anything to do with this loss.

Meanwhile, in Austria, the group's Klug and Company was quickly expanding its reach. It had a small fleet of almost thirty vehicles engaged in profitable trade with Italy.[6] They exported "wood, salt and hops" from Austria and imported "rice, macaronis, fruit" and other food from Italy.[7] While in Austria with Heidemann, Garms learned that Heidemann had valuable shares in Austrian firms (although Garms didn't know which firms) and a million marks in movie projectors.[8]

This last information explained why they were thinking about opening up a movie theater in Bremen. That particular business had seemed quite random given that the other businesses mostly centered on transportation, food, fuel (coal), or on making better contacts with the occupying forces such as through an officers' bar. Some businesses just came about by happenstance when profitable opportunities materialized before Heidemann, such as this film equipment left over from the Third Reich.

On September 22, Agent Reis followed up on Agent Nordheim's contact with Heidemann's associates in Munich. These representatives of the Tessmann concern had first pretended to try to rent a building from the CIC and then asked Agent Nordheim (whom they knew under a different name) if he might be interested in going into business with them. Nordheim had said he would get back to them about their offer of working together on an import-export business between Bavaria and the United States.

Now Agent Reis stopped by Tessmann's office on Trogerstrasse telling them the truth: his colleague in the CIC was heading back to the States soon, so he was interested in taking over any discussions with them. Reis used the alias of Mr. Matthews.

Heidemann himself was there this time, and he gave Reis a tour of their office. He also showed Reis samples of the Bavarian art he hoped to export to the United States. Their half-hour discussion covered the coal business, in which Heidemann was impressively knowledgeable, and his good relations with the American authorities.

Reis wrote in his report that "HEIDEMANN made one reference to the CIC when he said in mock fright that he never thought he would be visited by the American Gestapo. This Agent replied that anyone whose slate was clean had nothing to fear, with which HEIDEMANN agreed."[9]

While Heidemann was comfortable interacting with the CIC, he did worry about his new business partner, the black marketer and concentration camp survivor Hans Garms, finding out that Tessmann was run by Nazis. When two women showed up at one of their offices, one a high-ranking BDM leader and the other the wife of HJ *Oberbannführer* Simon Winter, he "was very worried because he was afraid that GARMS would find out and create a scene, or even have them all arrested."[10]

Heidemann quickly had these women sent to another location, but there was an ever-present danger that someone could show up from the ruins of occupied Germany and either say something incriminating or by their very presence suggest to Garms that his new business associates were high-ranking Hitler Youth leaders.

In order to avoid detection, "HEIDEMANN has confided in his associates that he wants to shift all former HJ members around in various firms so that they will be more or less evenly distributed and cause less suspicion, and on this he has already begun."[11]

Another issue arose for Heidemann when a group run by former HJ leaders contacted him in September. Based in northern Germany, in the British Zone, one of their leaders was Kurt Budäus. Budäus had been a district leader (*Gebietsführer*) in the Hitler Youth and a major (*Sturmbannführer*) in the SS. He had been the head of the Personnel

Office in the national HJ office (*Leiter der Personalabteilung der Reichs-jugendführung*) until the summer of 1944.

The other leader of this northern group was Willi Lohel, who had also been an HJ district leader (*Gebietsführer*) as well as a main office chief (*Hauptamtschef*) in the national leadership of the HJ.[12]

Based in Lübeck, Budäus and Lohel wanted to combine their operations with Heidemann's. While Heidemann and the others in the Tessmann organization were willing to entertain this possibility, the major sticking point was money. Heidemann's group had it, and Budäus wanted it. This increasingly led to tension and arguments between the two organizations.

Budäus had first reached out to Heidemann through one of his men in Bremen, a Mr. Dreblow. Heidemann in turn told Dreblow to "contact MEMMINGER who heads the political section of the undercover organization of former HJ officials and give him all information as to where this new group is to be reached. At present [this new group is] in the vicinity of BRAUNSCHWEIG."[13] Reis believed that this northern group would be invited to a meeting in Munich to "inform them of the new program in which NAZISM is to be reintroduced to the German masses under the guise of 'SAMMLUNG DIE ANSTANDIGEN.'"[14]

The CIC had not heard of Budäus's group until he made contact with Heidemann, and they still knew very little about it. Finding out more was now a top priority.

Jack Hunter continued going undercover as Hans Jaeger in order to learn more about the Tessmann concern.

At one point while he was in the field undercover, an unknown party sabotaged his vehicle. As a friend of his remembers the story, "He was driving from Munich to another town in Germany and had to stop for gas. While the attendant was filling his tank, Hunter used the men's room. When he came out, the attendant said, 'Apparently somebody doesn't like you.' He pointed out that the lug nuts on all four wheels were very loose. Hunter was driving mountain roads with hairpin curves over huge chasms. If a wheel had come off on those roads, he would have been killed."[15] Hunter never did find out who did this. It could have been someone who just wanted to kill an American, or who picked up on the fact that he was an intelligence agent.

Another incident occurred while Hans Jaeger had his gun drawn. As a friend of Hunter's explained, Hunter "was in a hotel trying to sneak up on one of the bad guys. Suddenly he saw motion to one side, turned, and fired six times. Only he was firing at his reflection in a mirror. Fortunately he could laugh about it later, but I'll bet it wasn't funny at the time."[16]

In September 1945, Artur Axmann readied himself to leave his hiding place in the Soviet Zone. His journey from a small village in northern Germany to Berlin would be a perilous one. He did not have transit papers, and his fake ID had a stamp on it that he had forged himself. By avoiding checkpoints whenever possible, and with a bit of luck, he managed to make it back to Berlin.

It was too dangerous to make contact with his wife (Ilse Bachstein) and their young son. Even though he was separated from Ilse and had a girlfriend whom he would later marry, he still wanted to visit Ilse and his son. He had not seen either of them since before the fall of Berlin. As far as he knew, they were still living in the city.

He worried that if he approached them the Russians would capture him.[17] So all he could do was stare across the distance at his former home in the Kladow district of the Spandau borough of Berlin. He wondered how his wife and son were doing with the Soviets controlling the city. Only later did he find out that they had imprisoned his wife for a few weeks.

He had arrived in Berlin at the train station at Wannsee. From this station, he walked the short distance to the edge of the water that separated him from his family in Kladow.

After a reflective moment, he quickly made his way north to the heart of Spandau. This would normally have been about a three- to four-hour walk, but Axmann ran when possible to minimize the amount of time he spent in Berlin. A fence behind the houses along Brunsbütteler Damm, a street in Spandau, separated the backyards there from a rail line.

Rumor was that it was possible to stowaway aboard a freight train here and ride it out of the Soviet Zone. Axmann could not travel through a checkpoint from one zone to another with the paperwork he had. He needed to sneak across.

Once at Brunsbütteler Damm, Axmann crept around people's backyards looking for a way through the fence. Eventually, he located a hole in the fence that someone else had cut. He was disappointed to find that although there were freight cars there, none of them had the necessary locomotive attached.

While snooping around this train yard, he ran into a fellow traveler. A former soldier, this man knew which train was heading west next. He assured Axmann that they were safe from the local train staff, who did not go after people hopping freights. This meant that they could safely go on the train now, instead of waiting until it started moving and then jumping on board at the last minute.

This was much safer, as boarding a moving train was a dangerous affair. Those who rode the rails in America during the Great Depression, for example, generally had to avoid the guards hired by the railroads (known as bulls) to prevent freight hopping. And so, they had to make last-second running leaps onto moving trains, resulting in countless deaths and injuries.

As Axmann rode the train through to the British Zone, he was nervous, but despite his concerns, he made it safely out of Soviet-controlled territory. He got off at the end destination of Brunswick. Then he made his way about two hundred miles northeast to the industrial city of Gelsenkirchen. It was here that his girlfriend, Erna Vieckariesmann, lived with her family.

In his first year as *Reichsjugendführer*, Axmann had traveled throughout Germany visiting various HJ groups. In the town of Gelsenkirchen, then known for its coal mining and oil refining, he saw a sixteen-year-old BDM member named Erna Vieckariesmann play the violin. He was in his late twenties. As he later wrote, "The beauty of her playing also corresponded to her appearance."[18] They stayed in touch and later ended up in a romantic relationship. During the chaos of the war, he had not felt it appropriate to formally divorce his wife. So they separated and he dated Erna toward the end of the war.

It turned out that Erna had arrived at her parents' place just a few days before Axmann returned to Gelsenkirchen, so Axmann's luck had held. They met up in front of a local hospital for a joyous reunion. Erna had already heard that he had survived the end of the war— former soldiers that Axmann had met while in the Soviet Zone had successfully brought her word.

Axmann's journey though was far from over. He still had his promises to Mayor Bleckmann and to the farm family back in Lansen to fulfill. First, he traveled to Heilsbronn in Bavaria, about three hundred miles southeast of his current location.[19] From there, he made local trips to visit close relatives of the farm family.[20] They were overjoyed to receive the news that their loved ones were alive and well in the Soviet Zone. This was the first they had heard anything about them. They gave Axmann supplies for his trip and alcohol to bring back to the farm.

Now he had a journey to make of more than four hundred miles due north to the Baltic port city of Lübeck in northern Germany. Axmann was not going there to sample Lübeck's famous marzipan treats or to gawk at its historic architecture, but to join his girlfriend again. They had made plans to rendezvous in Lübeck, so she had traveled there to see him after he made his trip south. While staying in Lübeck, Axmann met up with Gustav Memminger for the first time since the fall of the Third Reich.

They had worked together in the HJ national office, where Memminger had been Axmann's propaganda chief. Now Memminger was one of the leaders of the Tessmann-based organization of former HJ personnel. While Heidemann ran the economic section, he was responsible for implementing the political ambitions of this group.

According to Axmann, it was a random encounter.[21] Axmann's version of events is that he spotted Memminger on the streets of Lübeck and was shocked to see him. As Memminger had not noticed him, Axmann decided to have a bit of fun with this reunion. Instead of just calling out his name or openly approaching him, Axmann came from behind and placed his prosthetic device on Memminger's shoulder. The Third Reich's secret police (the Gestapo) had been famous for stopping people with just such a tap on the shoulder. Axmann thought it would be fun to give Memminger a bit of a fright.

Memminger was surprised to see his former boss standing in front of him in this northern German city. Instead of the clean-cut uniformed man with a military poise he was used to, Memminger faced a bearded fellow dressed like a civilian. According to Axmann, Memminger said, "Artur, you are here. We thought you fell in Berlin."[22]

They caught up on what had happened to each of them during the last days of the war and since the Allies had occupied Germany. Axmann wanted to know about his mother (Emma Axmann); he had not seen her since before Berlin was captured. Memminger informed him that she was alive and well, having moved from Berlin to Upper

Bavaria. Axmann's underlings from the HJ's national office were looking out for her.

Axmann explained his promise made to Lansen Mayor Bleckmann and that he had to go back there. Axmann, Memminger, and Axmann's girlfriend, Erna, arranged to meet up again in November, when Axmann would again leave the Soviet Zone.

It may have been that this was an arranged meeting and that Axmann portrayed a different version of events as he wanted to minimize his involvement with Heidemann's postwar activities. He clearly did try to spin the events in an innocuous direction when he was later interrogated by the CIC. Even though much of this story comes from his writings later in life, Axmann may have been less than honest in his account of how he came to meet with Memminger in Lübeck. If not, it was an amazing coincidence that of all the millions of people in Germany at that time, he happened to run into Gustav Memminger.

If Axmann had arranged this meeting with Memminger, then it would have been so he could get back in touch with his former underlings at the HJ national office to see what they had done with the Tessmann Corporation since the end of the war. He also would have wanted assistance with checking on his mother, obtaining high-quality false identification, and money.

From Lübeck, Axmann went to a town about forty miles to the south called Lauenburg. He knew that Mayor Bleckmann's daughters lived there, but he did not have an actual address for them. Despite this impediment, he managed to locate them. He explained that their father wanted them to travel back home to Lansen with him. Despite the dangers that this trip entailed, and that it meant moving to the Soviet Zone, they wanted to go. They asked to bring their cousin with them, to which Axmann agreed.

This journey back was fraught with more peril than Axmann's

journey from Lansen. While he was a trained and experienced soldier, he was traveling with civilians now. Moreover, they were young women, which meant that soldiers might detain them and try to rape them, and maybe end up hurting or killing Axmann if he tried to protect the girls, or if the soldiers didn't want a witness to their misdeeds.

First, they headed south and slightly east to a town about two hundred miles away called Hornburg. Here, they crossed on foot from the British Zone to the Soviet Zone. The border crossing was where they were most likely to run into troops. Although the Soviets were still officially allies with the West, tensions continued to rise between the parties.

Around midnight, Axmann led his charges through forests and a field in order to avoid checkpoints and troops guarding the border. Here, his luck ran out when one of the girls tripped and fell, making so much noise that some Soviet soldiers heard it. The soldiers quickly captured Axmann and the rest of his traveling party. The soldiers marched their prisoners to a hut in the forest, and then proceeded to go through their belongings, but they were not looking for contraband or evidence or otherwise operating in any sort of official capacity. These soldiers were common highwaymen, yet another pitfall of the road.

Having their belongings stolen was the least of their worries. Axmann fell into the automatic arrest category. If these soldiers figured out his identity, he might never see the outside of a Soviet jail cell again. His adjunct Weltzin, for instance, who had been captured by the Russians in Berlin during their escape together, died while in Soviet custody.

Even if these lowly border soldiers didn't recognize Axmann, if they decided to send him on for further detention, it was likely that somebody would eventually ID him, due to his low-quality fake papers and his highly recognizable war injury.

Things took a turn for the worse when the soldiers discovered the alcohol Axmann had been carrying and drank it. Adding alcohol to an already volatile situation made it more unstable and dangerous. This was the last thing Axmann needed.

The soldiers separated their prisoners along gender lines, putting the women into their own room. This was a frightening development; the girls started screaming as loud as they could. Axmann had previously instructed them to do so if they were in danger of being raped, in the hopes that it could bring them attention and so stop an attack. However, as they were in the middle of the woods in a border area, it was unlikely any passersby would help them. But perhaps, if they were lucky, an officer might hear these screams and do something to stop the situation.

Axmann felt helpless to do anything. But despite all their worries, nothing bad happened to the women during the night.

In the morning, they were all taken to the yard of a nearby military facility. There a Soviet major in a good mood asked them if they preferred the Russians or British (as an occupying force). They went with the obvious answer of Russians and were then waved on their way.

In this respect, it may have helped that they were sneaking into Soviet territory and not out of it. The general flow was in the other direction, with millions migrating from the east to the west.[23]

Perhaps the Soviet major interpreted their movements as indicating that they'd rather live under the Soviets than the British. During this incident, no one had bothered to check Axmann's papers. For now he was free.

The rest of the trip was uneventful, now that they were in Soviet-occupied territory. Back in Lansen, Mayor Bleckmann was overjoyed to have his daughters back home. And the farm family was pleased to hear that their relatives were well.

And so, Lansen continued to be a good place for Axmann to lay low. Only a few people knew that he was there. Also, he had a job, a place to stay, and the protection of an extremely grateful mayor.

TWELVE

THE SETUP

It was like being a worm working your way into a rotten apple.

PAUL SOAMES IN THE MOVIE *SHANGHAI*[1]

The CIC wanted to learn all they could about the northern group led by Kurt Budäus and Willi Lohel. Toward this end, Agent Reis went on an almost three-week-long road trip with his informant Kulas to northern Germany during October 1945. They took Kulas's car, a Volkswagen, after having received permission from the CIC brass at Frankfurt (including Jack Hunter) to make this exploratory trip.

Agent Reis later wrote about this trip. "We stopped at the little office [for Tessmann & Sons] in Feucht, a village near Nuremberg the first night and met some of the office help and two men who were in charge. One of the girls in this office was with Jutta Ruediger in her hideout in the Austrian mountains and whose picture I had taken with my Leica from a distance. She didn't recognize me, of course. On this trip I had assumed a false identity, a GI on furlough out for a good time and some travelling and not too worried about getting back to my outfit. During the night our VW was stolen and stripped by Russian DPs [displaced persons]. We were now without a vehicle but our newly found 'friends' got busy and with a little money encouragement provided us with a good vehicle to continue our trip, but with one catch, we had two passengers that wanted to travel to Bremen also. We couldn't refuse so we took them along but I arranged by phone for all of us to be arrested at a road block just outside of Kassel. We left our two friends languishing in the local jail and [Kulas][2] and I continued on into the British zone. We visited places [Kulas] remembered and came away with various bits of information usually from the wives of prominent HJ leaders."[3]

There was no coercion involved in extracting intelligence from these women, Kulas simply talked with them. Siegfried Kulas was a trusted member of Tessmann at this point, and his credentials as a Nazi were strong, as they included membership in the SS. When he talked privately with these wives, they trusted him enough to gossip about what they knew.

As Agent Reis later recalled, "After arriving in Bremen and checking in with CIC, [Kulas] paid a visit to the [Tessmann] firm's Bremen branch. After several visits over several days [Kulas] said there had been a meeting of northern HJ leaders but there were many others of HJ high rank floating around in the area. He said that he was invited to a meeting the next day at which [one of the northern group's leaders, Willi] Lohel was to be present . . .[4]

"Reporting on the meeting which Lohel attended, [Kulas] said someone had asked the whereabouts of Artur Axmann, HJ leader and Lohel had replied 'It is best to believe that he fell with the Fuehrer in the Reichs' Chancellery.' (We knew that Axmann's chauffeur was alive and living in the foothills in Bavaria because we had found him and questioned him regarding the last hours at the Chancellery and the possibility of Axmann having survived. The chauffeur had told us that he was present at the bunker where Hitler and Eva Braun were last seen, and that when he left the bunker area Axmann was still there fighting and that was the last time he saw Axmann. The chauffeur thought he was either captured by the Russians or killed.) Now this statement by Lohel seemed to open a door to the past and it spurred us on for more information about Axmann."[5]

From Bremen, Agent Reis and Siegfried Kulas traveled northeast. As Reis later recounted, "[Kulas] and I drove on to Hamburg and scouted around a few days and I enjoyed the hospitality of the British MI for a place to stay and rations. At one of the meetings [Kulas] attended [the northern group's other leader, Kurt] Budaus was present and asked [Kulas] to relay a message to [Heidemann] to meet at Goettingen [a college town due south of Hamburg] on November 5th with Budaus, Memminger and [Heidemann]. According to [Kulas] this signified that [Heidemann] would be taking care of the commercial and business end, Memminger the political and Budaus the regimentation of the rank and file, into an organization much as it had been before the war's end. Budaus, [Kulas] said, was champing at the bit because of inactivity and remarked 'we shouldn't wait too long (to get together an organization) but to get going and, on one day's reign of terror hang 50 or 60 people such as Buergermeisters [mayors] and other German bureaucrats all over Germany to show that the Nazis were still powerful and that anti-Nazis should fear them and be afraid to carry out or enforce anti-Nazi laws.' [Kulas] said he cautioned Budaus against such outbursts and urged him to stay in hiding but he said this was typical of the Budaus temperament."[6]

Budäus was still stuck on the idea of conducting Werwolf activities that the other HJ leaders had already abandoned. The others felt that killing Allied troops or German collaborators in big displays like this would only result in their own capture. They had instead adopted more subtle long-term strategies to gain political and economic power.

The only killings the other leaders were still considering were for their own disciplinary purposes as part of Overbeck's proposed Feme courts.

During this trip, when "Siegfried [Kulas] and I journeyed to Bremen and Hamburg, we had a double purpose—to get information on the HJ AND to find 120 liters of white rum hidden in a small town southwest of Bremen. We got both and brought back the rum in two vehicles but found it was ersatz rum (synthetic) and it would make you break out in little red dots like hives. [We] experimented and found that using GI grapefruit juice as a mixer eliminated this minor irritant and [Jack Hunter was] there and drank some of same."[7]

Reis and Kulas's road trip ended in Munich on October 29. They had some free time before the meeting that one of the leaders of the northern HJ group, Kurt Budäus, had set up for November 5. During this break, Agent Reis spent his time briefing Jack Hunter and others in the Farben Building (including General Sibert) about his trip and recent developments in the case. He also had a similar meeting in Heidelberg with General Keyes, then the commander for the U.S. Seventh Army, which was headquartered there.

In early November, as Reis later wrote, "[Kulas] and I kept a date at Goettingen (near Kassel) because Budaus had issued a call for a meeting between himself, [Heidemann] and Memminger, on November 5th and [we] were anxious to see who would show. We briefed the local [police] to pick up Budaus if he made an appearance and hold him for the MP's. [Heidemann] had instructed [Kulas] to tell Budaus that he, [Heidemann], couldn't come to this meeting. [Heidemann] told [Kulas] that all Budaus wanted was to stir up trouble and try to pry some funds out of him, and [Heidemann] didn't want to accommodate Budaus on either [trouble or money] at this time. [Kulas] and I were in the hopes that Memminger would show up and we could possibly get a lead on where Axmann was, if he were still alive. Budaus showed on

November 5th but spooked before the [police] could get him and gave them the slip. Memminger didn't show."[8]

Reis was now partnered with Special Agent George Hochschild. His old partner, Werner D. Nordheim, had left the military and returned to the States.

While working on an unrelated case, Hochschild stumbled upon some of the money Willi Heidemann had stashed away. This happened when Agent Hochschild traveled to the small Upper Bavarian village of Oberammergau, near the Austrian border, to do some counterintelligence work.

This village was famous for the large-scale passion play that started in 1634 and had been put on almost every ten years since then. This tradition started during an outbreak of the plague, when the villagers "swore an oath that they would perform the 'Play of the Suffering, Death and Resurrection of Our Lord Jesus Christ' every ten years."[9]

Oberammergau was also home to a large military facility used by the U.S. Army as the Information and Education School (today it is used by NATO). Hochschild's assignment took him there to interrogate the locally hired German cooks. It was suspected that some of them were using their presence at this school to learn details about its classified curriculum. Agent Hochschild confirmed this to be the case: some of the kitchen staff were indeed guilty of spying.

As Hochschild recalled in 2010, "While I was down there, somebody told me that Mrs. Heidemann [Willi Heidemann's wife] was in Oberammergau and that they were hiding some money with her. So, I hunted around and lo and behold, I found her. She was living in a rented apartment and I talked to her and she was very, very scared. She was very worried about the whole thing. I said, 'I understand that you've had some dealing with some money.'

She said, 'Oh, yes, yes, I wish you'd get rid of it.'

I said, 'What is it?'

'Well it's in a barracks bag.' And it was under her bed, and she gave me the barracks bag [what we now call a G.I. duffel bag]. I took it, opened it and it was full of money—mostly British stuff and non-German currency, paper money. So I didn't want any part of it. There was an outfit, I think it was an infantry outfit, a small group in Oberammergau . . . I went to their CEO, I think he was a captain. I told him, I have a bag full of money. Could he guard it for me? He said, no, he doesn't want any part of it. Get out of here. I don't want to talk to you; I don't even want to see the damned thing. So, the only thing I could see, I put it in the jeep and drove it to Frankfurt. Well I had to get rid of it. I told whoever was in Frankfurt the story. And they said we have to find out how much it is. And they assigned a staff sergeant and he and I counted the money. It took us two days to get to the same amount. He counted independently from me and I counted. And it was quite a bit of money; it took a long time. Like I said about two, three days before we both agreed on the amount. I turned it in to the MI [Military Intelligence] staff and I have a receipt from it. I kept that receipt for a long time. It was over two hundred thousand dollars. It was a lot of money."[10]

Using the Consumer Price Index, the estimated value of this haul today would be slightly less than $2.5 million.[11]

Normally people are drawn to money, and it may be hard to understand why those who came into contact with this lucre back then wanted nothing to do with it. It was dangerous though to have so much cash. If you were caught with it, there was no legitimate explanation for having it. And so why risk temptation by having anything to do with this money? Once the money was confiscated, those in the military were worried that if any of the money were ever stolen, anyone who had access to it at any point would be under suspicion.

Hochschild disclosed, "I didn't inquire where it came from and how it got there. I was trying to get rid of the goddamned stuff."[12]

While the money had originally been in reichsmarks when Heidemann had taken it from Berlin, somehow he had exchanged it on the black market for other currencies. Hochschild explained, "I don't know how they changed it into British pounds, French francs, and quite a bit of U.S. dollars. In that barracks bag was no German money, it was foreign currency."[13]

If Willi Heidemann's only consideration was selecting someone he could trust not to steal this money, then his wife was the right move. But Hochschild felt that Willi Heidemann should have picked someone else to hold on to these funds. As Hochschild recounted, "Willi Heidemann gave it to her to safeguard. She was very, very scared. She was the wrong choice altogether. She was crying half the time. She didn't know what to do with it. She was worried, it was dangerous, and somebody was going to shoot her and all this kind of garbage. She was trying to get rid of it, but she couldn't find anybody to take it. I don't blame her."[14]

While Hochschild was focused on dealing with the money, and he was not interested in punishing Mrs. Heidemann for hiding it, she could have ended up in a situation where she faced a lengthy prison sentence for holding on to these illicit Nazi funds. Or, as she was very aware, someone could have killed her for the money. Willi Heidemann would have been much better off if he had just buried this stash somewhere and not troubled his wife with it.

Separate from the ongoing Nursery operation, the Rosenheim CIC office obtained its own informant who would play a key role in this case.

Rosenheim is a picturesque town in Upper Bavaria where the Inn and Mangfall Rivers come together. It is only about forty miles southeast of Munich, the spiritual birthplace of Nazism, which the Nazi

Party referred to as the "Capital of the Movement" (*Hauptstadt der Bewegung*).

Rosenheim was also the physical birthplace of *Reichsmarschall* Hermann Göring. Göring though was now in Nuremberg, on trial at the International Military Tribunal.

CIC Special Agents Irving J. Lewis and Walter Kaufman ran their new informant out of Rosenheim.[15] Lewis had chiseled features with a sharp jaw, short curly hair, and a pronounced nose. His partner Kaufman had more of a scholarly look with his wire-frame glasses and smaller build. Kaufman's ears stuck out a bit and his dense hair lacked a real part.

Lewis and Kaufman had developed this informant through his relationship with his Polish girlfriend, who had helped the CIC turn him.

Codenamed "Slim," his real name was Günter Ebeling and he had been a senior unit leader (*Oberstammführer*) in the HJ. He had also been a department head in the General Government of Poland (*Leiter der Hauptabteilung III im Generalgouvernement*). Ebeling had been active in HJ activities (in Krakow, Poland), and so, through his past work with the HJ, he had the trust of HJ leaders.

As Agent Reis later wrote, Ebeling "had no known knowledge of the existence of the transportation firm or any of its other facets, but seemed to have an in with [Gustav] Memminger and [Simon] Winter through some past connection."[16] This connection appears to have been his friendship with Overbeck.[17]

Ebeling used the resources of the Rosenheim CIC to become close to Gustav Memminger and Ernst Overbeck. He was able to supply them with false papers (courtesy of his CIC handlers), and he had a vehicle, travel papers, and gasoline. With the help of the CIC, he had even arranged for safe houses for former HJ leaders.

Up to now, the CIC had not known Axmann's location. Even Kulas, as trusted as he was by those running Tessmann, could not obtain this information. Instead, it was Ebeling who was about to be introduced to Axmann and so could then inform the CIC exactly where to find him. His cultivation of Memminger and Overbeck was about to pay off.

The CIC was careful to keep Ebeling unaware of their other main informant, Kulas. And vice versa. Their handlers, though, shared information, and Hunter received both sets of reports at his desk in the Farben Building. Hunter now had two sets of agents working with him as the case officer in charge. During his handling of Operation Nursery, he was promoted to the rank of first lieutenant.

Artur Axmann spent October 1945 on the farm in Lansen. He observed that the Soviets were recruiting former German soldiers into their own forces. Watching what was happening around him in the Soviet Zone, Axmann felt that the Soviets were preparing for a possible confrontation with their erstwhile allies to the west.

On October 18, the International Military Tribunal in Nuremberg issued an indictment against twenty-four leading Nazi war criminals.[18] This tribunal was made up of judges from the Allied Powers—the Soviet Union, the United Kingdom, the United States, and France. Each country had one judge and one alternate. This trial was a huge news story throughout occupied Germany. Axmann knew many of the defendants personally—for instance, his mentor and predecessor as *Reichsjugendführer*, Baldur von Schirach, was among them. Von Schirach was indicted for conspiracy to wage aggressive war (count I) and crimes against humanity (count IV).[19]

In what must have been a humorous surprise to Axmann, Martin Bormann was among those the International Military Tribunal indicted. He was being tried in absentia. Axmann had seen Bormann's dead body with his own eyes during their breakout from Hitler's bunker. Since the Allies didn't know for certain if Bormann was dead, they weren't taking any chances.

The International Military Tribunal charged Bormann with conspiracy to wage aggressive war, war crimes, and crimes against humanity. His lawyer's main defense was rather unusual—that Bormann was already dead. He was eventually found guilty of these last two charges and sentenced to death by hanging.

In early November, the time had come for Axmann to leave Lansen. The month before, when he'd been in Lübeck, he had arranged with Gustav Memminger to meet him again. He'd also planned to meet up with his girlfriend there. He needed to start traveling immediately in order to get to Lübeck, which was in the British Zone, on schedule to meet them.

This time, Axmann's trip was relatively easy; he already knew the way. In Berlin, he met up with a young woman from Lansen, who had previously arranged to cross out of Soviet controlled Germany with him. Her name was Gerda, she was only twenty, and unlike Axmann, she had never made this trip before. As Gerda recalled in 2012, they met up late at night, and along with another man, went to "a pub close to the freight yard" to warm themselves.[20]

She went on to describe their trip together: "There was bright moonlight, as we made our way to the freight depot. . . . We were lucky that the patrolman who ran the station was a German. He had noticed us and asked us where we wanted to go. By two in the morning, the roofless freight train started to move. . . ."[21]

"At the border, the train had to stop. We heard voices and knew that therefore we were not alone on the train. Then suddenly two Russian soldiers looked into our wagon, but they said nothing. Later we learned that their platoon leader had been instructed to respect this no man's land. The train drivers were simply gone. . . . In Helmstedt, [which was the inner-German border crossing between the Soviet and British

Zones] our journey together ended. . . . That my companion was the former Hitler Youth leader Artur Axmann, I did not learn until later." [22]

Although this trip went as planned, once in Lübeck, Axmann was in for a shock.

Instead of meeting up with Memminger again, two other former subordinates of his from the national leadership office of the Hitler Youth were there. Ernst Overbeck and Simon Winter surprised him at his pension in Lübeck. Memminger had sent them. While Axmann was overjoyed to see them, he was concerned about them having a man with them that he did not know.

This unknown figure was Günter Ebeling, who had driven Overbeck and Winter to meet Axmann. In his later writings, Axmann claimed that the fact that Ebeling had his own vehicle made him suspicious.[23] Despite any reservations Axmann may have had about trusting a stranger who somehow had access to a car, he let Ebeling drive them around.

He should have been very suspicious of Ebeling. It was true that a German who had travel papers, a car, and gasoline in November 1945 was a rare thing. If Tessmann had sent one of their work vehicles that had travel papers and gasoline based on their legitimate transportation business, it would have made sense. But this was a private individual who had all these things.

However, the same things that made Axmann suspicious of Ebeling also made him too valuable for Axmann to ignore. Besides, Winter and Overbeck trusted him.

In actuality, the CIC office in Rosenheim had supplied Ebeling with everything he needed. And now the CIC knew exactly where Axmann was hiding. This was huge; while there had been speculation that Axmann might still be alive and running things, the CIC had lacked solid leads about this. The Soviets seemed to believe that he was dead, and despite all the hard work by those involved in Operation Nursery, no one knew for certain what had become of Axmann.

Axmann talked about how he wanted to move to the American Zone, but he needed somewhere safe to stay and papers good enough to stand up to scrutiny.[24] Ebeling said he could provide all these things—he had already done so for others in their organization. Of course, the CIC was the actual source of such papers.

The plan was for Axmann to move in early December to the small town of Oberaudorf in the district of Rosenheim, which was part of Upper Bavaria. At an elevation of more than fifteen hundred feet, this mountain town was just north of the border between Germany and Austria. Here Axmann could escape into the Alps if need be, or cross the border into Austria.

Ebeling was to arrange an apartment there and get high-quality papers in the name of Erich Siewert. The CIC would be the ones to provide Axmann with his housing in Oberaudorf; Ebeling would then pretend that he had found it. Special Agents Lewis and Kaufman had already arranged with the Third Army's chief of intelligence to arrest Axmann once he was living in Oberaudorf. Ebeling would be far away when the arrest happened, so as to minimize the danger that anyone at Tessmann would think he had anything to do with Axmann's capture.

Axmann received some good news at this meeting. His mother was still doing well and she was living safely in Wackersberg, the village near Bad Tölz where Tessmann had at one time run their operations.

On December 1, Axmann left Lübeck on his own. He hitched a ride in the back of a truck with a bunch of German veterans. They didn't know who he was, but during their conversations about the war and life in Nazi Germany, they happened to mention his name repeatedly. It must have felt surreal to Axmann to be surrounded by people who talked about him, while he pretended to be just another injured veteran.

Travel in the back of an open truck, in the chill December air of northern Germany, was far from comfortable, but as Axmann later noted, he and his fellow travelers had already experienced much worse. It was a near universal experience of former German soldiers to have slept rough with little protection from the elements.

It was a harsh winter that year, which was terrible for a continent that had just emerged from a brutal war. As a well-known journalist, William L. Shirer, wrote in his journal, "For even though the fighting has stopped, the peoples of Europe this winter are hungry and cold."[25]

On December 4, Axmann arrived in the village of Oberstaufen, in the Bavarian Alps, just north of the border with Austria. Here, he met up with Memminger and Winter again at the town train station.[26] They took him to meet his mother, who had come there with Heidemann the day before.

It was the first time Axmann had seen his mother since the war. They were close, as his father had died when he was young. She had raised him and his siblings on her own. This was an emotion-filled reunion—they had both managed to survive the end of the war and to find each other. Given the chaos and destruction they had lived through, this was no small feat.

BDM *Bannführerin* Melita Maschmann recalled of Axmann's mother, "One sometimes saw [her] at meetings, an old woman dressed in black who looked simple and likeable, and who gave the impression that she detested being displayed in public."[27]

The next day, December 5, was Overbeck's birthday. A big meeting was held in a cabin outside of town to bring Axmann up to date on their activities so far. Other leaders from the national office of the HJ were there as well, including Willi Heidemann and Heinrich Hartmann. They discussed the goals of their organization, including whether resistance of any kind against the occupying forces was futile and what their future goals should be.

Even the most die-hard Nazis, including the likes of Axmann, who had been with Hitler until the end, could see that Werwolf-style active resistance to the Allied Forces would do nothing to rid Germany of the occupying forces or restore it to a National Socialist form of government. Attacking occupation forces would instead result in their being hunted down and captured.

While there was talk of some kind of passive resistance, the plan in place to pursue clandestine political power while growing economically seemed to be the consensus position.

A major topic of discussion was whether to risk reaching out to those young men in Germany who now had nothing. Many former HJ members had coped with the hardships of living in postwar Germany by becoming tramps, living on the road without hope for their future.

Heinrich Hartmann convinced Axmann and the others that they would need to do what they could for these young men. He argued, "We must now do everything we can to protect the youth against nihilism."[28]

This main meeting was held in the large downstairs area. A much more intimate meeting took place upstairs, when Heidemann debriefed Axmann on all of the group's business activities. This organization had expanded so quickly into so many different enterprises that Axmann had to draw a diagram to keep things straight.[29] This meeting consisted of only the two of them.

For the week and a half that Axmann stayed in Bavaria, he lived in this two-story cabin. One night, Ebeling came by and talked with him. Ebeling was concerned that Axmann had not followed the plan to move to Oberaudorf. Axmann said he still wanted to move there, but he now wanted to travel around Germany before settling down sometime after Christmas.

Axmann told Ebeling that he wanted to return to Lübeck to meet with a man the CIC considered the "liaison representative with the

Wehrmacht for the underground."[30] The *Wehrmacht* had been the combined military of Nazi Germany.[31]

Ebeling offered to drive Axmann for the trip north. Ebeling still had his car, travel papers, and gasoline. After this meeting, Ebeling informed the CIC about Axmann wanting to travel more before going to Oberaudorf.

The CIC was worried that Axmann might change his plans again and so avoid falling into the trap they had set for him in Oberaudorf. It would have been easy to arrest him there, as they were the ones finding him a place to live.

They were afraid to wait and see if Axmann did end up moving there. If Axmann came up with a new destination again, they might lose him.

Under the original plan, Ebeling would be long gone when Axmann was arrested in Oberaudorf, so no one would suspect him of being the traitor. Now the CIC wanted to arrest Axmann before he left Third Army territory during his upcoming trip. They had already coordinated with the Third Army higher-ups to make this arrest happen and if Axmann traveled into a different military jurisdiction, they would not be prepared to coordinate with the local military authorities to capture him.

CIC Special Agents Lewis and Kaufman asked Ebeling exactly where Axmann expected to go on this trip and when. They didn't want to tell him about their new arrest plans for Axmann until everything was in place and it was too late for Ebeling to back out.

But Ebeling was no fool; he quickly deduced the reason for these questions. The CIC planned on arresting Axmann during this trip and they were not going to wait around in the hopes he would still eventually move to the apartment in Oberaudorf.

Ebeling freaked out. If Axmann were arrested while Ebeling was driving him, it could expose Ebeling as a traitor. He wanted out; this was not the plan they had agreed on, and the last thing he wanted was the Nazi underground regarding him as a traitor to their cause. And so Ebeling said that he quit. That was that.

But of course, the CIC had other ideas and explained to him that they were going to arrest Axmann with or without his help. As very few people knew Axmann's location and plans, even if Ebeling made an excuse to back out of driving him and washed his hands of this operation, he would still risk the suspicion of his fellow Nazis. He had to go along with the plan, and the CIC promised that they would do what they could to protect him.

During the very early morning hours of December 12, Ebeling met with CIC and Third Army representatives to come up with a plan for Axmann's upcoming arrest. Three different possible arrest locations were discussed for further consideration. They agreed to pick one based on additional reconnaissance. After considering all the things that could go wrong, they eventually went with the one they called "Plan C."

While in Munich, Ebeling picked up Ernst Overbeck and some belongings of Memminger's. On the drive from Munich, they were stopped at a checkpoint and almost arrested. This was narrowly avoided, and they were able to drive to their lodging. They spent the night and then got up in the morning to meet up with Axmann and the others.

Axmann, Overbeck, and Memminger had no idea that their driver, Ebeling, was going to deliver them into a trap carefully arranged by the CIC.

THIRTEEN

CAPTURE

I remember one German to whom Nazism meant midnight
arrests and rubber truncheons, while to another it meant
Autobahns and parades and good jobs.

JACK HUNTER[1]

Christmas came early for the CIC in 1945. On December 15, agents
were in place along with soldiers from the Third Army to arrest
Axmann and two of his top men. Jack Hunter and the other CIC agents
had carefully prepared for this moment.

CIC Special Agent Irving J. Lewis was one of the agent's handling
the informant Günter Ebeling from the CIC office in Rosenheim,
Bavaria. He wrote that the "Third Army established a series of inter-
locking road blocks covering all possible road exits, including the
borders of French-Occupied Germany and Austria. Blocks were
instructed to allow the vehicle driven by SLIM [Ebeling's codename]
to pass into the area unhindered, but to arrest all passengers on the
exit. CIC/Rosenheim provided descriptions of passengers and the
vehicle."[2]

The CIC wanted Axmann to enter their trap, and then not be able to leave it. These soldiers stationed on roadblocks were there as precautions, nothing more. If things went according to plan, they wouldn't be involved other than to let the target into the area. But if things went wrong, and Axmann somehow evaded them despite his driver working for the CIC, then they would be ready to arrest him. The same was true for his fellow passengers—Gustav Memminger and Ernst Overbeck, both high-level leaders of the HJ.

Agent Walter Kaufman (from the CIC office in Rosenheim) and a partner were in disguise as skiers. A thick layer of snow covered the buildings, roads, and trees equally. The Bavarian Alps were popular with skiers, and with all this snow on the ground, the agents looked like just another pair of tourists up for the weekend from Munich to hit the slopes.

Their job was to keep an eye on things in Oberstaufen, the village from where Axmann would be leaving. With the help of local American soldiers, they had secured a room from which they could monitor the situation starting December 14, the day before the arrest. They monitored the situation until Axmann left the following morning.

Agent Reis was there as well, to provide Kaufman with support. This was Third Army territory, and Reis was with the Seventh Army, but he was still a key part of this operation. During the day of the operation, he would help tail Ebeling.

Kaufman's usual partner, Lewis, was with another agent that day. It made sense to divide these agents up so that those who had experience with this operation could work with those who did not. This way at least one person would be familiar with what their targets looked like. Lewis also had an important job—to follow Ebeling from Oberstaufen as he drove Axmann to his final destination. Since the driver, Günter Ebeling, was in on it, this would most likely be an easy task.

The CIC told Ebeling that it was important for him to drive in a manner that made it simple for the trailing agents to stick with him.

While the CIC did this primarily to keep track of their targets, Ebeling was told that the trailing agents were also there to provide him with protection if something went wrong.

These agents wore civilian clothes in case Axmann spotted them.

Having a tail proved useful before Axmann had even entered the vehicle. While driving on the morning of December 15, Ebeling was stopped by an American military checkpoint that was unrelated to this operation. He was nearly arrested for carrying American gasoline, which the soldiers assumed he had obtained illegally on the black market. Gasoline was dyed red at the time to signify that it belonged to the occupying authorities; a German civilian should not have been driving around with it.

This was a tricky situation, though, as Ebeling was not alone—Ernst Overbeck was also in the car. However, the trailing CIC agent managed to get Ebeling released from this roadblock without raising Overbeck's suspicions.

Another problem arose before the trap could be sprung. Once near Oberstaufen, Ebeling's car got stuck in the snow. Agent Reis had been trailing him and so got out and pretended to be a Good Samaritan. He helped Ebeling and Overbeck out of the snow so that they could continue on their way. He even talked a bit with Overbeck. As Reis later recalled, "Overbeck thanked me courteously and seemed to have no suspicion of me."[3]

Yet another close call occurred at a roadblock when instructions got confused, and the soldiers manning the checkpoint thought that they were supposed to arrest Ebeling. Fortunately, they didn't have his full plate number, and they let him through.

If they had had his correct plate number, it would have spelled disaster for the operation. The soldiers would have arrested him and Overbeck. Then it would have been difficult to explain why Ebeling no longer had Overbeck with him. Perhaps the CIC would have then simply arrested Axmann and Memminger before they could begin their planned road trip. However, such an outcome would have been less than ideal, as the CIC preferred to make these arrests in a controlled, isolated environment.

While waiting for Axmann to show up, those in the arrest area started to panic. They later reported that "As the hours passed, tension naturally mounted, for AXMANN had been at 1000 hours in OBERSTAUFEN. . . . Eventually word was received that AXMANN had come into town. Speculated plans for climbing the mountain were dropped immediately and all forces were alerted for the departure from OBERSTAUFEN."[4]

While Axmann was taking his time to arrive in town, there had been talk of going into the Alps to look for him at his lodging there. Plus, there was a fear that Axmann might have gotten wind of their scheme and retreated into the mountains, in which case soldiers would have to comb through these snow-filled heights to try to find him. This would have been a difficult search operation with the Alps providing a fugitive many places in which to hide. If Axmann had panicked and fled away from civilization, and into the mountains, he would have had a very good chance of getting away.

Once in Oberstaufen, Ebeling was unable to locate Axmann. This problem was also averted. An undercover CIC agent, wearing civvies, surreptitiously let Ebeling know that Axmann was waiting for him nearby. In fact, Axmann was very close by, but he was behind Ebeling, and somehow they had missed seeing each other.[5]

To make his passengers more comfortable, Ebeling showed up with fake IDs for Overbeck and for Axmann's brother Kurt. They had previously requested them from Ebeling, so it was not a surprise that he had them. Kurt Axmann had earlier made contact with Artur Axmann through the Tessmann group, and Artur Axmann knew that his brother needed a good cover identity. The Rosenheim CIC was only too happy to provide these documents, as they knew they would get them back shortly if everything went according to plan.

Around 1 P.M., later than expected, Ebeling was finally on the road out of Oberstaufen with his three passengers—Artur Axmann, Gustav Memminger, and Ernst Overbeck. Two sets of CIC agents tailed them. The signal went out over the radio that things were in motion with the code: "Christmas is coming."[6]

As the CIC dryly noted, "Christmas came for Arthur [sic] AXMANN, former Reichsleiter and Reichsjugendfuehrer, leader of the planned revival of the Hitler Jugend, at 1410 hours, 15 December 1945."[7]

It was then, about four miles south of Kempten, that the trap was sprung. Ebeling had just passed the small village of Waltenhofen. Once Ebeling drove around a curve on the road from Oberstaufen, a road-block checkpoint stood in front of them. They had driven about twenty miles since starting their trip. Ebeling stopped the car and everyone got out.

Agent Reis noted that "although the roadblock check was not used as often as immediately after [the] cessation of hostilities, the German populace had been so regimented and indoctrinated during Hitler's regime they were not surprised at anytime for identity check. This attitude served us well."[8]

Near this checkpoint stood an inn that the army had taken over. It was below freezing outside, so it made sense that travelers would be escorted inside to have their papers inspected and answer questions. The Americans had previously emptied out this inn; now the only ones inside were soldiers and CIC agents, including Jack Hunter.[9]

With the notable exception of Ebeling, these Germans had no idea that they were about to step into the command post of the operation planning their arrest.

As Reis later wrote, "We passed by [Ebeling] and hurried into the building to make certain that our medic friends were ready. Axmann was one of the first to be brought into the building and as he entered, the two medics stepped forward, one on each side of him, and thrust their fingers into his mouth and searched for cyanide tablets and on other areas of his body."[10] The others "were also given the same treatment."[11]

This blitz attack as soon as they entered the building surprised the arrestees before they had time to react. The CIC was especially worried that Axmann might try to kill himself using a cyanide pill.

While Axmann did not have a suicide pill, having long ago given his to Mrs. Goebbels, the CIC didn't know that. Also, Axmann had no interest in killing himself. If he was the sort to kill himself, rather than risk capture, he would have already done it in the bunker after Hitler and Goebbels did. Or when Bormann took his own life when faced with the overwhelming dangers posed by the Russians during the breakout attempt.

The Allies had learned the hard way though not to take any chances with high-ranking Nazis. *Reichsführer-SS* Heinrich Himmler had famously used a cyanide pill to kill himself after the British captured him. The CIC took every precaution with *Reichsjugendführer* Artur Axmann. Axmann remembered what happened a bit differently; he felt that the medics had "immediately attacked my lower jaw."[12]

Ebeling and his three passengers were stripped and thoroughly searched. With the exception of Axmann's prosthetic arm, all of their belongings were taken away, including a stash of documents. Axmann had on him the diagram he'd drawn based on Heidemann's explanations of the group's business interests. During the arrest, Ebeling was treated the same as the others in an attempt by the CIC to conceal from them that he was an informant.

Axmann later wrote that during this strip search, "Ebeling was standing next to me and protested loudly and indignantly. I felt that this outrage was phony. He was our betrayer."[13]

Two blurry photographs exist of Artur Axmann taken during his capture. He was stripped down to his white long johns and surrounded by CIC personnel. In well-known portraits of him from his time in charge of the Hitler Youth, he had always been clean-shaven. Now, he had a thick mustache. In one of the photos, a gag has been put into his mouth. It looks like a large white cloth that has been stuck in there and allowed to hang out, like he is throwing up an oversized white sock.

After this search, the captives were taken upstairs and put into American military uniforms. They were even given helmets to wear. Axmann tried to argue that his fake ID was legitimate and that he was not Artur Axmann. Of course, no one believed him.

Hunter and Axmann finally came face-to-face when Axmann entered into the requisitioned inn. There was no time for introductions though—it was a quick operation and specialized interrogators would question Axmann later.

The goal at this point was to keep these arrests secret so that the Tessmann operation didn't receive word of what had happened. Even if a local saw one of the prisoners being spirited away from the inside of the building to the street, they would just see someone in a U.S. uniform with part of his head covered.

The prisoners were rushed away. Axmann and Memminger were taken to Third Army territory. A soldier kept a Tommy gun trained on Axmann while he entered a light tank in the middle of a convoy.[14] The CIC was not taking any chances with the former *Reichsjugendführer*.

Overbeck went to the Seventh Army at Heidelberg; Agents Reis and Hochschild escorted him there personally.[15] Decades later, Reis remembered this trip well: "Overbeck was silent on the ride to Heidelberg except when Agent George [Hochschild] asked him if he knew who had helped him push his vehicle out of the snow in Allgau. When

Overbeck replied that he didn't but thought it was one of the natives in Allgau, George enlightened him by pointing to me, and then Overbeck said he had badly underestimated the Americans. He seemed to be in shock."[16] Overbeck told them that he now had the deepest respect for the CIC.[17]

Ebeling, of course, was free to go on his way. He would tell his erstwhile comrades at Tessmann that he'd experienced serious car troubles on the road from Oberstaufen to Lübeck. In what would have been about a six-hundred-mile journey, Ebeling would claim that he'd only made it as far as Stuttgart. This was about a quarter of the way.

As his story went, his passengers had then taken a train the rest of the route. In order to help protect Ebeling, CIC Agents Lewis and Kaufman asked that when Axmann's arrest was announced someday, that the date and location of his capture be kept secret.[18] Otherwise, Ebeling would be exposed.

The CIC had managed to pull off arresting the former leader of the Hitler Youth along with two of his top men. Despite some hiccups, this carefully planned operation was a resounding success.

FOURTEEN

THE ROUNDUP

Only the dead have seen the end of war.

GEORGE SANTAYANA[1]

Now that Axmann had been captured along with some of his top men, the CIC worked in overdrive to bring down the conspiracy of former HJ leaders still dedicated to the Nazi cause.

Axmann, Memminger, and Overbeck were all intensively interrogated. They tried to give as little information as they could, sticking to what they thought their interrogators already knew and trying to spin those facts that they couldn't deny in such a way that their activities would seem innocuous.

After being captured, Axmann was asked repeatedly about the deaths of Hitler and Bormann.[2] At one point Axmann even helped make a diagram showing the locations of Hitler and Eva Braun's bodies as he found them. He also assisted with a diagram of where he came upon Bormann's body.

Axmann and Memminger were transferred to Oberursel, while

Overbeck was held in Heidelberg.[3] The message from the USFET HQ to the Third Army troops holding Axmann and Memminger that requested the prisoners be moved to Oberursel included the following: "Since subjects are desperate men, request they be held incommunicado and placed under heavy guard during transfer."[4]

The town of Oberursel is northwest of Frankfurt, in the German state of Hesse. Here the U.S. Military Intelligence Service Center was located. It was informally known as Camp Sibert after General Edwin Sibert (the G-2 for USFET).[5] During World War II, this facility had been used by the Germans to interrogate prisoners of war, primarily captured Allied pilots and flight crews. This is where Axmann and Memminger were held.

While he was being admitted to Camp Sibert, Axmann's prosthetic arm was taken away from him, never to be returned. He later speculated that "it landed on either the garbage heap or as a souvenir in America."[6] This prosthetic had helped him during his breakout from the bunker, when the Russian soldiers he ran into were fascinated by it. But now, it was gone, and he was without his Dr. Strangelove–like appendage.

Axmann was held in solitary confinement. Christmas was the same as all his other days in Camp Sibert with one exception—he heard singing from outside that faintly made its way into his cell.[7]

The documents found on these prisoners were carefully analyzed. Especially helpful was the diagram Axmann had drawn, of Heidemann's various business enterprises, during their one-on-one meeting in the cabin outside of Oberstaufen.

Meanwhile, the CIC did what it could to keep the arrests secret. They didn't want to spook their remaining targets or expose their informants.

The CIC's plan for concluding Operation Nursery was to coordinate a massive operation to make as many arrests as possible simultaneously. Until then, isolated high-level members of this conspiracy would be picked up when possible. The idea was to grab people in such a way that their comrades would not know what had happened to them, or at the very least, would not know the real reason why they had been detained.

The CIC had already done this successfully when they arrested Reichs Deputy of the BDM (*Reichsreferentin des BDM*) Dr. Jutta Rüdiger at a hospital and pretended that she had just been randomly identified. While eventually word reached the others that she had been arrested, the real reason why remained secret. She had been arrested because an informant, Siegfried Kulas, had delivered her into the hands of the CIC, but her comrades believed the cover story that she had been picked up because of bad luck.

This approach worked, and in short order other key figures were arrested. Willi Heidemann, Walter Bergemann, and Simon Winter were picked up. As Agent Hochschild recalls it, Seventh Army MPs arrested Heidemann from his third-floor residence near the Bavarian resort town of Garmisch-Partenkirchen.[8]

By January 9, U.S. forces had arrested twenty Nazi operatives as part of this operation.[9]

Among the documents confiscated from Simon Winter was an interesting letter from a Hilde Merklein. It had been sent using a courier, which was illegal during the occupation as it allowed Nazis to send messages without going through the post. Merklein had been Winter's secretary and later became an officer under his command in the national leadership office for the HJ in Berlin.

As this letter revealed, since the war ended she had obtained employment as the secretary to an up-and-comer in German politics. She worked for Professor Carlo Schmid, then the minister of education for the area of Württemberg, appointed by the French. The letter from Merklein to Winter "disclosed some inside information concerning the formation of the new Landesregierung [state government] which then was a topic of discussion . . . especially the new choice for Minister of Education and his assistant for political questions."[10]

While other BDM plants in secretarial positions were often in Military Government offices, this was an amazing position from which Merklein could spy. Although education at first might sound like a relatively unimportant ministry, the education of young people was something that those who had run the HJ and BDM understood to be of the utmost importance in influencing the country's future.

Moreover, they had placed a BDM officer with someone who was a rising star in German politics. Professor Schmid went on to great prominence in the shaping of the modern West German state. In his 1979 obituary, the *Los Angeles Times* referred to him as "one of the founding fathers of the West German state and a man described as Germany's most articulate spokesman for progressive socialism."[11]

As it was, the CIC now knew about this spy Professor Schmid had unwittingly hired, so they resolved to have her fired (if she was still working for him).

Despite the disappearances of key figures such as Axmann, Memminger, Winter, Heidemann, and Bergemann, the rest of the group did not go to ground, but continued about their business.

The first New Year's celebration in occupied Germany came and went. On January 8, 1946, the prosecution at the International Military Tribunal at Nuremberg started its case against the individual defendants. Until then, the trial had focused on six organizations—the Reich Cabinet, the Leadership Corps of the Nazi Party, the Security Service (SD), the secret police (Gestapo), the Stormtroopers (SA), and the General Staff and High Command of the German Armed Forces.

Surprisingly, Axmann was never called to testify at Nuremberg. He had firsthand knowledge of the death of Martin Bormann, and Bormann's lawyer's main defense was that his client was dead. Also, he knew Baldur von Schirach well and could have testified on his behalf.

Axmann wrote in his memoirs that it was "incomprehensible" to him that he was "not called to the International Military Tribunal [at Nuremberg] in the trial of Martin Bormann. . . . It must indeed have been known I am here in the central warehouse of the American Intelligence in Oberursel. But I've still no explanation for this."[12] He also found it "incomprehensible" that he "was not called as a witness at the trial of Baldur von Schirach" at the IMT at Nuremberg.[13] At this trial, Axmann's predecessor as head of the Hitler Youth, Baldur von Schirach, admitted that he had "educated the youth of Germany for a man who murdered millions."[14]

The interrogation of suspects picked up during Operation Nursery continued. A report on January 2, 1946, stated that "none of the prisoners has been broken so far, and the information obtained is far from a complete picture. OVERBECK has categorically refused to furnish any names and addresses."[15] This report goes on to explain that Axmann and Memminger pretended to cooperate a bit while only giving old, out-of-date contact information for their Nazi colleagues.

For the things that the prisoners couldn't deny (because the CIC had documented them well), like the meeting in Lübeck between Axmann and Memminger, they tried to spin the facts as best they could. Instead of this having been a trip to meet with others who wanted to bring back National Socialism to Germany, it was simply a series of social visits. As the interrogation document notes, "MEM-MINGER claims that the trip was not undertaken, in order to organise groups, but only in order to find out what had become of old friends during the past few months. The conversation with AXMANN in LUEBECK for instance concerned only a general exchange of experiences according to him."[16]

The CIC had an informant (Günter Ebeling) present in Lübeck when Axmann and Memminger met up. So they knew that Memminger was not telling the truth about what happened there.

During an interrogation, "AXMANN hinted that possibly EBEL-ING might have had some connection with his arrest, since everything went like clockwork."[17] His interrogator tried to address these suspicions by pointing out a couple other possibilities for how he was caught. Meanwhile, Memminger wasn't suspicious of Ebeling at all.[18]

Far from giving up while in captivity, Axmann tried to bargain in exchange for answering questions. He wanted to send a message out before he would cooperate fully. Military Intelligence interpreted this request as having a threefold purpose. First, it was an attempt to stall the interrogations and slow down this process. This would be the case even if this condition were never met; as long as it was considered, it would cause delay.

Second, Axmann was trying to warn the others that the CIC was after them. Third, Axmann wanted to try to gain the assistance of people with some kind of influence, who might be able to help him out.[19] The interrogators at Camp Sibert did not fall for this and promptly refused his request.

An example of how the prisoners tended to react to evidence against them is Gustav Memminger's take on the "list of traitors" found among his personal papers. The title of this paper seemed straightforward, and the meaning of it difficult to deny, but Memminger still tried to spin it. According to notes on his interrogation, "he was afraid that this entry might be 'misinterpreted' and gives the following 'explanation': It had come to the attention of their group that some of the HJ people had turned informer and were working for the CIC. . . . It was considered advisable to compile a list of all such cases. Again MEMMINGER asserts this should only warn their friends not to trust the 'traitors,' but was not meant as a basis for repressive and retaliatory action."[20]

Military Intelligence did not buy such excuses for a second. They were well aware of the group's plan to set up a Feme court, and it was not credible that they would simply want to warn people about traitors in their midst and not plan on eventually doing harm to them.

The prisoners spent the month of January undergoing further interrogations. U.S. Military Intelligence believed that these "prisoners seem to have realised that we possess a great amount of factual information on their activities. Therefore, they seem to have adopted the practice of giving factual information (e.g. trips, meetings with friends etc.) accurately, but [to] concentrate on an attempt to interpret these activities as harmless and innocent. They are still quite security conscious when it comes to names, addresses and future plans."[21]

Axmann confirmed that his intended destination was Lübeck, where he was heading when he was arrested en route. He then admitted to having had plans to use members of their group who "had served as officers at the front in order to maintain liaison with former army officers. The purpose of this liaison is twofold: a. positive liaison with Army and Air force units and their staffs in the British Zone . . . b. negative work in the Russian Zone, i.e. to discourage former officers from working for the Russians directly or from joining German units under Russian supervision."[22]

A rare moment of candor happened as a result of an interrogator surprising one of the prisoners with unexpected evidence: "When OVERBECK was shown the sheet, on which AXMANN had jotted down the structure of HEIDEMANN's various firms and enterprises, he forgot himself for a moment and lost his usual composure exclaiming 'For Heavens sake, you've got that one too. At least, I had hoped that these notes would have been destroyed.'"[23] As First Lieutenant Leo Barton, the writer of these interrogation notes, pointed out about Ernst Overbeck's outburst: this was "a reaction which would not have taken place, if HEIDEMANN had really 'just been running a business.'"[24]

Military Intelligence noted that a "point has been raised by every one of the prisoners so far, whether they are part of the political or of the business group, that is their professed preference for Americans and British and their uncompromising rejection of the 'Bolshevists.' True, their 'love' for the Americans has been slightly tempered by the fact that we have continued to arrest their friends and to denazify according to Law No 8. But they still hope to convince us that former Nazis are actually the most reliable friends."[25]

Memminger had extensive papers that military intelligence viewed as "a good example of the camouflage under which Nazi propaganda is being continued."[26] One of the ideas the group was trying to spread was that "the past 12 years were not in vain, since so many principles and achievements of the National Socialists were incorporated into the programs of the parties now in existence."[27] They wanted to bring back National Socialism, but were smart enough to understand that given the circumstances, they would need to be careful about how they presented their platform.

It was not enough merely to inspire others to nostalgia for the fallen regime; they wanted to be in control of whatever new Nazi party emerged. The method (*"Utiser Weg"*) to achieve their goals emphasized that "in order to count on the strength of the National Socialists for the future, their cohesion and solidarity must be maintained. This requires the organisation of all good German elements in solidarity which will receive their directives from one headquarters"[28] that would have to be "camouflage[d] . . . in order to exist in illegality."[29]

Conveniently, the high-ranking Nazis already captured "cannot be counted upon for this reconstruction work."[30] This meant that Axmann and his men would comprise the new, secret leadership of a covert Nazi Party. Axmann would not have to hand over power to men who had held more power than him during the Third Reich (like the last president of Germany, Karl Dönitz). When Memminger's documents were drawn up, the Allies already held prisoner Dönitz and other key Nazi figures.

By the time Willi Heidemann was brought to Camp Sibert, Military Intelligence already knew all about him and had plenty of facts with which to confront him. He tried to deny as much as he could, even his rank in the HJ. His interrogator decided to run with this and get Heidemann to sign a sworn document containing his lies. He did, in front of three witnesses.

So now they had a straightforward perjury charge they could bring against Heidemann. They could use this as leverage to get him to cooperate once they confronted him with the evidence that he'd perjured himself.

A Military Intelligence report details two pages, single-spaced, of proof that Heidemann lied under oath. This evidence included statements from Axmann and other prisoners captured as part of Operation Nursery.

The report also includes that "HEIDEMANN had erased what presumably was a Party or HJ badge from the photos in his Wehrpass [military identification] and Kennkarte [identity document]. His Wehrpass also shows a hole which—accidentally, of course—obliterates the space where his former occupation was entered. . . . It may be noted that HEIDEMANN was asked where his Wehrpass was; instead of answering the question, he immediately explained how the hole in his Wehrpass was caused by strafing from a plane; reminded that he had not been asked about this, but whether he had his Wehrpass with him in [Munich], he pretended not to know for sure."[31]

It was an absurd story—a plane flying low to the ground shooting bullet after bullet in automatic firing at people below somehow managed to punch a hole in just the spot in his identity document where it would obliterate his job information, all without injuring Heidemann. He would have had to have been running from fire with his ID card out in his hand, away from his body, when a bullet happened to hit it.

Bill Salzmann, an attorney who currently investigates and

prosecutes high-profile fraud cases for the U.S. federal government and "sometimes gets lied to for a living," observed that "the nonsense of the content of the lie is secondary to the Intelligence report." Instead, the tipping point, at least from the perspective of the CIC officer drafting the report, was that "when asked where the pass was, Heidemann instead argued for its authenticity. This could be an indicator of Heidemann's consciousness of guilt. The non-responsiveness of his answer, alone, would have alerted a trained interrogator."[32]

Rosenheim CIC Agents Kaufman and Lewis continued to run their informant Günter Ebeling. They met with him in Bad Oeynhausen, a spa town in northwest Germany, in early January 1946, as part of their investigation into Tessmann operations in the British Zone.[33] Meanwhile Agents Reis and Hochschild continued handling Kulas along with their other, lesser informants.

Plans were being put in motion for a roundup of all the remaining members of this conspiracy. As Agent Reis later recalled, "All the names, addresses and detailed instructions for the picking up and placing these individuals under arrest in a proper sequence in both the U.S. and British Zones took some doing. We picked up or caused to be picked up HJ officials who were not a part of a given group or wouldn't be missed immediately, from time to time, to whittle down piece by piece the 'big pie.' . . . There were approximately 2000 HJ leaders and forty were equal in rank to Memminger and Winter and Overbeck."[34]

A major raid would take place simultaneously in the British and American Zones, during the early hours of Sunday, March 31, 1946. In order to prepare for this raid, debriefings were held at local counterintelligence offices in mid-March.

Bruce Haywood, who was stationed in Bremerhaven, remembers this well: "The Region's head man began with a warning that not a word of what we were about to hear could leave the room; it was top, top secret. Then he introduced my boss . . . [who] quickly held everyone's attention with his solemn delivery. What he briefed us on was the evident setting up of an underground organization of members of the Hitler Youth and its companion girl's organization . . . whose members were chosen for their utter commitment to Nazi ideology."[35]

The briefing officer did not know the inner details of Operation Nursery, or if he did, he didn't share them with the personnel gathered together on the second floor of this former police station.[36] Instead, he just gave them the broad overview that some kind of Nazi conspiracy centered on former HJ and BDM was afoot. And he explained what this meant to the local agents—a list had been drawn up of names and addresses of suspects for them to pick up in this subregion.

Haywood was a British warrant officer in the 92 Intelligence Team but was working with the CIC. There was an usually high level of cooperation between the British and American occupying forces in Bremerhaven, owing to it being part of an American enclave located within the British Zone.

At this meeting, Haywood was told that "on a certain night two weeks hence, between midnight and five in the morning, every person named in the lists would be arrested. We were to take in those in our territory and deliver them promptly to Bremen for interrogation. We were not to question them. It was crucial that not one of them have warning of what was to happen, so only one person of those present at our meeting would be entrusted with the names of the suspects in our territory."[37]

Captain James Draycott (British but like Haywood assigned to work with the American CIC)[38] announced to the room that "I am now turning over to Mr. Haywood a sheet of paper with six names and addresses on it. Between now and the time for the arrests he will have to ascertain whether the people are in fact at those addresses. He will not reveal those names to anybody else."[39] Afterward, he gave Haywood "a sealed envelope and, smiling, said 'Don't let this out of your sight.'"[40]

His list had an even 3-3 split between men and women. A more crucial distinction to Haywood was between those living in Bremerhaven and those on the outskirts. Five of the names would be easy, as they lived in the city, but the sixth would be trickier.

For those in the city, as Haywood recalled, "the German police had accurate, up-to-date housing lists. But I wouldn't dare to consult those in the file room with Germans about. Playing safe, I had the police deliver to my office the files for all the streets in the town, not just the five streets where my targets were thought to be. I gave no explanation for why I wanted the files."[41] All five names checked out, and Haywood was hopeful that the targets would be home during the raid as a curfew was then in effect.

Along with a partner, he did a drive-by of the addresses in town to get a sense of where they were, and of all the ways they could go in and a suspect could flee out. As for the BDM suspect in the countryside, he needed a different approach. He later wrote, "I couldn't possibly go to the policeman in her community and ask him to tell me where she lived. Nor could I ask to see files at the mayor's office, lest someone gossip about my interest."[42]

He even worried about using his own car to drive around, as someone might recognize it. So he borrowed a car and drove around the village, looking for the target address. He decided that rather than risk tipping off his suspect, he would not investigate whether she actually lived there, and instead he would hope for the best. So far, the five names and addresses he had looked into had checked out.

Such matters as how to check up on the accuracy of the list they were given and how to conduct the actual raid were up to the local agents. Haywood's plan "would have two teams of four men, each team to use two jeeps. Another agent would stay by the phone, just in case a call from Bremen came in. We would begin immediately after midnight."[43]

Just after midnight, now the early morning of Sunday, March 31, 1946, the raid began. In Bremerhaven, they divvied up the suspects in town into two groups and picked them up first. Four of the suspects were at home. The fifth, a woman, was not; she was at her boyfriend's place. The team that went to pick her up threatened the mother with arrest unless she coughed up his name and location.

The arresting agent told Haywood what happened next. It turned out that the mother had sent them to the housing for single officers. They found their suspect with her boyfriend, an American officer who worked in the same building as the arresting agents.

They still had one left to pick up though—the woman in the country. Once there, they were able to make an arrest at the address on their list, of a girl named Inge.

The arrestees were taken to the local jail, to be held in isolation.[44] Later, the Americans drove them to a detention center in Bremen for interrogation.[45]

The large-scale raid of March 31, 1946, was primarily to pick up the rank and file of the HJ underground movement. The leaders had already been arrested—Axmann and his top men in December. During the time between the two raids, the British and the Americans had captured about two hundred of the Nazi underground's leadership.

As the head of intelligence in the American Zone said in a press release, "In today's round-up of suspects, [General] Sibert pointed out that many, if not all personalities may be unaware of the real intentions of the ringleaders and as such would later be released, provided they do not fall into existing automatic arrest categories."[46]

Thousands of American and British soldiers provided support for their counterintelligence services in picking up suspects. In some areas, armor was used to provide protection in case they encountered heavy resistance.[47]

The Associated Press reported that "gun battles between Nazi fanatics and American and British troops broke out at scattered points in Western Germany early today as an estimated 7000 Allied soldiers cracked down on a Nazi attempt to regain power and re-establish Nazism in Germany. Early reports of a vast dragnet thrown over Germany and Austria said that firing occurred at a number of points as combat troops, counterespionage agents and constabulary forces swooped down on almost 1000 suspects."[48]

This figure included the two hundred or so suspects that had already been arrested. Brigadier General Edwin Sibert, who had been in charge of intelligence for the American Zone since its establishment, told the press that "the movement's long-range plan, designed to revive the Nazi ideology in Germany, was the most dangerous threat to our security encountered since the war."[49]

While this raid took place in the British and American Zones, the CIC did have information about some activities by these personalities in the Soviet Zone, which they shared with the Soviet authorities.[50]

When the official press release went out from the USFET, Hunter's name was omitted. He was originally credited in the press release at the very end as follows: "1st Lt. Jack D. Hunter, Claymont, Del., of the Counter Intelligence Branch as the officer in charge of the case."[51]

Hunter believed that this omission was the result of political infighting at the CIC headquarters in Frankfurt, where another, high-ranking officer had earlier wanted to take over the Nursery case from him.

As Hunter later wrote, "At the beginning, few at headquarters gave the Nursery case any real importance, especially a ranking career officer on the rim of the affair who obviously couldn't have cared less that a lowly second-John [second lieutenant] reservist had been put in charge. Later, though, when the case picked up momentum and drew the personal interest of General Eisenhower, he arranged to move closer to the loop and inch his way into prominence.

"It made no difference to me. Everybody was higher in rank and importance than I was, so what's to fret about one more careerist maneuvering to beautify his resume? But Colonel Culp, the CIC top dog, doggedly kept me in charge on the grounds that I seemed to be doing okay, so what the hell was all the fuss? This, of course, did little to endear me to the careerist, and the man's jealousy and pettiness became evident when he saw my name at the tag end of the news release to be issued by General Sibert. He demanded that it be removed, because, in his words, 'I will not have the names of our agents publicized. It's too dangerous.' Which, of course, was silly, because my name, as chief of the German Desk, was carried openly in the phone book for Ike's headquarters—as available as the day's Stars and Stripes newspaper. And it was also specifically retained in General McNarney's official citation. But somewhere in all this palace wrangling somebody threw the petulant careerist a bone and authorized the removal of my name from the news release distributed to the international media."[52]

In April 1946, the following commendation came from General Joseph McNarney himself, then the military governor for the American Zone and head of all American forces in Europe (USFET):

HEADQUARTERS
U.S. FORCES, EUROPEAN THEATER
Office of the Commanding General

12 April 1946

SUBJECT: Commendation
TO: Chief, Counter Intelligence Corps, European Theater
(THRU: Assistant Chief of Staff, G-2, United States
Forces, European Theater.)

The successful completion of Operation NURSERY climaxes a long record of splendid performance on the part of the Counter Intelligence Corps in this Theater. In that operation, by good judgment and efficient functioning, the Regional and Sub-Regional offices have eliminated a dangerous element from German life.

The achievements of the Counter Intelligence Corps in this connection gain all the greater significance when the nature of the organization just smashed is taken into account. Here was no fly-by-night scheme of harassment, concerned with chalking swastikas on buildings or with cutting wires. It was an organization planned in terms of years, not of months, whose ultimate aim was subversion designed to upset the aims of the occupation, to keep alive the spirit of National Socialist ideals and to undermine subtly whatever new German leadership may emerge from the country's downfall.

With patience and resourcefulness, the Counter Intelligence Corps agents under the case direction of Lt. J.D. HUNTER developed the slimmest of leads and by close and careful surveillance of the key personalities recorded the growth of an underground organization since its inception in June 1945. Since the scope of this operation transcended the borders of the occupational zones, these agents had to secure the cooperation of other occupying powers. Such a task called for tact, detailed knowledge of the situation, and sure judgment. That the development of this operation in all its ramifications proceeded without compromise is a tribute to the security-mindedness of the agents; a single leak of important information would have alerted the subversive organization and driven it out of reach, even further underground, with its potential danger to the occupation greatly increased. The agents were opposed by men with demonstrated records of ruthlessness. These men had money, arms, organization. The agents not only risked their own lives on numerous occasions; they had to persuade indispensable German informants to take innumerable risks, for which they could not even expect recognition.

The success of the operation in the face of such formidable handicaps reflects the greatest possible credit on the Counter Intelligence Corps. The vigilance and resourcefulness shown and the experienced gained augur well for the success of such future operations as will unquestionably arise.

It is desired that you express to the members of the Counter Intelligence Corps who participated in Operation NURSERY, no matter in how humble a capacity, the contents of this message and my personal appreciation of their accomplishment.

/S/ JOSEPH T. McNARNEY
/T/ JOSEPH T. McNARNEY
General, U.S. Army, Commanding

Brigadier General Edwin Sibert, McNarney's G-2, in charge of all U.S. Army intelligence operations in Europe, forwarded on the above commendation with his own congratulations:

1st Ind. ELS/rje
Assistant Chief of Staff, G-2, Hq. U.S. Forces, European Theater (Main), APO 757, U.S. Army, 16 April 1946
TO: Chief, Counter Intelligence Corps, Hq. U.S. Forces, European Theater (Main), APO 757, U.S. Army

It gives me great pleasure to forward the above commendation. My congratulations on a job well done.

/S/ EDWIN L. SIBERT
/T/ EDWIN L. SIBERT
Brigadier General, GSC
A.C. of S., G-2

And finally, the acting chief of the CIC in turn forwarded on the above communications:

2nd Ind. CMC/aee
Headquarters, 970th CIC Detachment,
Headquarters United States Forces,
European Theater, APO 757, U.S. Army, 19 April 1946
TO: All individuals of the 970th Counter
Intelligence Corps Detachment

1. Attention is invited to basic communication and 1st Ind.
2. Although I cannot participate in its credit, I am proud, indeed, to find myself in command of an organization whose personnel has won such high praise from the Theater Commander. You have my heartiest congratulations on your success and its recognition.

C.M. Culp
Colonel, Infantry
Acting Chief, CIC

EPILOGUE

Some people are larger than life. Hitler is larger than death.

DON DELILLO[1]

After the roundup, the first sign that Bruce Haywood had a problem with one of his arrests was when a reliable source told him that the locals were complaining that the girl he had picked up in the countryside had not been a Nazi supporter.

In contrast to this girl, Haywood was told that her mother was "a Party member of long standing and a notorious loudmouth whose late husband had been in the SS."[2] It turned out that she too was named Inge. He worried that he'd screwed this up and captured the wrong woman, but he didn't admit it to anyone.[3] As he remembers it, "I couldn't bring myself to acknowledge my mistake to my boss, and I hoped fervently that my suspicions would turn out to be correct, namely that none of the persons we had arrested was a conspirator. My boss's report on the release of all the arrestees and their ignorance of any plot took a huge weight off my shoulders."[4]

Of course, just because the other people they had picked up in this subregion were released didn't mean that the proper Inge would have been released as well. But the odds would have been in her favor because, as Brigadier General Sibert had acknowledged in the initial press release for the raids, it was anticipated that "many if not all" of those being picked up would be released as long as they were "unaware of the real intentions of the ringleaders" and did "not fall into existing automatic arrest categories."[5]

And so the majority of the low-level figures captured during this raid were released after being held briefly. Most of them did not fall into the automatic arrest categories.

As for Artur Axmann, he sat in jail. In addition to questions related to Operation Nursery, he continued to face interrogations about Hitler, Eva Braun, Bormann, and the final days in the bunker. There was also some interest in his experiences in the Soviet Zone. Eventually, he was allowed to interact with other prisoners, including Memminger.

In October 1946, Axmann was transferred to British custody, where he lived with about twelve thousand other prisoners, many of them former Nazis. Although conditions were generally worse than they had been in the American detention center, Axmann preferred it here as he was free to spend his time with his fellow prisoners instead of being cooped up in a cell.

Here, he had access to news from the outside world and so learned the results of the International Military Tribunal at Nuremberg. On October 1, 1946, the court announced its verdicts: nineteen of the defendants were found guilty of at least one count, while the court acquitted three. As for those convicted, twelve were sentenced to death, including Martin Bormann. Three received life sentences. The court sentenced Albert Speer and Baldur von Schirach to twenty years. One defendant received fifteen years, and the final president of Nazi Germany, Karl Dönitz, received a ten-year sentence.

On October 16, 1946, the condemned were hanged with two notable exceptions. Hermann Göring had cheated the executioner's noose by committing suicide the night before. And, as Axmann was well aware, Bormann had been dead for a year and a half now.

Axmann knew all of those executed personally.[6] Not surprisingly, considering that he was a true believer in Hitler and a former high-level Third Reich official, Axmann did not see what happened at Nuremberg as a triumph of international law and a documentation of the terrible wrongs committed by the Nazis, but as a form of victor's justice.[7]

A most pleasant surprise for Axmann happened one day during a visit to the camp dentist. He ran into Gisela Hermann, the BDM woman he had last seen injured in the Reich Chancellery before he fled from the bunker. It was a joy to find her alive and well, having been rescued from the Soviets by her fellow BDM members. She had been a patient in a hospital in Soviet territory in which some former BDM women worked as nurses. They used Red Cross uniforms and a wheelchair to spirit her to safety, although she was later picked up in the West after turning in her *Fragebogen*.[8]

In July 1947, Axmann was transferred to Nuremberg, which was in the American Zone. On March 15, 1949, he was allowed out of jail, but had to remain in this city and report back for his upcoming denazification proceeding.

On April 29, 1949, he was sentenced to 3.25 years imprisonment in a labor camp as a major offender who had militarized young people, but was given credit for time served, so he was a free man. As for why he was given so little time, by 1949, the focus for many had shifted from prosecuting Nazis to the intrigues of the Cold War. And, as far as former high-ranking Nazi officials went, Axmann's crimes were comparatively minor. For example, he had not used slave labor or been part of the machinery of the holocaust. The court did have these harsh words for him though, "Axmann acted unconscionably during this senseless situation and demonstrated that he was, until the last minute, a devoted servant of National Socialism."[9]

He received a fine of 18,000 deutsche marks and faced a host of restrictions on his rights, including voting, working certain kinds of jobs, and even having a driver's license. He also lost his pension and the ability to join a "trade union or economic or professional association."[10]

Among the many rights that he lost was that for a period of ten years he could not hold the kind of white-collar jobs for which he might be qualified, such as writer. The idea generally with such restrictions was that the convicted person could still do something like manual labor, but this was not something anyone would hire him for as he only had one hand. However, through his contacts he did manage to get a job in the coffee trade.

With the war over, and his no longer hiding from the Allies, Axmann was able to divorce his first wife and marry his longtime girlfriend, Erna Vieckariesmann. They stayed together the rest of their days and had one son and two daughters of their own.

One day, another ghost from Axmann's bunker days appeared. Armin Dieter Lehmann, the boy who had been his courier in the bunker and who he thought had died during the breakout attempt, was alive and well. He had tracked Axmann down. Lehmann traveled the world and eventually settled down in the United States to work in the travel industry. He had been given the Iron Cross by Hitler himself on Hitler's last birthday, as part of the ceremony in the Reich Chancellery garden. But he had also seen the chaos of the last days of the bunker, and he later became an activist for nonviolence, nuclear disarmament, and peace.

In August 1958, Axmann faced a second denazification proceeding, this time in Berlin. As an expert on these proceedings, Professor Toby Thacker, explained in 2011, "It was possible to go through a number of different [denazification] proceedings."[11] So even though Axmann had already been the subject of a denazification proceeding almost ten years before, in 1949, he now faced another one.

In this second, and final, proceeding, Axmann received a fine of 35,000 deutsche marks. United Press International converted this to $8,333 in 1958 U.S. dollars.[12] The proceeding ruled that he had held a prominent position in the Nazi regime, with the task of indoctrinating the youth into becoming "obedient followers of the Nazi system."[13]

As a former HJ member wrote, "It's revealing that [Artur Axmann] was never charged with war crimes, although he sent tens of thousands of boys into battle and death."[14] Besides using child soldiers, another serious crime that he committed, and was not charged with, was his involvement with the rounding up of Swing Kids.

Axmann apparently never recovered the gun he'd hidden during his escape from the bunker. He once said about this historic pistol, "I sometimes read about agents and spies being exchanged between East and West at the Sandkrug Bridge. And I wonder what they would think if they knew that the gun with which the Führer took his own life might lie beneath their feet!"[15]

Axmann's views had changed little by the time he wrote his memoirs, *This Cannot Be the End*, fifty years after the events in the bunker, in 1995. The title came from what he said to Hitler during their final conversation. He dedicated the book to his "fallen comrades."[16] In it, he remained a Nazi, a man who still had admiration for Hitler and had excuses for everything. He explained his refusal to criticize Hitler, saying, "As far as my personal relationship with [Adolf Hitler], I can only say that he has treated me like a son, and please do not expect that a son speaks ill of his father."[17]

As Dagmar Reese put it in *Growing Up Female in Nazi Germany*, a book about the BDM, Axmann's memoir "must be considered part of the literature of justification."[18]

Axmann argued that militarizing the German youth was a good thing as it led them to be better soldiers when they became adults and joined the military and so more likely to survive in battle. In regards to those who fought as child soldiers, he depicted them as volunteers who wanted to fight.

He admitted to facts that didn't incriminate anyone (like details of his breakout), and admitted facts that were already known, but in the book, he put his own self-serving spin on everything.

As he did during his interrogations, he denied that a conspiracy had existed to try to bring back a Nazi regime, but instead insisted that it was merely a series of business enterprises run by like-minded people trying to help one another out. So people could stay in touch and work toward helping the large population of homeless youth in Germany.

Of course, this explanation did not convince his interrogators and it did not explain the documents found during the December 1945 arrests that detailed the group's goals and operational methods.

On October 24, 1996, at the age of 83, Axmann died in Berlin. According to news reports, "His death was announced only on Monday after his burial at a secret location to prevent his tomb from becoming a neo-Nazi shrine."[19]

A paid obituary notice in a major German newspaper proclaimed, "His social commitment to the youth was exemplary. We thank him for that."[20] It was signed by BDM *Obergebietsführerin* Gisela Hermann, who was the injured girl Axmann had left behind when fleeing the bunker; Eberhard Grüttner, who had been in charge of the *Kinderlandverschickung* ("KLV") and a Berlin youth leader; Werner Kuhnt, who was a former Nazi Party member and politician in a far right party; and Dr. Jutta Rüdiger, the last head of the BDM.[21]

An article in the popular German magazine *Der Spiegel* wrote of this with a bit of sarcasm. As for what Axmann did to deserve praise as a model to the youth, they asked if he had worked for the "down-trodden and disenfranchised." They answered their own question with a definite negative: "No, he drove 15 year olds into futile battles."[22]

Those on the other side of Operation Nursery celebrated their victory in style. They managed to consume seven bottles of Hennessy Three Star Cognac (the equivalent of today's Hennessy Very Special aka V.S.). A group photo (with a notation on it) shows many of them together during this celebration: First Lieutenant Jack Hunter (under the name "The Prince of Vom Rath Strasse"—after the street he lived on); infor-mant Siegfried Kulas ("a German personality whose name cannot be revealed"); Captain Donald Allen (chief of the CIC Balkan Desk whom Hunter turned to for advice); Fritz Hauser (a German civilian who drove Hunter at times and broke into houses for him at other times); Lieutenant Tuure Tenander (a fellow G-2 officer at USFET Hq and friend of Hunter's who was not part of Operation Nursery); Agent Reis; Agent Kaufman; and Agent Lewis.

The army awarded the Legion of Merit to Agent Reis and Agent Hochschild for their work on Operation Nursery. Brigadier General Edwin Sibert himself pinned the Bronze Star on Jack Hunter. Accord-ing to Hunter, he had originally been cited for the Legion of Merit but his administrative boss had blocked it. He also blocked the British from awarding Hunter an Order of the British Empire on the grounds that an American intelligence agent shouldn't be getting awards from the British.[23]

As Hunter explained what happened next, "Sibert was too busy to notice and the British didn't give a damn, so I somehow ended up with Sibert pinning the Bronze Star on me in his office one day before boat-time, thanks to the intervention of a big gear in Ike's office who thought I was being shafted."[24]

Hunter's time in the army was coming to an end, and the War Department wanted him to stay in Germany as CIC chief of operations for the region centered on Munich. As he later explained, "I would be a civilian with all the perks of Top Brass, have an impressive salary and be allowed to bring along my family and live in a handsome house that went with the post."[25] At first he and his wife were excited about this prospect, "but then sanity prevailed. I was finally struck with the truth. I would be returning to a country that was still in smoldering ruins and more intensely smoldering hatreds. I would be resuming a job filled with danger, not only to myself but to my family, who could become hostages on the half-shell for some of the creeps I'd be working against."[26]

And so, Hunter left Europe on June 25, 1946, and arrived back in the States on the holiday of July 4. In late August, he was officially discharged from the army. After working as a newspaper reporter, then a congressional speechwriter, and finally a public relations man for DuPont, Hunter became a professional author.

While working as the editor of *DuPont Magazine*, Hunter penned his first novel by writing at night. This book, *The Blue Max*, was named for the prestigious award for German officers, which became famous during World War I. The award's formal name was the *Pour le Mérite*, but its nickname was the Blue Max, and the book's main character (fighter pilot Bruno Stachel) desires the distinction greatly.[27] He copes with his own raging alcoholism while he does whatever it takes to get this blue-and-gold Maltese cross.

The book combines Hunter's childhood love of World War I aviation dogfighting with the firsthand observations that he'd made as the case officer for Operation Nursery. He used the insights that he'd gained from spending time with those who were part of the Tessmann operations to help him create the characters in *The Blue Max*, especially the antihero Stachel.[28]

The book came out in 1964 and was a huge success—it eventually sold over a million copies. A 1966 film was made with the same name starring George Peppard as Bruno Stachel. The film was a hit as well. For his next book, Hunter followed the suggestion of his editor and wrote a fictionalized account of his work in Operation Nursery. *The Expendable Spy* came out in 1965. It too sold well and received strong reviews.

Despite his color-blindness, Hunter also developed a second career as a WWI aviation painter. He had his colors carefully labeled so he knew which ones to use. He considered his first sale to be the cover he painted for his debut novel, *The Blue Max*.

He eventually settled down in a small compound in the heart of St. Augustine, Florida. St. Augustine calls itself "the nation's oldest city"[29] as it is "the oldest continuously occupied settlement of European and African-American origin in the United States."[30] It is a lovely town with an ancient fort on the water, a walkable historical district, and the use in some of the architecture of a limestone filled with the fossils of ancient seashells (known as coquina).

Hunter continued to paint and to write throughout his life, altogether publishing seventeen novels. Jack Hunter died in St. Augustine, Florida, on April 13, 2009, at the age of eighty-seven. Unlike Axmann's, there was no need to hide Hunter's grave from the public. Hunter is buried, along with other American veterans, at the Jacksonville National Cemetery in Florida.

Siegfried Kulas and Jack Hunter kept in touch long after Nursery was wrapped up. Even though Kulas had claimed to the CIC and Hunter that he had turned against the Nazis and so wanted to work against their resurgence, Hunter eventually realized that he remained a Nazi. Siegfried Kulas visited Hunter in the United States in 1976, but he couldn't make a return visit after a law was later passed that prohibited certain Nazis from entering the United States.[31]

Hunter was glad that Kulas couldn't come back again. He later wrote, "I simply couldn't rid myself of my hatred for what he and his colleagues had done to the world. And he made [my wife] Tommy nervous, the way he would stand silently and look over her and her home with those codfish eyes."[32]

Hunter added a postscript to Kulas's 1976 visit: "I did hear from him again, though. His postcard, sent from a vacation resort in Spain, was addressed: 'To Jack D. Hunter, Turkey Point Road, Chesapeake Isle, Md., United Jewish States of Reagan.' I was very sad. Some six years of war, with tens of millions slain, and all we'd learned was that you can't kill an idea. I tore up the card and dropped it into the garbage can."[33]

After Operation Nursery wrapped up, Kulas had hoped that the CIC would protect him from punishment for his activities during the Third Reich. While the CIC did protect him during the operation, despite his falling into the automatic arrestee category for his SS activities, afterward he was on his own with regards to the Germans.

The West German government didn't care what assistance he had provided to the Americans, they still tried him for something he did while he was a part of *Einsatzgruppen* 1b.[34] He only served in this mobile death squad from June to August 1941, as he was shot through his right knee in August of that same year.

The West Germans arrested him in November 1960 and held him prisoner until he was acquitted a year later. The charge against him arose out of activities of *Einsatzgruppen* 1b in Latvia in July 1941. Kulas had been tasked with observing while Latvian auxiliary police slaughtered over sixty unarmed, civilian Jewish men, women, and children. However, the court acquitted him on the basis that he had not actually participated in this slaughter.

As for Hans Garms, the concentration camp survivor who was brought into the Tessmann operation to help conceal that Nazis ran it, he eventually ran into trouble for his black market activities. In 1948, a Munich court sentenced him to three years imprisonment and a fine.[35]

U.S. Army Intelligence Chief Brigadier General Edwin L. Sibert turned his attention from Nazis to Communists. He became an assistant director of the CIA and then returned to the army as chief of staff of the Far East Command before retiring in January 1954. During his many years of service, he was awarded three Distinguished Service Medals, the Legion of Merit, and the Bronze Star. He died on December 16, 1977.

Timothy Reis returned to his job at a Gambles Hardware Store in Idaho when he left the army. He worked in sales and retail management for many years, eventually owning two Gambles Hardware Store franchises that he operated with his longtime wife, Melva.[36] They had met before the war, while Reis had been "trying to sell a washing machine to Melva's mother at the Lewiston Gambles store, when Melva walked in. Tim took one look at her and completely forgot what he was doing."[37]

Reis also went into real estate, operating his own company in Kamiah, Idaho, called Reis Realty. He and Hunter stayed in touch throughout their lives. Reis died on June 22, 2007.

ACKNOWLEDGMENTS

I'd like to thank my family: my brother Todd (aka "The Selby"); my parents, Richard and Rikki; Maria Olga Vargas and her son Christopher; my girlfriend Mandy Jonusas and her mother, Kerstin Jonusas; and my cousins Marc Goldstone and Mitch Goldstone.

Additional thanks go out to my literary agent, Scott Miller of Trident Miller Group, and his assistant at the time, Alexander Slater. Thanks to everyone at the Berkley Caliber imprint of Penguin, including my editor, Natalee Rosenstein, and to Robin Barletta, Pam Barricklow, Courtney Wilhelm, Rick Willet, and Pete Garceau.

To my friends who provided me with suggestions and edits, thank you. They include Jennifer Brody, Laura Dawson, Felize Diaz, Janet Dreyer, Kikki Edman, August Evans, Catherine Culvahouse Fox, Leor Jacobi, Kate Klonick, Michael Maggiano, Rachel McCullough-Sanden, Gabriel Meister, Annabel Raw, William Salzmann, Jeremy Sirota, Alfred ("Dave") Steiner, Nader Vossoughian, and Abigail Wick. For help with translations: Lina E. Johansson and Bettina Wirbladh.

For help related to the research for this book: Chris Crawford; Gabriel Garcia; Martin Krabbe; Kim Lehmann; Bruce Haywood; David Rosenberg of the Center for Jewish History; Former CIC special agent George Hochschild; Amy Gieske, Deborah Idema, and Bill Lewis (for help regarding their father); Professor Torsten Schaar (for sharing his doctorate thesis on Axmann and answering questions about him); former CIC special agent Werner Michel; Dr. Kurt Schilde; Randall Bytwerk; Jim Cate of the National Counter Intelligence Corps Association (NCICA); Stan Solin of "Agent Report"; for help with the National Archives, William Cunliffe (special assistant, Office Records Services), Eric Vanslander, and Wilbert Mahoney; Robert Hunter for the stories about his brother Jack; Professor Blair Worden and the Dacre Trust for their assistance with Hugh Trevor-Roper's archives; at the United States Holocaust Memorial Museum, Edna Friedberg, PhD, and Megan Lewis; Professor M. David Osselton for his help with information on cyanide poisoning; Professor Toby Thacker for help with my questions about denazification proceedings; Staff Sergeant Brandon Moreno (U.S. Army) for my questions about the military; Iris Heisel of *Amt Seenlandschaft Waren* for information about the former mayor of Lansen; Bob Mueller and Robin Mueller, whose relative, CIC agent Robert Mueller, served in the 970th Detachment of the CIC; ScanMyPhotos.com for a superb job of scanning old photo albums that I used during my research.

For the map illustrating Axmann's escape route: Johan Stenbeck.

I'd also like to thank Sarah McNally and all the staff at one of my favorite independent bookstores, McNally Jackson in New York City.

Some of those who helped tremendously with the research for this book preferred anonymity. I'd like to thank them nonetheless for their invaluable assistance.

FOR FURTHER READING

Ambrose, Stephen E. *The Supreme Commander: The War Years of Dwight D. Eisenhower*. Jackson, MS: University Press of Mississippi, 1999.

Antill, Peter. *Berlin 1945: End of the Thousand Year Reich*, Campaign 159. Oxford, U.K.: Osprey Publishing, 2005.

Axmann, Artur. *Das kann doch nicht das Ende sein: Hitlers letzter Reichsjugendführer erinnert sich*. Schnellbach, Germany: Verlag Siegfried Bublies, 1995.

Beevor, Antony. *The Fall of Berlin 1945*. New York: Viking, 2002.

Eberle, Henrik, and Matthias Uhl. *The Hitler Book: The Secret Dossier Prepared for Stalin from the Interrogations of Otto Guensche and Heinze Linge, Hitler's Closest Personal Aides*. Philadelphia: PublicAffairs, 2006.

Fest, Joachim. *Inside Hitler's Bunker: The Last Days of the Third Reich*. New York: Picador, 2005.

Haywood, Bruce. *Bremerhaven: A Memoir Of Germany, 1945–1947*. Raleigh, NC: Lulu, 2010.

Hunter, Jack. *The Expendable Spy*. New York: Bantam Books, 1966.

Junge, Traudl. *Until the Final Hour: Hitler's Last Secretary*. London: Phoenix, 2005.

Kater, Michael H. *Hitler Youth*. Cambridge, MA: Harvard University Press, 2004.

Knopp, Guido. *Hitler's Children*. Gloucestershire, U.K.: Sutton Publishing, 2004.

Lehmann, Armin D., and Tim Carroll. *In Hitler's Bunker: A Boy Soldier's Eyewitness Account of the Fuhrer's Last Days*. Edinburgh: Mainstream Publishing, 2004.

Lepage, Jean-Denis. *Hitler Youth, 1922–45: An Illustrated History*. Jefferson, NC: McFarland & Company, 2009.

Linge, Heinz. *With Hitler to the End: The Memoir of Hitler's Valet*. New York: Skyhorse Publishing, 2009.

MacDonogh, Giles. *After the Reich: The Brutal History of the Allied Occupation*. New York: Basic Books, 2007.

Melchior, Ib. *Case by Case: A U.S. Army Counterintelligence Agent in World War II*, Novato, CA: Presidio Press, 1993.

Melchior, Ib, and Frank Brandenburg. *Quest: Searching for the Truth of Germany's Nazi Past*. New York: Presidio Press, 1994.

O'Donnell, James P. *The Bunker*. Cambridge, MA: Da Capo Press, 2001.

Petrova, Ada, and Peter Watson. *The Death of Hitler*. New York: W.W. Norton, 1996.

Rempel, Gerhard. *Hitler's Children: The Hitler Youth and the SS*. Chapel Hill, NC: UNC Press Books, 1990.

Ryan, Cornelius. *Last Battle: The Classic History of the Battle for Berlin*. New York: Simon & Schuster, 1995.

Shirer, William L. *The Rise and Fall of the Third Reich: A History of Nazi Germany*. New York: Simon & Schuster, 1990.

Speer, Albert. *Inside the Third Reich*. New York: Avon Books, 1971.

Thacker, Toby. *Joseph Goebbels: Life and Death*. Basingstoke, U.K.: Palgrave Macmillan, 2009.

Trevor-Roper, Hugh. *The Last Days of Hitler*. Chicago: University of Chicago Press, 1992.

ABBREVIATIONS

BDM	*Bund Deutscher Mädel* (League of German Girls, female version of HJ)
CIC	U.S. Army Counter Intelligence Corps
FDR	Franklin D. Roosevelt
HJ	*Hitler Jugend* (Hitler Youth)
IMT	International Military Tribunal
KLV	*Kinderlandverschickung* (sending of children to the land)
MG	Military Government
MITC	Military Intelligence Training Center
NSDAP	*Nationalsozialistische Deutsche Arbeiterpartei* (Nazi Party)
OCS	Officer Candidate School
OSS	Office of Strategic Services
ROTC	Reserve Officers' Training Corps
SHAEF	Supreme Headquarters, Allied Expeditionary Force
SS	*Schutzstaffel*
U.K.	United Kingdom
USFET	United States Forces, European Theater
U.S.S.R.	Union of Soviet Socialist Republics (the Soviet Union)
V-E DAY	Victory in Europe Day
V-J DAY	Victory over Japan Day

NOTES

DRAMATIS PERSONAE

1 The convention this book uses with German characters is to replace the character "ß" (Eszett) with a double "ss." So for example, the German word for street, Straße is written as Strasse. This book uses umlauts for these German characters: ä, ö, and ü. When quoting documents that follow other conventions regarding German characters, this book leaves such characters as they were in the original.

PROLOGUE

1 George Orwell, "Review of *Mein Kampf* by Adolf Hitler," *New English Weekly,* March 21, 1940.

2 There were actually two connected bunkers that I refer to as "Hitler's bunker" or "the bunker." The upper or forward bunker (*Vorbunker*) and the lower bunker (which was the *Führerbunker* proper).

3 Axmann's Command Post (CP) at this point was at Wilhelmstrasse 64. Artur Axmann, *Das kann doch nicht das Ende sein: Hitlers letzter Reichsjugendführer erinnert sich* (Schnellbach, Germany: Verlag Siegfried Bublies, 1995), 429, 433, and 435. Axmann's headquarters were in this building's cellar, which also served as an air-raid shelter. Unless otherwise noted, when using quotes from sources in German, translations have been obtained by the author. As a general rule, if the title of a source is in English, the quote from it was in English. If the title is in German, such as with Axmann's memoir, the source material was in German and the author had it translated.

4 From Traudl Junge's diary entry for April 26, 1945: "All around us death and ruins. On the Wilhelmsplatz is a dead horse, starving people carve it up, and pretty soon there is only the skeleton left." Page 3 of translated version of Junge's diary attached to Interrogation of Traudl Junge by Michael Musmanno, March 21, 1948, Munich.

5 *See* Artur Axmann, "*Das Ende im Führerbunker,*" *Stern,* May 2, 1965, 75. For a

mention of the Soviets using phosphorous shells in Berlin, see e.g., Antony Beevor, *The Fall of Berlin 1945* (New York: Viking, 2002), 161. Note that white phosphorous can be used for illumination or to produce cover smoke, but it also creates toxic fumes.

6   Armin D. Lehmann and Tim Carroll, *In Hitler's Bunker: A Boy Soldier's Eyewitness Account of the Fuhrer's Last Days* (Edinburgh: Mainstream Publishing, 2004), 148–149.

7   Axmann's CI Arrest Report lists him as having a height of 1.7 meters. Axmann CI Arrest Report, December 17, 1945.

8   Color reported in the CI Arrest Report for Axmann, December 17, 1945.

9   Axmann, *Das kann doch nicht*, 438.

10   Ibid.

11   This book uses HJ as the abbreviation for Hitler Youth based on the German name of the organization (*Hitler Jugend*).

12   This book uses the terms Soviet and Russian interchangeably for the troops serving the Soviet Union.

13   Interrogation of Artur Axmann by Michael Musmanno, January 7, 1948, Nuremberg, 2.

14   Axmann nicknamed them "tank crackers." Guido Knopp, *Hitler's Children* (Gloucestershire, U.K.: Sutton Publishing, 2004), 271.

15   Artur Axmann, *Völkischer Beobachter*, March 28, 1945, quoted in and translated by Brenda Ralph Lewis, *Hitler Youth: The Hitlerjugend in War and Peace, 1933–1945* (Osceola, WI: MBI Publishing, 2000), 171. Note that I've changed the spelling of "honour" to the American spelling of "honor."

16   Vienna HJ leader Ralf Roland Ringler. Michael H. Kater, *Hitler Youth* (Cambridge, MA: Harvard University Press, 2004), 220–221, Endnote 235 (on page 332), quoting from (and translating) Ralf Roland Ringler, *Illusion einer Jugend: Lieder, Fahnen und das bittere Ende: Hitlerjugend in Österreich: Ein Erlebnisbericht* (Sankt Pölten, Austria: Verl. Niederösterr. Pressehaus, 1977), 149.

17   There was talk by Hitler of miracle weapons, rescue by German military forces, and the Western Allies turning against the Soviets, but such non-reality-based ideas of rescue became increasingly absurd as the Battle of Berlin progressed.

18   Axmann made this offer to Hitler around 6 P.M. on April 28, 1945. Lehmann and Carroll, *In Hitler's Bunker*, 192. See also Henrik Eberle and Matthias Uhl, eds., *The Hitler Book: The Secret Dossier Prepared for Stalin from the Interrogations of Otto Guensche and Heinze Linge, Hitler's Closest Personal Aides*, trans. Giles Mac-Donogh, (Philadelphia: PublicAffairs, 2006), 262. Hitler's valet, Heinz Linge, also mentions this in his memoirs, along with the detail that a tank (panzer) would have accompanied them. Heinz Linge, *With Hitler to the End: The Memoir of Hitler's Valet* (New York: Skyhorse Publishing, 2009), 197.

19   Eberle and Uhl, *The Hitler Book*, 262.

20   Interrogation of Artur Axmann by Michael Musmanno, January 7, 1948, Nuremberg, 23.

21 "I personally was firmly convinced that [Hitler] would take his own life and I had the same impression of Goebbels." Ibid., 18.

22 "Might of the Soviet, Impressive Parade on May Day," A.A.P., *The Age* (Melbourne, Australia), May 2, 1945.

23 Axmann, *Das kann doch nicht*, 79–80.

24 Gerd was the short form of Gerhard. Weltzin's name is listed as Gerhard in the *SHAEF Basic Handbook on the Hitler Jugend* (Annexe C), but Axmann in his memoir refers to him as "Gerd Weltzin." See, e.g., Axmann, *Das kann doch nicht*, 427. I have followed Axmann's lead and referred to him as Gerd.

25 Artur Axmann, "Das Ende im Führerbunker," 75. Note that this overall story about Axmann's last meeting with Hitler is taken from two sources—this article written by Axmann and his later memoir. Each quote though is cited to its source.

26 Ibid.

27 Axmann, *Das kann doch nicht*, 443–444.

28 Ibid., 444. Axmann used his statement to Hitler ("This cannot be the end"; in German "Das kann doch nicht das Ende sein") for the title of his memoirs.

29 Ibid.

30 Ibid.

31 Artur Axmann, "Das Ende im Führerbunker," 75.

32 Axmann, *Das kann doch nicht*, 444.

33 Interrogation of Artur Axmann by Michael Musmanno, January 7, 1948, Nuremberg, 19–21.

34 The HJ doctor was *HJ-Hauptbannführer* Professor Dr. Liebenow.

35 The source for this entire paragraph is the Interrogation of Artur Axmann by Robert Kempner, October 10, 1947, 7–8.

36 "The Wilhelmsplatz looks bleak, the [Hotel] Kaiserhof has collapsed like a house of cards; its ruins reach almost all the way to the Reich Chancellery." Traudl Junge's diary entry for April 22, 1945, Traudl Junge, *Until the Final Hour: Hitler's Last Secretary* (London: Phoenix, 2005), 161.

37 Lehmann and Carroll, 154.

38 Artur Axmann, "Das Ende im Führerbunker," 75.

39 Interrogation of Artur Axmann by Michael Musmanno, January 7, 1948, Nuremberg, 26.

40 Ibid., 27.

41 James P. O'Donnell, *The Bunker* (Cambridge, MA: Da Capo Press, 2001), 224.

42 Ibid., 225.

43 For example, Hitler's secretary (Traudl Junge) thought she heard a shot [Junge, *Until the Final Hour*, 187], but as an endnote in her own book explains, experts came to the conclusion that "at this point Frau Junge was far away, on the stairs from the lower to the upper part of the bunker. What she thinks she heard . . . was probably an illusion caused by the running diesel generator and the constant heavy firing on the Reich Chancellery." Junge, *Until the Final Hour*, n111, on page 215.

Also, Axmann recalled Goebbels saying "I believe I heard a shot" although Axmann himself "heard nothing." Interrogation of Artur Axmann by Michael Musmanno, January 7, 1948, Nuremberg, 28. See also Axmann, *Das kann doch nicht*, 445.

44 O'Donnell, *The Bunker*, 224. Axmann's memoir has him in the map room waiting with others, not right outside the door, but as his memoir was written much later than this statement about being near the door, in so far as there is conflict between the two, this statement seems more reliable. In neither account does Axmann claim he heard a shot.

45 Ib Melchior and Frank Brandenburg, *Quest: Searching for the Truth of Germany's Nazi Past* (New York: Presidio Press, 1994), 256.

46 See e.g., Interrogation of Artur Axmann by Michael Musmanno, January 7, 1948, Nuremberg, 29.

47 Interrogation of Artur Axmann by Hugh Trevor-Roper, Military Intelligence Service Center (MISC), USFET, January 14, 1946, 2. It is possible that Hitler bit down on a cyanide capsule in addition to shooting himself. "Axmann stated that he also believe [sic] that Hitler took poison first and then shot himself." Notes on the Interrogation of Artur Axmann written by Walter Rapp (director, Evidence Division, Office of Chief of Counsel for War Crimes), October 16, 1947, 5. But see "Hitler had shot himself through the right temple (whether he also took poison could not be determined)." Interrogation of Artur Axmann by Hugh Trevor-Roper, January 14, 1946, 2. Despite what is written in the notes of this interrogation, in *The Last Days of Hitler*, Trevor-Roper quotes Axmann saying that he believed Hitler "shot himself through the mouth, and that the concussion of such a blast resulted in the blood on the Fuehrer's temples." Axmann quoted in Hugh Trevor-Roper, *The Last Days of Hitler* (Chicago: University of Chicago Press, 1992), 46.

48 "AXMANN states that HITLER was sitting at one of the end of the sofa (the left end from the viewpoint of the observer), leaning slightly to the outside. Eva Braun's body was to Hitler's left, towards the middle of the sofa, leaning against Hitler's body." Leo Barton, Military Intelligence Service Center, USFET, "Supplement to interrogation of KEMPKA etc. on brief received from Major TREVOR-ROPER," January 25, 1946, 2.

49 Trevor-Roper, *The Last Days of Hitler*, 207.

50 "Axmann was not present during this wedding." Notes on the interrogation of Artur Axmann written by Walter Rapp, October 16, 1947, 3. Axmann was present at the party/gathering to say congratulations afterward.

51 The number of guests is from Traudl Junge, *Until the Final Hour*, 183.

52 James E. Combs and Dan D. Nimmo, *A Primer of Politics* (New York: Macmillan, 1984), 359.

53 Traudl Junge's diary, April 22, 1945. Translated version of Junge's diary attached to Michael Musmanno's March 21, 1948, interrogation of Traudl Junge in Munich.

54 "One of these days I shall speak to him about this." Ibid.

55 Interrogation of Artur Axmann by Michael Musmanno, January 7, 1948, Nuremberg, 34.

56 "Axmann did not personally witness the burning as this was too horrible for him to witness but he knows as a matter of fact that it did take place." Notes on the interrogation of Artur Axmann written by Walter Rapp, October 16, 1947, 5.

57 According to Eberle and Uhl, *The Hitler Book*, 272, instead of giving the pistol directly to Axmann, Günsche handed it to "Axmann's adjutant, Lieutenant Hamann. He also gave him Hitler's dog-whip. Hamann wanted to keep them safe as relics for the Hitler Youth." It would appear that if Hamann had first received the gun, he gave it over to Axmann. Otto Hamann, though, was not Axmann's adjutant, Weltzin was. Hamann had been the leader of the HJ Berlin region, and he died from wounds he received while trying to cross from Axmann's CP on Wilhelmstrasse. Axmann, *Das kann doch nicht*, 434. Axmann wrote that he received the gun from Günsche. Axmann, *Das kann doch nicht*, 446.

58 Axmann, *Das kann doch nicht*, 446. Günsche and Axmann had been "on very close terms because [Günsche] once had been a Hitler Youth leader." Interrogation of Artur Axmann by Michael Musmanno, January 7, 1948, Nuremberg, 38.

59 Junge said when interrogated that "I know from Günsche that [Hitler's] ashes were collected into a box, which was given to the Reichsjugendführer Axmann, about the further fate of Axmann I do not know, I saw him for the last time on 2nd May, when I left the Reichschancellory." CIC Special Agent Karl Sussman, Memorandum for the Commanding Officer, Garmisch Sub-Region, Subject: Interrogation of JUNGE, GERTRUD, August 30, 1946, (Secret), 6.

60 Axmann denied this, but Trevor-Roper wrote that "nevertheless, if I were to hazard a guess, I should guess that the ashes were given to Axmann." Hugh Trevor-Roper, *The Last Days of Hitler* (London: The Macmillan Co.,1952), page xxxiii. Also, on page 226 of this edition, Roper wrote, "Perhaps, as Guensche is said to have stated, [Hitler's] ashes were collected in a box and conveyed out of the Chancellery. Or perhaps no elaborate explanation is necessary." All other citations of this book are to the 1992 edition. See also O'Donnell, *The Bunker*, 302. (Axmann "was suspected of being a 'keeper of the flame,' perhaps even the custodian of Hitler's ashes.")

61 Artur Axmann, "Das Ende im Führerbunker," 75.

62 Axmann, *Das kann doch nicht*, 509.

63 O'Donnell, *The Bunker*, 222.

CHAPTER ONE

1 Brenda Ralph Lewis, *Hitler Youth: The Hitlerjugend in War and Peace, 1933–1945* (Osceola, WI: MBI Publishing, 2000), 39. (I added the umlaut to *Führer*.) The boys were joining the Jungvolk organization of the HJ, which was for boys ten to fourteen years old. The blood banner referred to here was "a Nazi 'icon' said to have been soaked in the blood of those who had died in the failed putsch of 1923. At the Nuremberg rallies, all new flags were touched to this grim relic." Ibid.

2   Those HJ boys in the government sector at the end were part of Axmann's breakout group.

3   Armin D. Lehmann and Tim Carroll, *In Hitler's Bunker: A Boy Soldier's Eyewitness Account of the Fuhrer's Last Days* (Edinburgh: Mainstream Publishing, 2004), 76.

4   See e.g., Kater, *Hitler Youth* (Cambridge, MA: Harvard University Press, 2004), 23.

5   A similar ceremony had been held a month before, when Hitler (again accompanied by Axmann) had awarded twenty members of Hitler Youth (HJ) the Iron Cross.

6   Artur Axmann, *Das kann doch nicht das Ende sein: Hitlers letzter Reichsjugendführer erinnert sich* (Schnellbach, Germany: Verlag Siegfried Bublies, 1995), 418.

7   Ibid.

8   Lehmann and Carroll, *In Hitler's Bunker*, 87. In quotes like this where there was no umlaut in the original, I have left it out in the quote.

9   Ibid.

10 See e.g., Axmann, *Das kann doch nicht*, 418.

11 *Oberscharführer* Peter Hartmann, quoted in Ada Petrova and Peter Watson, *The Death of Hitler* (New York: W.W. Norton, 1995), 10.

12 Lehmann and Carroll, *In Hitler's Bunker*, 88–89.

13 Joachim Fest, *Inside Hitler's Bunker: The Last Days of the Third Reich* (New York: Picador, 2005), 48.

14 Lehmann and Carroll, *In Hitler's Bunker*, 89. Immediately prior to this quote, Lehmann talks about how Axmann tried to present what happened that day in a different light. "After the war I talked to Axmann at great length about those dark days. He claimed to me that he had presented us to Hitler to show just how weary and beaten we were, to convince him that the struggle was over and it would be futile to sacrifice our young lives. That was not the impression I had at the time."

15 Axmann, *Das kann doch nicht*, 12.

16 Max Wiedemann, "Aufstieg und Fall des Artur Axmann," *Sozial Extra*, October 15, 1985, Nr. 10.

17 Axmann joined the Nazi Party in September 1931. Interrogation of Artur Axmann by Robert Kempner, October 10, 1947, German version, 2. The age limit to join the party was later lowered.

18 Another translation of his position is "head of the social branch of the Reichsjugendfuehrung." Ibid., 3.

19 Most groups were banned promptly, some Catholic groups lasted longer. See e.g., "Germany: Swastikas, Man & Boy," *Time*, March 5, 1934.

20 Ibid.

21 Interrogation of Artur Axmann by Robert Kempner, July 22, 1947, 1. See also, Axmann, *Das kann doch nicht*, 233.

22 Axmann, *Das kann doch nicht*, 233.

23 Interrogation of Artur Axmann by Robert Kempner, October 10, 1947, German version, 5.

24 Axmann, *Das kann doch nicht*, 234.

25 Ibid.

26 Ibid., 234–235.

27 The position of *Reichsjugendführer* was created by Hitler on June 17, 1933.

28 Baldur von Schirach testimony on May 23, 1946, International Military Tribunal, *The Trial of German Major War Criminals: Proceedings of the International Military Tribunal Sitting at Nuremberg, Germany*, Part 13, (London: H. M. Stationery Off., 1947), 354. Von Schirach kept his title as "Reich Leader of Youth Education" and also received the title of "Inspector of Youth" (Ibid.). Although he had those titles and tried to take responsibility at his trial in Nuremberg for "Youth Leadership" to protect Axmann so "that no other Youth Leader will be summoned before a court for actions for which I have assumed responsibility," in reality once Axmann took the post of *Reichsjugendführer* he was effectively in charge of the Hitler Youth and BDM. Von Schirach was busy with his new job as the district leader of Vienna.

29 "As Reich Youth Leader of the NSDAP and Youth Leader of the German Reich, the Führer has named the Obergebietsführer Arthur [*sic*] Axmann." Max Domarus, *Hitler: Speeches and Proclamations, 1932–1945*, (English Volume III: 1939–1940) (Wauconda, IL: Bolchazy-Carducci Publishers, 1997), 71, quoting translated material from *Deutsches Nachrichtenbüro* (German News Bureau) text, August 7, 1940.

30 Axmann put Helmut Moeckel in charge while he was gone.

31 Interrogation of Artur Axmann by Michael Musmanno, January 7, 1948, Nuremberg, 1.

32 The information in this paragraph comes from Interrogation of Artur Axmann by Robert Kempner, October 10, 1947, 10, and Axmann, *Das kann doch nicht*.

33 Melita Maschmann, *Account Rendered: a dossier on my former self*, trans. Geoffrey Strachan (New York: Abelard-Schuman, 1965), 147.

34 Stephen E. Ambrose, *The Supreme Commander: The War Years of Dwight D. Eisenhower* (Jackson, MS: University Press of Mississippi, 1999), 630. See e.g., Peter Antill, *Berlin 1945: End of the Thousand Year Reich, Campaign 159* (Oxford, U.K.: Osprey Publishing, 2005), 30–31. This is a complicated topic; there is literally an entire book just about Eisenhower's decision not to go to Berlin: Stephen E. Ambrose, *Eisenhower and Berlin, 1945: The Decision to Halt at the Elbe* (New York: W.W. Norton, 2000).

35 Ambrose, *The Supreme Commander*, 630.

36 From a letter General Eisenhower sent to General George Marshall, August 31, 1944 (Top Secret). Text of this letter kindly provided to the author by Herbert L. Pankratz, archivist, Eisenhower Presidential Library & Museum, Abilene, Kansas.

37 Antill, *Berlin 1945*, 18.

38 Field Information Agency, Technical (FIAT), USFET, Intelligence Report No. EF/Min/3, October 1, 1945, "SPEER Ministry Report No. 19, Part III: ADOLF HITLER," (Restricted), 46.

39 Goebbels "dictated a short 'Appendix' to Hitler's Private Testament," which included "For the first time in my life, I must categorically refuse to obey a command of the *Führer*." Toby Thacker, *Joseph Goebbels: Life and Death* (Basingstoke, U.K.: Palgrave Macmillan, 2009), 301.

40 James P. O'Donnell, *The Bunker* (Cambridge, MA: Da Capo Press, 2001), 261–262.

41 Ibid., 270.

42 Richard Holmes, *The World at War: The Landmark Oral History from the Previously Unpublished Archives* (London: Ebury Press, 2008), 552.

43 CIC Special Agent Karl Sussman, Memorandum for the Commanding Officer, Garmisch Sub-Region, Subject: Interrogation of JUNGE, GERTRUD, August 30, 1946, (Secret), 6.

44 Earl F. Ziemke, *The U.S. Army in the Occupation of Germany, 1944-1946* (Washington, DC: U.S. Government Printing Office, 1975), 380.

45 Jonathan Huener and Francis R. Nicosia, *The Arts in Nazi Germany: Continuity, Conformity, Change* (New York: Berghahn Books, 2006), 47.

46 Kater, *Hitler Youth*, 152.

47 Officially, Hitler gave Axmann the Gold Cross "in recognition of his unique service in directing the efforts of German youth in the Reich and now in the struggle for Berlin." "Fuehrer Awards Cross of Gold to Axmann," *North German Home Service*, 5 P.M., April 27, 1945, recorded and translated by BBC Monitoring, 5:38 P.M., April 27, 1945 (document in the National Archives of the U.K.).

48 The other holder of the Gold Cross of the German Order to survive past 1945 was *Reichsarbeitsführer* (Reich labor leader) Konstantin Hierl. Another recipient, Karl August Hanke, lived a month after Germany's surrender; he died on June 8, 1945.

49 "Fuehrer Awards Cross of Gold to Axmann," North German Home Service, 5 P.M., April 27, 1945, recorded and translated by BBC Monitoring, 5:38 P.M., April 27, 1945 (document in the National Archives of the U.K.).

50 Axmann, *Das kann doch nicht*, 445.

51 Lehmann and Carroll, *In Hitler's Bunker*, 221.

52 Office of Chief of Counsel for the Prosecution of Axis Criminality, Dept. of State, United States, and War Dept., United States, International Military Tribunal, *Nazi Conspiracy and Aggression* (D.C.: U.S. Government Printing Office, 1946), 577.

53 Ibid.

54 Paul Lemberg, *Be Unreasonable: The Unconventional Way to Extraordinary Business Results* (New York: McGraw-Hill Professional, 2007), 40.

55 This number is according to Lehmann, who was part of this breakout group. Eberle and Matthias Uhl, eds., *The Hitler Book: The Secret Dossier Prepared for Stalin from the Interrogations of Otto Guensche and Heinze Linge, Hitler's Closest Personal Aides*, trans. Giles MacDonogh, (Philadelphia: PublicAffairs, 2006), page 275, has the number at 200.

56 See Lehmann and Carroll, *In Hitler's Bunker*, 220.

57 Ibid.

58 As Trevor-Roper noted in his comments on the interrogation of Axmann: "Axmann appears reliable in regards to facts, but not dates . . . Almost all AXMANN's dates are wrong. In the circumstances this is not unnatural and in fact very few of such witnesses have been accurate in these matters." Major Trevor-Roper, CI War Room, "Special Interrogation of AXMANN AND KEMPKA," Addressed to USFET, AC of S, G-2, CIC, February 11, 1946. I've checked times with other sources as Axmann appears to have become confused as to exact times regarding the final days in Hitler's bunker and the breakout. Given all the confusion back then, and the long, strange hours kept by Hitler, it is not surprising that Axmann's sense of time was thrown off. As for Axmann's factual accuracy, additional evidence for it came decades after Trevor-Roper's above analysis when the verification of Bormann's remains proved Axmann's account of Bormann's death to be reliable.

59 Lehmann and Carroll, *In Hitler's Bunker*, 223.

60 "Hitlers Höllenfahrt: Das Ende im Bunker und die lange Reise des Leichnams / Teil II," *Der Spiegel* (Hamburg), April 10, 1995, 176.

61 Axmann, *Das kann doch nicht*, 449.

62 Lehmann and Carroll, *In Hitler's Bunker*, 223.

63 O'Donnell, *The Bunker*, 304.

64 Lehmann and Carroll, *In Hitler's Bunker*, 224.

65 O'Donnell, *The Bunker*, 304.

66 Testimony of Erich Kempka on the last days of Hitler, Berchtesgaden, June 20, 1945.

67 Cornelius Ryan, *Last Battle: The Classic History of the Battle for Berlin* (New York: Simon & Schuster, 1995), 398.

68 Ibid.

69 In his memoirs, Axmann had various justifications for his use of HJ in fighting. His main arguments centered on their service being voluntary. As for the boys who fought to hold bridges in Berlin, his argument centers on this being an order from Hitler and his need to obey his leader. Colonel Hans-Oscar Wohlermann (chief of artillery for General Helmuth Weidling's LVIth Panzer Corps headquarters) went on to say that "he had no doubt that Axmann had given the promised counterorder" with his thinking that it either "did not get through in time" or that the HJ ignored it. It appears though that Axmann did not give such a counterorder. Tony Le Tissier, *Zhukov at the Oder: The Decisive Battle for Berlin* (Mechanicsburg, PA: Stackpole Military History Series edition, 2009), 220.

70 Le Tissier, *Zhukov at the Oder*, 220.

71 Lehmann and Carroll, *In Hitler's Bunker*, 120.

72 Axmann, *Das kann doch nicht*, 420.

73 See e.g., Lehmann and Carroll, *In Hitler's Bunker*, 80.

74 Second Execution Order to the Law of the Hitler Youth (Youth Service Regulation) of March 25, 1939, Article 9(3), "Induction into the Hitler Youth takes place on 20

April of every year." *Nazi Conspiracy and Aggression,* Volume IV, Office of the United States Chief Counsel for Prosecution of Axis Criminality (D.C.: United States Government Printing Office, 1946), Translation of Document No. 2115-PS.

75 Lehmann and Carroll, *In Hitler's Bunker,* 80.

76 Max Wiedemann, "Aufstieg und Fall des Artur Axmann," *Sozial Extra,* October 15, 1985, 37. Quoting from *Panzerbär,* the *"Kampfblatt für die Verteidiger Berlins,"* April 22, 1945.

77 Melita Maschmann, *Account Rendered: a dossier on my former self,* trans. Geoffrey Strachan (New York: Abelard-Schuman, 1965), 157.

78 Artur Axmann, "Nazis Through and Through," *Völkischer Beobachter,* September 3, 1944, quoted in and translated by Jost Hermand, *A Hitler Youth in Poland: the Nazis' program for evacuating children during World War II,* trans. Margot Bettauer Dembo, (Evanston, IL: Northwestern University Press, 1997), 77–78.

79 Maschmann, *Account Rendered,* 158.

80 Ibid.

81 Guido Knopp, *Hitler's Children* (Gloucestershire, U.K: Sutton Publishing, 2004), 273.

82 Ibid.

83 Ibid., 273–274.

84 Antony Beevor, *The Fall of Berlin 1945* (New York: Viking, 2002), 270.

85 Jean-Denis Lepage, *Hitler Youth, 1922–45: An Illustrated History* (Jefferson, NC: McFarland & Company, 2009), 153.

86 Chris Bishop, *The Encyclopedia of Weapons of WWII: The Comprehensive Guide to Over 1,500 Weapons Systems, Including Tanks, Small Arms, Warplanes, Artillery, Ships, and Submarines* (New York: Sterling Publishing Company, Inc., 2002), 16.

87 Ibid.

88 Axmann recalled the explosion being at "a point about 300 meter [*sic*] north of Weidendammer Bruecke." Leo Barton, Military Intelligence Service Center, USFET, "Interrogation of AXMANN on special brief by Major TREVOR-ROPER," January 14, 1946, 3.

89 O'Donnell, *The Bunker,* 304.

90 Erich Kempka testimony on July 3, 1946, International Military Tribunal, *The Trial of German Major War Criminals: Proceedings of the International Military Tribunal Sitting at Nuremberg, Germany,* Part 18 (London: H. M. Stationery Off., 1946), 73–74.

91 Ibid., 74.

92 Lehmann and Carroll, *In Hitler's Bunker,* 236.

93 Ibid., 305.

94 Ibid.

95 Hans Baur on Bormann: "His face was little known in those days. No one would have recognized him." Ib Melchior and Frank Brandenburg, *Quest: Searching for the Truth of Germany's Nazi Past* (New York: Presidio Press, 1994), 29.

96 Ibid., 28.

97 Ibid., 29.

98 Kurt Schilde, *"Artur Axmann auf der Spur: Aktivitäten des letzten Reichsjugend-führers nach 1945,"* in *Deutsche Jugend im Zweiten Weltkrieg,* ed. Ingo Koch (Rostock, Germany: Verlag Jugend und Geschichte, 1991), 99.

99 O'Donnell, *The Bunker,* 310

100 Interrogation of Axmann by Hugh Trevor-Roper, January 14, 1946, 3.

101 Ibid.

102 Dr. Reidar F. Sognnaes, "Dental evidence in the postmortem identification of Adolf Hitler, Eva Braun, and Martin Bormann," *Legal Medicine Annual,* 1976: 173–235.

103 Professor M. David Osselton (director, Centre for Forensic Sciences, the School of Conservation Sciences, Bournemouth University) email to author, July 4, 2011. Osselton noted that he consulted the following references: R. H. Dreisbach, *Handbook of Poisoning* (Lange Medical Publications); M. Ellenshorn, *Ellenhorn's Medical Toxicology: Diagnosis and Treatment of Human Poisoning* (Elsevier Science).

104 Professor M. David Osselton, email to author, July 4, 2011.

105 Ibid.

106 Here is another account Axmann gave of his encounter with Bormann's body: "I could see him clearly in the moonlight. There was not a mark on him and I assumed he had taken poison. I knew he carried a cyanide vial. I did not stay long enough to examine him." Melchior and Brandenburg, *Quest,* 255. Note that Axmann told Trevor-Roper a different assumption for what had happened to Bormann: "The bodies showed no signs of life; AXMANN did not see any wounds and no signs of a shattering explosion. He assumed therefore that the two were hit by rifle fire in their backs." Interrogation of Axmann by Hugh Trevor-Roper, January 14, 1946, 3.

107 O'Donnell, *The Bunker,* 306.

108 Albert Krumnow, a retired postman, in 1965 "said he and two other mailmen were ordered by Soviet troops on May 8, 1945, to bury two bodies which showed no signs of injuries. On one of them they found identity papers of . . . Dr. Stumpfegger. . . . The other body, he said, was of the same build as Bormann." Reuters, "Police Dig at Berlin Wall Seeking Body of Bormann," *Montreal Gazette,* July 22, 1965, 5. The police searched for these bodies in 1965, but Krumnow did not know their exact location and they were not found at that time.

109 "In 1972, during construction work near the Lehrter railway station, the skeletal remains of two males were found. By investigating the teeth and the bones and comparing the results with notes from the doctor and dentist of Bormann, experts from the police dental clinic of Berlin and the Institute of Legal and Social Medicine in Berlin concluded at the time that one of these was Bormann." K. Anslinger et al., "Identification of the skeletal remains of Martin Bormann by mtDNA analysis," *International Journal of Legal Medicine* 114 (2001): 194–196, 194. These bodies were only fifteen yards away from where police had dug in 1965 based on Krumnow's information. Otto Doelling, "Painstaking Work Explodes Bormann Myth," AP, *Tri-City Herald,* April 15, 1972, 8.

110   K. Anslinger et al., "Identification of the skeletal remains." "An 83-year-old female cousin of Bormann provided a sample for comparison." Ibid.

CHAPTER TWO

1   Gordon Gaskill, "G-Men in Khaki," *American Magazine,* Vol. 139 (New York: Crowell-Collier Pub., January, 1945): 33.

2   Victor Greto, "At 87, Writer Still Flies High," *News Journal* (Wilmington, DE), March 1, 2009.

3   Robert "Bob" Hunter (Jack Hunter's younger brother), email to author, September 13, 2011.

4   *History and Mission of the Counter Intelligence Corps in World War II* (Fort Holabird, MD: CIC School, CIC Corps, U.S. Army, 1951), 11.

5   Ibid. for the change in policy after Germany was defeated. As for exceptions to this policy, one example is Jack Hunter's friend during his military intelligence training, Werner Michel.

6   Tanya Perez-Brenna, "Jack D. Hunter is flying high; Love of airplanes turned novelist into artist, too," *Florida Times Union* (Jacksonville, FL), November 7, 2003.

7   It appears that young Jack Hunter was not aware that an English translation of this book existed then, or he did not have access to a copy. It had been translated in 1918 as *The Red Battle Flyer.*

8   Jack Hunter, *Spies, Inc.* (New York: Dutton, 1969), 13. The main character, who tells this joke ("a decorated ex-Army counter-intelligence agent") appears to be based on Hunter himself.

9   Perez-Brenna, "Jack D. Hunter is flying high."

10   Bob Hunter, conversation with author, January 15, 2011.

11   Ibid. Bob Hunter was also color-blind. He joined the military as an electronics technician, but he was not able to do tech duty as he needed to see the color of lights, which indicated whether a ship was going away or coming toward one. When the military found out, they put him in electronics duty.

12   Ibid.

13   Greto, "At 87, Writer Still Flies High."

14   Richard Prior, "'Blue Max' Author Relives War," *St. Augustine News,* July 23, 2007.

15   Letter from the Adjunct General's Office, War Department, subject "Temporary Appointment," letter effective as of Jack Hunter's graduation date of August 4, 1944.

16   Jack D. Hunter, "The Blue Max Revisited," *Over the Front,* Vol. 13, no. 3, (Fall 1998).

17   Jack Hunter, unpublished material.

18   John Schwarzwalder, *We Caught Spies* (New York: Duell, Sloan and Pearce, 1946), viii.

19   Thomas M. Johnson, *The Golden Sphinx: The Army's Counter-Intelligence,* reprinted in *Secrets & Spies: Behind the Scenes Stories of World War II* (Pleasantville, NY: Reader's Digest Association, 1964), 365.

20   *History and Mission of the Counter Intelligence Corps,* 11.

21 Werner Michel, correspondence with author, November 14, 2010.

22 Ibid., January 3, 2011.

23 Gaskill, "G-Men in Khaki," 33.

24 AR 381-100 quoted in John Mendelsohn, *The History of the Counter Intelligence Corps (CIC):* Vol. 1 (New York: Garland, 1989), 114.

25 Ib Mechior, *Case by Case: A U.S. Army Counterintelligence Agent in World War II* (Novato, CA: Presidio Press, 1993), 27.

26 Schwarzwalder, *We Caught Spies*, vii.

27 William Attwood, "The Germans Call It a Gestapo," *New York Herald Tribune*, March 7, 1947.

28 Schwarzwalder, *We Caught Spies*, 262.

29 "No Soldier shall, in time of peace be quartered in any house, without the consent of the Owner, nor in time of war, but in a manner to be prescribed by law." U.S. Constitution amendment III.

30 Alan Dundes and Carl R. Pagter, *Work Hard and You Shall Be Rewarded: Urban Folklore from the Paperwork Empire* (Detroit, MI: Wayne State University Press, 1978), 109.

31 Supreme Headquarters Allied Expeditionary Force (SHAEF) Evaluation and Dissemination Section, G-2 (Counter Intelligence Sub-Division), Compiled by MIRS (London Branch), *The Hitler Jugend (The Hitler Youth Organisation)*, Basic Handbook, 1944, E.D.S./G/5, Foreword, 1.

32 Ibid.

CHAPTER THREE

1 Adolf Hitler, speech given at Elbing, Germany, November 1933, quoted in Office of Chief of Counsel for the Prosecution of Axis Criminality, Dept. of State, United States, and War Dept, United States, International Military Tribunal, *Nazi Conspiracy and Aggression*, Vol. 4 (Washington, DC: U.S. Government Printing Office, 1946), 313.

2 Artur Axmann, *Das kann doch nicht das Ende sein: Hitlers letzter Reichsjugendführer erinnert sich* (Schnellbach, Germany: Verlag Siegfried Bublies, 1995), 451. A slightly different location for the gun's burial is given in a German magazine article which quotes an unnamed source: "Hitler's gun [Axmann] had, he told a confidant, deposited under the ballast stones of a track near the Lehrter station— before he ran into a squad of Red Army soldiers." Mathias Müller von Blumencron, "Trophäen des Sieges," *Der Spiegel*, February 1, 1999.

3 Ib Melchior and Frank Brandenburg, *Quest: Searching for the Truth of Germany's Nazi Past* (New York: Presidio Press, 1994), 256.

4 Interrogation of Axmann by Hugh Trevor-Roper, January 14, 1946, 4.

5 Axmann, *Das kann doch nicht*, 451.

6 Interrogation of Axmann by Hugh Trevor-Roper, January 14, 1946, 4. See also Axmann, *Das kann doch nicht*, 452.

7   Artur Axmann, *"Meine Flucht mit Bormann,"* Stern, May 9, 1965, 58.

8   Ibid.

9   Peter Antill, *Berlin 1945: End of the Thousand Year Reich, Campaign 159* (Oxford, U.K.: Osprey Publishing, 2005), 83.

10 Ibid.

11 Hendrik C. Verton, *In the Fire of the Eastern Front: The Experiences of a Dutch Waffen-SS Volunteer, 1941–45* (Mechanicsburg, PA: Stackpole Books, 2010), 66.

12 Ibid. Those with the SS tattoo often tried to remove it, see ibid., 212–213, where the author had his removed using ice and a razor blade. The trick at that point came for Allied authorities to look not only for the tattoo itself, but for a telltale scar of its removal.

13 Vasily Grossman, quoted in Antony Beevor, *The Fall of Berlin 1945* (New York: Viking, 2002), 394.

14 Ibid., 395.

15 William L. Shirer, *The Rise and Fall of the Third Reich: A History of Nazi Germany* (New York: Simon & Schuster, 1990), 1137.

16 See ibid.

17 *Stars and Stripes*, May 2, 1945, 1, extra edition.

18 Ibid.

19 Karl Dönitz, *Memoirs: Ten Years and Twenty Days* (New York: World Pub. Co., 1959), 443–444.

20 For this section on the April activities in Bad Tölz, see the "Memorandum to the Officer in Charge," the 307th CIC detachment at the Headquarters of the Seventh Army, Munich subsection, June 11, 1945.

21 Axmann, *Das kann doch nicht*, 426. Axmann just wrote the meeting place in Upper Bavaria, he didn't write down the name of the actual town in Upper Bavaria—Bad Tölz.

22 The Nazi Party then was called the *Deutsche Arbeiter Partei*, the beer hall was Hofbräukeller, and the date was October 16, 1919.

23 Correspondence with Silvia Schurz, Tourist-Information, Bad Tölz, April 12, 2011.

24 "Memorandum to the Officer in Charge," June 11, 1945, 1.

25 Ibid., 1–2.

26 John Schwarzwalder, *We Caught Spies* (New York: Duell, Sloan and Pearce, 1946), 256.

27 Klaus Neumann, *Shifting Memories: The Nazi Past in the New Germany* (Ann Arbor: University of Michigan Press, 2000), 51.

28 Hugh Trevor-Roper, *The Last Days of Hitler* (Chicago: University of Chicago Press, 1992), 94.

29 Hans-Adolf Prützmann's title was the general inspector of special defense *(Der Generalinspekteur für Spezialabwehr)*. Arno Rose, *Werwolf: 1944–1945* (Stuttgart, Germany: Motorbuch-Verlag, 1980), 26.

30 Charles Whiting, *Hitler's Werewolves: The story of the Nazi resistance movement, 1944–1945* (New York: Stein and Day, 1972), 146.

31 "Werewolves to Fight for Reich," Associated Press, London, April 2, 1945.

32 David Stafford, *Endgame, 1945: The missing final chapter of World War II* (New York: Little, Brown, 2007), 136.

33 Trevor-Roper, *Last Days of Hitler*, 94.

34 Schwarzwalder, *We Caught Spies*, 258.

35 Ibid., 256.

36 Trevor-Roper, *Last Days of Hitler*, 93.

37 "Termed a 'Truce,'" *Evening Post*, Vol. CXXXIX, Issue 106, May 7, 1945, 5.

38 Charles Whiting, *Hitler's Werewolves*, 192.

39 It was either April 25 or April 26. The CIC was not sure. "Memorandum to the Officer in Charge," June 11, 1945, 2.

40 Ibid.

41 Progress Reports on Nursery Case, USFET, OSS Mission For Germany, X-2 Branch, July 28, 1945, Appendix 2.

42 USFET Release No. 1406, Security Release Time–0001 hours, March 31,1946. 1.

43 "Memorandum to the Officer in Charge," June 11, 1945, 2.

44 Ibid., 4.

45 Christian Tessmann & Soehne GmbH, registered at the Amtagericht Berlin.

46 "Memorandum to the Officer in Charge," June 11, 1945, 2. See also Progress Reports on Nursery Case, Appendix 2.

47 Jean-Denis Lepage, *Hitler Youth, 1922–45: An Illustrated History* (Jefferson, NC: McFarland & Company, 2009), 124.

48 Ibid., 125.

49 "Flint Kaserne," Special Forces Association Rocky Mountain Chapter 4-24, accessed June 21, 2011, http://sfa4-24.org/index.php?option=com_content&view=article&id=8&Itemid=11.

50 Ibid.

51 Diana Zinkler, *"Wir waren doch noch Kinder,"* *Hamburger Abendblatt*, May 7, 2005.

52 Ibid.

53 Ibid.

54 Ibid.

55 Ibid.

56 Ibid.

57 Ibid.

58 Clifford H Peek, ed., "The Last Ten Days of the War, XIV," *Five Years, Five Countries, Five Campaigns with the 141st Infantry Regiment* (San Antonio, TX: 141st Infantry Regiment Association, 1945).

59 "Dachau was the first concentration camp which was established for a long period. It was opened on March 21, 1933. Other concentration camps were opened some

days earlier. But all these were short time camps for several weeks. They were established in houses, prisons or working halls. But Dachau was the first one with barracks, watch towers, ditch and barbed wire." Albert Knoll, Archive, the Dachau Concentration Camp Memorial Site, email to author, July 8, 2011.

60 Ibid.

61 Richard Marowitz, interviewed by Matthew Rozell at Hudson Falls High School on May 3, 2002, as part of a "small town high school history project," transcribed by Sean Connolly and Nick Wildey. "April 29th, 1945. The Liberation of Dachau," accessed November 9, 2010, www.teachinghistorymatters.wordpress.com/2011/04/25/april-29th-1945-the-liberation-of-dachau/.

62 "The Dachau death train consisted of nearly forty railcars containing the bodies of between 2,000 and 3,000 prisoners who were evacuated from Buchenwald on April 7, 1945. The train arrived in Dachau on the afternoon of April 28." United States Holocaust Memorial Museum, Photo Archives, notes on Photograph #16988.

63 Richard Marowitz interview at Hudson Falls High School.

64 "World Battlefronts: Battle of Germany: The Man Who Can't Surrender," *Time*, February 12, 1945.

65 DeWitt MacKenzie (AP war analyst), "The War Today," AP, *Lawrence Journal-World*, April 3, 1945, 4.

66 Omar N. Bradley and A. J. Liebling, *A Soldier's Story* (New York: Modern Library, 1999), 536.

CHAPTER FOUR

1 George Orwell, *Orwell: the Observer Years*, (London: Atlantic Books, 2003), 41.

2 Artur Axmann, "*Meine Flucht mit Bormann*," *Stern*, May 9, 1965.

3 Artur Axmann, *Das kann doch nicht das Ende sein: Hitlers letzter Reichsjugendführer erinnert sich* (Schnellbach, Germany: Verlag Siegfried Bublies, 1995), 452. The rest of the material in this chapter about Axmann's escape from Berlin is largely based on the facts in his memoir and his articles in *Stern* magazine.

4 Ibid.

5 Ibid.

6 Axmann, "*Meine Flucht mit Bormann*."

7 Interrogation of Artur Axmann by Robert Kempner, October 10, 1947, 8.

8 Twice in his book, *Das kann doch nicht*, Axmann mentions having been broke. On page 454, he wrote that after having escaped the bunker into the ruins of Berlin, he didn't have a single penny. On page 461, he again mentioned being broke, when he left the village he'd been hiding out in, in Soviet-controlled territory in northern Germany. In an interrogation, he'd claimed to have had some money when he left Berlin, but that appears to have been a lie to cover up that he had later received money from Heidemann.

9 Armin D. Lehmann and Tim Carroll, *In Hitler's Bunker: A Boy Soldier's Eyewitness Account of the Fuhrer's Last Days* (Edinburgh: Mainstream Publishing, 2004), 223.

10 Ibid.

11 Ibid., 225.

12 Interrogation of Axmann by Hugh Trevor-Roper, January 14, 1946, 4.

13 Berlin is comprised of boroughs, which are in turn made up of localities.

14 A second unconditional surrender document was signed before midnight on May 8 in Berlin at the behest of the Soviets.

15 The Soviets waited until the Berlin signing ceremony. Besides, the time the first surrender document called for German forces to cease operations was 11 P.M. CET on May 8, which was May 9 in Moscow.

16 Alex Singleton, "Proclaim V-E Day Today," AP, *Lewiston Daily Sun* (Lewiston, ME), Tuesday morning, May 8, 1945, 23. Byline London, May 7.

17 "*Life* Goes to Some V-E Day Celebrations," *Life,* May 21, 1945, 119.

18 Kenneth Bourne, D. Cameron Watt, Paul Preston, and Anita Prazmowska, "British documents on foreign affairs: reports and papers from the Foreign Office confidential print: From 1940 through 1945. Series A: The Soviet Union and Finland, Part 3," (Frederick, MD: University Publications of America, 1997), 189.

19 President Harry S. Truman, "Broadcast to the American People Announcing the Surrender of Germany," 9 P.M. May 8, 1945, Harry S. Truman Library and Museum.

20 Zero hour is a phrase traditionally used in English to indicate the scheduled starting time of a military operation. For an analysis of the cultural meaning of this phrase, see Stephen Brockmann, *German Literary Culture at the Zero Hour* (Rochester, NY: Camden House, 2009). For the different meanings associated with this expression, see also James F. Harris, "A Critical View of 'Stunde Null, in Comparative Perspective,'" *Different Restorations: Reconstruction and "Wiederaufbau" in Germany and the United States, 1865, 1945, and 1989,* edited by Norbert Finzsch and Jürgen Martschukat (Providence, RI: Berghahn Books, 1996), 39–40.

21 I converted this from meters to feet: "400 million cubic metres of rubble," which is "equivalent to a country the size of Great Britain completely covered in rubble to a height of several meters." Deborah Ascher Barnstone, *The Transparent State: Architecture and politics in postwar Germany* (London: Routledge, 2005), 28.

22 "Memorandum to the Officer in Charge," the 307th CIC detachment at the Headquarters of the Seventh Army, Munich subsection, July 5, 1945, 2.

23 Ibid.

24 Werner Michel, correspondence with author, January 3, 2010.

25 Kevin Conley Ruffner, "The Black Market in Postwar Berlin: Colonel Miller and an Army Scandal, Part 1," *Prologue,* Vol. 34, no. 3 (fall 2002).

26 Military Government of Germany, "Fragebogen," Form MG/PS/G/9a, Revised May 15, 1945.

27 Ibid.

28 One former CIC agent wrote that CIC agents "resent bitterly being called 'G-Men in Khaki.'" John Schwarzwalder, *We Caught Spies* (New York: Duell, Sloan and Pearce, 1946), viii.

29 Judge Advocate General's Office, War Crimes Office, "Memorandum for Dossier File No. 100-587," August 2, 1945. File No. 100-587 was for subject Artur Axmann, although his first name was misspelled as "Arthur."

30 This comes from Ib Melchior, *Case by Case: A U.S. Army Counterintelligence Agent in World War II* (Novato, CA: Presidio Press, 1993), 157–158.

31 Alexander Kozak and Duval A. Edwards, "38th CIC Joins in Liberating Bataan and Corregidor," in Duval A. Edwards, ed., *Jungle and Other Tales: True Stories of Historic Counterintelligence Operations* (Tucson, AZ: Wheatmark, 2008), 96.

32 Werner Michel, email to author, January 4, 2011.

33 Ib Melchior, *Case by Case*, 30.

CHAPTER FIVE

1 Winston Churchill, *The Grand Alliance* (New York: Houghton Mifflin Company, 1950), 370.

2 *The Times* Military Correspondent, "Wehrmacht's Hope of Survival," *The Times* (London), May 17, 1945, 4.

3 Albert Speer, *Inside the Third Reich* (New York: Avon Books, 1971), 627.

4 Ibid.

5 Giles MacDonogh, *After the Reich: The Brutal History of the Allied Occupation* (New York: Basic Books, 2007), 70.

6 Albert Speer, *Inside the Third Reich*, 630.

7 See e.g., "Himmler Poison Suicide," UPI, *Lodi News-Sentinel* (CA), May 25, 1945, 1.

8 "The Representatives of the Supreme Commands of the United States of America, the Union of Soviet Socialist Republics, the United Kingdom and the French Republic." From "Declaration Regarding the Defeat of Germany and the Assumption of Supreme Authority by Allied Powers," June 5, 1945.

9 Ibid.

10 Robert McKenna, *The Dictionary of Nautical Literacy* (New York: McGraw-Hill Professional, 2003), 301.

11 Martin Kidston, *From Poplar to Papua: Montana's 163rd Infantry Regiment in the Pacific in World War II* (Helena, MT: Farcountry Press, 2004), 16.

12 Ibid.

13 "The Queen Mary Carries 14,000 Troops Home," *The Times* (London), June 21, 1945, 4.

14 Werner Michel, email to author, January 4, 2011.

15 Ibid.

16 Ibid.

17 Werner Michel, letter to author, November 14, 2010.

18 Werner Michel, email to author, January 4, 2011.

19 Werner Michel, letter to author, November 14, 2010.

20 Ibid.

21 *Interessen Gemeinschaft Farbenindustrie Aktiengesellschaft.*

22 The IG Farben Trial was also known as *U.S. v. Carl Krauch et al.*

23 "IG Farben-Haus," *Institut für Stadtgeschichte Karmeliterkloster,* Frankfurt am Main, accessed March 31, 2011, http://www.stadtgeschichte-ffm.de/service/geden ktafeln/ig_farben_haus.html.

24 Jack D. Hunter, communication with a confidential source, who provided it to the author.

25 Jack D. Hunter, unpublished material.

26 Ibid.

27 Bob Hunter, conversation with author, January 15, 2011.

28 Ibid.

29 Ibid.

30 Hunter, unpublished material.

31 Lansen is now Lansen-Schönau. It was combined with the municipality of Alt Schönau in 2005. "*Namens- und Grenzänderungen vom* 01.01. *bis* 31.12.2005," *Statistisches Bundesamt Deutschland.*

32 Timothy Reis, unpublished memo, June 10, 1979.

33 Ibid.

34 Ibid.

35 Hunter, unpublished material.

36 CIC Special Agent (ret) George Hochschild, interview with author, October 25, 2010.

37 Hunter, unpublished material.

38 Captain FC Grant, SCI, Seventh Army, "Operation NURSERY, 1st Report," June 25, 1945, 1.

39 Andreas Pretzel, Gabriele Rossbach, *Wegen der zu erwartenden hohen Strafe . . .* (Berlin: Verlag Rosa Winkel, 2000), 36 and 42 n78.

40 While those of Jewish descent were forced to wear yellow triangles, concentration inmates deemed homosexual had to wear a pink triangle.

41 These facts about Kulas come from his later criminal trial. LG Karlsruhe on 12/20/ 1961, VI Ks 1 / 60 BGH of 05.28.1963, 1 StR 540/62.

42 With many minor variations, this is a cliché used by police and prosecutors when explaining why their informants themselves have extensive criminal records.

43 "The International Military Tribunal in its decision of October 1, 1946 declared that the Einsatzgruppen and the Security Police, to which the defendants belonged, were responsible for the murder of two million defenseless human beings, and the evidence presented in this case has in no way shaken this finding." *Trials of War Criminals Before the Nuernberg Military Tribunals Under Control Council Law No. 10, Nuernberg October 1946–April 1949,* vol. 4, *U.S. v. Otto Ohlendorf et. al.* (Case 9: "Einsatzgruppen Case") (D.C.: U.S. Government Printing Office, 1950), 411–589, 412.

44 Ibid., 412. This trial was presided over by Michael Musmanno whose interrogation of Artur Axmann is quoted elsewhere in this book.

45 Ibid., 414.
46 Ibid., 415.
47 Ibid., 448–449.
48 From the criminal trial of Kulas, which included other criminal defendants. LG Karlsruhe on 12/20/1961, VI Ks 1 / 60 BGH of 05.28.1963, 1 StR 54.
49 A. I. Goldberg, "Germans in Munich are Irked by Food, Prices, Treatment," AP, *Milwaukee Journal*, June 2, 1945, 9.
50 Ibid.
51 Grant, "Operation NURSERY," 1.
52 Ibid.

CHAPTER SIX

1 *Shanghai* (2010). Film written by Hossein Amini.
2 Timothy M. Reis, "Memorandum for the Officer in Charge," 307th CIC Detachment, HQ 7th Army, APO 758, June 11, 1945.
3 John Schwarzwalder, *We Caught Spies* (New York: Duell, Sloan and Pearce, 1946), 260.
4 Reis, unpublished memo.
5 "Patton chose a code name for Third Army headquarters: Lucky. That portion of headquarters consisting of himself and his key officers was Lucky Forward, while the administrative section was Lucky Rear." Alan Axelrod, *Patton* (Basingstoke, U.K.: Palgrave Macmillan, 2009), 124-125.
6 Timothy Reis, unpublished memo, June 10, 1979.
7 Ibid.
8 General George Patton, June 5, 1944, from Charles M. Provence, *The Unknown Patton* (New York: Hippocrene Books, 1983), 36.
9 Ibid., 37.
10 Major W. H. Prentice, Cover Letter to CO, OSS/X-2, June 25, 1945, 2.
11 Reis, unpublished memo.
12 Reis, "Memorandum for the Officer in Charge," July 5, 1945, 1.
13 Werner Michel explained the term "Special Agent" in the CIC context as follows: "Concerning the term Special Agent, during my 11 years in CIC all operational individuals who had been rated as qualified, were designated as special agents and signed agent reports (AR's) as s/a CIC." Werner Michel, email to author, January 4, 2011.
14 They were not the first spies (or counterspies) to use journalism as a cover for their activities, and they would not be the last. This practice is one that occasionally causes serious problems for legitimate journalists because people then suspect them of being spies. As a recent example, in 2009, two French spies pretended to be journalists in Somalia and were subsequently kidnapped. The International News Safety Institute, an organization "dedicated to the safety of news media staff working in dangerous environments," issued a press release condemning "any practice of government security agents posing as journalists." As they explained,

"this directly affects the safety of all journalists in Somalia—currently the most dangerous country in the world for the news media—and elsewhere. Journalists are already in great danger in many parts of the world and actions that fuel suspicion of their true identities and roles must be condemned." "Government agents posing as journalists threaten safety of news media, INSI says," INSI, July 16, 2009.

15 Reis, "Memorandum for the Officer in Charge," July 5, 1945, 4.

16 Reis, unpublished memo.

17 Reis, "Memorandum to the Officer in Charge," July 5, 1945, 4. Note, I corrected the spelling of "Tessmann" in this quote.

18 CIC reports listed him as a dispatcher (*Fahrdienstleiter*). Ibid., 6. His bio, though, in an attachment to this report, listed him as "chief of the repair shop" at Tessmann. Ibid., 8 (Appendix III). A later CIC report, on August 26, 1945, again lists him as a dispatcher.

19 Ibid., 6.

20 Ibid.

21 Ibid., 8 (Appendix III).

22 Reis, "Memorandum for the Officer in Charge," July 4, 1945.

23 Reis, "Memorandum for the Officer in Charge," July 10, 1945, 3.

24 Robert Hemblys-Scales of the British Army of the Rhine (BAOR).

25 Hunter, unpublished material.

26 These numbers come from Jack Hunter's receipt when he turned these items in on June 12, 1946, to the personnel officer.

27 Hunter, email to a confidential source, who provided it to the author.

28 This street name changed while Hunter was living on it. It was "vom-Rath-Straße" but changed slightly in February 1946 to become "Walter-vom-Rath-Straße." Email to author from K. Rheinfurth, *Institut für Stadtgeschichte, Stadt Frankfurt am Main*, June 16, 2011. Today it is "Walter-vom-Rath-Straße."

29 Artur Axmann, *Das kann doch nicht das Ende sein: Hitlers letzter Reichsjugendführer erinnert sich* (Schnellbach, Germany: Verlag Siegfried Bublies, 1995), 458.

30 See e.g., Giles MacDonogh, *After the Reich: The Brutal History of the Allied Occupation* (New York: Basic Books, 2007). See also Peter Antill, *Berlin 1945: End of the Thousand Year Reich, Campaign 159* (Oxford, U.K.: Osprey Publishing, 2005), 84, and Norman M. Naimark. *The Russians in Germany: A History of the Soviet Zone of Occupation, 1945–1949* (Cambridge, MA: Belknap Press, 1995), 105–107.

31 Axmann said in an interrogation, in reply to "How many young people were under you as Reichsjugendfuehrer?": "I figure there must have been 9 million people." Interrogation of Artur Axmann by Robert Kempner, October 10, 1947, 1.

CHAPTER SEVEN

1 Peter G. Tsouras, *The Book of Military Quotations* (Zenith Imprint, 2005), 465. The quote was originally said on Armistice Day (November 1942), in the House of Commons.

2   Reis, "Memorandum for the Officer in Charge," July 5, 1945, 5. I've corrected the spelling of Zeppelin; this quote had it as "ZEPPERELIN," although it was spelled correctly elsewhere in this document.

3   Reis, "Memorandum for the Officer in Charge," July 10, 1945, 1. I fixed a typographical error in this quote, it used to say "the cooperate" when it should have read "he cooperate."

4   For example, one key document Pommerening copied listed all the drivers for the company and included when they were born.

5   Reis, "Memorandum for the Officer in Charge," July 10, 1945, 3.

6   Reis, unpublished memo.

7   Ibid.

8   Ibid.

9   Ibid.

10   Reis, "Memorandum for the Officer in Charge," July 10, 1945, 3.

11   Ibid., 4. Although this report has the wrong first name for "BOEHMER."

12   Frau Dr. Rüdiger, "*Sie haben sich während Ihrer Studienzeit 1931 der nationalsozialistischen Bewegung angeschlossen.*" Irmhild Boßdorf interviewed Dr. Jutta Rüdiger in *Junge Freiheit* (Berlin), March 24, 2000.

13   Jutta Rüdiger, *Ein Leben für die Jugend: Mädelführerin im Dritten Reich: das Wirken der Reichsreferentin des BDM* (Preussisch Oldendorf, Germany: Deutsche Verlagsgesellschaft, 1999), 131-132.

14   Ibid., 130.

15   Ibid., 132.

16   Reis, "Memorandum for the Officer in Charge," July 14, 1945, 1.

17   Ibid., 2.

18   Melita Maschmann, *Account Rendered: A Dossier on my Former Self*, trans. Geoffrey Strachan (New York: Abelard-Schuman, 1965), 179.

19   The CIC has different spellings for Dinglinger within the same document; they also spell it as Dingler and Dingliner. Reis, "Memorandum for the Officer in Charge," July 23, 1945, 1-2.

20   Reis, "Memorandum for the Officer in Charge," July 14, 1945, 3.

21   Ibid., 2.

22   Reis, "Memorandum to the Officer in Charge," July 23, 1945, 1–2.

23   Maschmann, *Account Rendered*, 177.

24   Ibid., 179.

25   Rüdiger, *Ein Leben für die Jugend*, 135-136.

26   From where the women had crossed, it was a bit more than four miles though.

27   Reis, unpublished memo.

28   Maschmann, *Account Rendered*, 179.

29   Ibid.

30   The source for this entire paragraph is Reis, unpublished memo.

31   Reis, "Memorandum for the Officer in Charge," July 14, 1945, Agents' Notes, 5.

32 Ibid.

33 Ibid.

34 Ibid.

35 "SHAEF Setup Comes to End—All Yanks In European Theater Placed Under USFET," *Sun* (Baltimore, MD), July 14, 1945, 3.

36 Bob Hunter, conversation with author, January 15, 2011.

37 Postcard from Jack Hunter to his wife at her Rocky River, Ohio, address. It has a U.S. postmark of July 25, 1945.

CHAPTER EIGHT

1 Hitler in a speech at the Reichsparteitag in 1935. United States Office of Chief of Counsel for the Prosecution of Axis Criminality, United States Dept. of State, Nazi Conspiracy and Aggression: Vol. 3, United States War Dept., 1946, 320.

2 "Work Contract Between Kulas and Tessmann," "Appendix I," "Memorandum to the Officer in Charge," July 23, 1945.

3 The source for this entire paragraph is Reis, "Memorandum to the Officer in Charge," July 23, 1945, 3.

4 Ibid., 6.

5 Reis, "Memorandum to the Officer in Charge," August 1, 1945, 2.

6 Ibid., 1.

7 Hunter, unpublished material.

8 Jäger means "Hunter." Jack is often short for John, while Hans can be short for the equivalents of John in German. Some people who knew him as Hans Jaeger called him Hansel as a nickname.

9 Hunter, unpublished material.

10 Ibid.

11 Hunter, email to confidential source, who provided it to the author.

12 Jack Hunter, *The Expendable Spy* (New York: Bantam Books, 1966), 128.

13 These leaders were, at first, Churchill, Truman, and Stalin. Churchill was replaced though by Clement Attlee as the election results announced on July 26 had Attlee as the new prime minister.

14 Peter Antill, *Berlin 1945: End of the Thousand Year Reich, Campaign 159* (Oxford, U.K.: Osprey Publishing, 2005), 32. In 1945, the United States was the only country in the world with the atom bomb.

15 Richard W. Cutler, *Counterspy: Memoirs of a Counterintelligence Officer in World War II and the Cold War* (Washington, D.C.: Brassey's, Books 2004), 57.

16 Protocol of the Proceedings, Berlin (Potsdam) Conference, (the "Potsdam Agreement"), Aug. 2, 1945, 3 Bevans 1207, sections II.A.3, II.A.3.(ii), and II.A.3.(iii).

17 Ibid., section II.A.3.(vi).

18 Theo Sommer, "New Life Blossoms in the Ruins. Germany after the surrender: a tough start into a new epoch," *Atlantic Times* (Germany), May 2005.

19 Of course, people in the United States celebrated the Victory over Japan and the

end of World War II when it was announced in the United States on August 14 local time. But for the United States, the official V-J Day, as proclaimed by the President, took place on September 2. Japan first announced its surrender during the day of August 15 in Japan (which was still August 14 in the United States), but September 2 was the day of the official surrender ceremony.

20   Potsdam Agreement, section II.B.19.

21   Ibid., section III.

22   Yalta Agreement, February 11, 1945, 59 Stat. 1823, 5(2)(c).

23   Statement by the Governments of the United Kingdom, the United States of America, the Union of Soviet Socialist Republics and the Provisional Government of the French Republic on Control Machinery in Germany, June 5, 1945.

24   Artur Axmann, *Das kann doch nicht das Ende sein: Hitlers letzter Reichsjugend-führer erinnert sich* (Schnellbach, Germany: Verlag Siegfried Bublies, 1995), 458.

25   Axmann, *Das kann doch nicht*, 459.

26   Ibid., 461.

CHAPTER NINE

1   Albert Camus, *The Rebel: An Essay on Man in Revolt* (New York: Vintage Books, 1984), 182. The word "Führerprinzip" was italicized in the original.

2   Reis, "Memorandum to the Officer in Charge," August 31, 1945, 3.

3   Artur Axmann, *Das kann doch nicht das Ende sein: Hitlers letzter Reichsjugend-führer erinnert sich* (Schnellbach, Germany: Verlag Siegfried Bublies, 1995), 455.

4   Ibid., 426.

5   Ibid., 455.

6   Reis, "Memorandum to the Officer in Charge," August 31, 1945, 2.

7   Ibid., 4.

8   Ibid., 4–5.

9   Baldur von Schirach testimony on May 23, 1946, International Military Tribunal, The Trial of German Major War Criminals: Proceedings of the International Military Tribunal Sitting at Nuremberg, Germany, Part 14, (London: H. M. Stationery Off., 1946), 333.

10   Ibid.

11   Supreme Headquarters Allied Expeditionary Force (SHAEF) Evaluation and Dissemination Section, G-2 (Counter Intelligence Sub-Division), Complied by MIRS (London Branch), *The Hitler Jugend* (The Hitler Youth Organisation), Basic Handbook, 1944, E.D.S./G/5, Annexe C.

12   Gerhard Rempel, *Hitler's Children: The Hitler Youth and the SS* (Chapel Hill, NC: UNC Press Books, 1991), 131.

13   Reis, "Memorandum to the Officer in Charge," August 31, 1945, Agents' Notes, 4–5.

14   Ibid., 5.

15   Reis, "Memorandum to the Officer in Charge," August 26, 1945, 3.

16 Reis, unpublished memo. While this memo said Gams was in the camps for seven years, Heidemann used the figure of eight years on another occasion. Reis, "Memorandum to the Officer in Charge," September 23, 1945, 3.

17 See Reis, "Memorandum to the Officer in Charge," September 8, 1945.

18 This could happen either from inadvertence, or an inability to control his anger toward these unrepentant Nazis.

19 See Reis, "Memorandum to the Officer in Charge," September 17, 1945, 3.

20 Hunter, unpublished material.

21 Ibid.

22 Ibid.

23 Axmann did not use the mayor's name in his memoirs, he only referred to him by his title. However, Herrmann Bleckmann was the mayor of Lansen at that time. Iris Heisel of Amt Seenlandschaft Waren, email to author, August 10, 2011.

24 Axmann, *Das kann doch nicht*, 459.

25 Axmann wrote "first-floor," but it was what most Europeans call the first floor and Americans call the second floor. As this is being written primarily for an American publisher, I've used the term "second-floor" in the text itself. See ibid., 460.

26 Ibid.

27 Ibid.

28 Ibid.

CHAPTER TEN

1 Don DeLillo, *White Noise* (New York: Penguin, 1986), 26.

2 For this section on Frankfurt, see Reis, "Memorandum to the Officer in Charge," September 8, 1945.

3 The source for this entire paragraph is ibid., 2.

4 Ibid.

5 Ibid., 1.

6 Reis, unpublished memo. Also, the subject line on the continuation reports filed by Agent Reis changed to "The NURSERY Case." Reis, Memorandum to the Officer in Charge, September 8, 1945, 1. The operation had previously been given this codename, but with this change in classification, so too came a change in the subject title. "In this report the Subject title (Suspicious Undercover Activities of HJ in Southern Germany) has been changed to read THE NURSERY CASE due to the change of classification of this case from SECRET to TOP SECRET. Future reports will carry the subject title as it now reads." Ibid. As such, Memoranda to the Officer in Charge, by Reis, related to this case, prior to September 8, 1945, were "Secret"; from this date on they were "Top Secret."

7 George Hochschild, interview with author, October 25, 2010.

8 Ibid.

9 Hunter was "the Officer in Charge of the case": see e.g., USFET Release No. 1406, March 31, 1946.

10 Hunter, unpublished material.

11 One of Jack Hunter's daughters told a newspaper that "her father named the sting after the birth of his twin daughters while he was in Germany." Peter Guinta, "Jack Hunter 1921–2009," *St. Augustine Record*, April 14, 2009.

12 Reis memo, unpublished.

13 International Military Tribunal, The Trial of German Major War Criminals: Proceedings of the International Military Tribunal Sitting at Nuremberg, Germany, Part 13, (London: H. M. Stationery Off., 1947), Part 14, 335.

14 For a discussion of the use of the term "chutzpah" in American legal decisions, see Judge Alex Kozinski and Eugene Volokh, "Lawsuit, Shmawsuit," Yale Law Journal 463 (1993), 103. Here is an excerpt: "The most famous definition of 'chutzpah' is, of course, itself law-themed: chutzpah is when a man kills both his parents and begs the court for mercy because he's an orphan. But there's another legal chutzpah story. A man goes to a lawyer and asks: 'How much do you charge for legal advice?' 'A thousand dollars for three questions.' 'Wow! Isn't that kind of expensive?' 'Yes, it is. What's your third question?'"

15 This incident is documented in Reis, "Memorandum to the Officer in Charge," September 8, 1945, 4–5.

16 Ibid., 4. Note that Hompeschstrasse was misspelled in the original; I corrected the spelling here after confirming that it had the same spelling in 1945. Gabriele Hopf of Landeshauptstadt München explained that "there has to be a typo in the American military documents. Since 1897, the year of the naming, the spelling of 'Hompeschstraße' has remained [the same]. The street is named [after] Johann Wilhelm Freiherr von Hompesch-Bollhei . . . and his brother Ferdinand Ludwig Joseph Anton Freiherr von Hompesch-Bollheim." Gabriele Hopf, email to author, July 8, 2011.

17 Ibid. Again, I've corrected the spelling of the Hompeschstrasse.

18 Ibid.

19 Ibid., 4–5.

20 Ibid., 5.

21 Ibid., 6, Agents' Notes.

22 Both sides had been clever enough to know that the old axiom about the best lies being close to the truth was a good one. Nordheim played a CIC agent who could not help them with the renting out of a building, while those he met with described their real need for a building to expand their business.

23 The CIC was not certain at first if this meeting was held on September 5 or 7, but Hermann Giesler confirmed it was on the 7th when he was interrogated by the CIC on September 20, 1945. Reis, "Memorandum to the Officer in Charge," September 23, 1945, 2.

24 Reis, "Memorandum to the Officer in Charge," September 17, 1945, 6, Agents' Notes.

25 Agent Reis wrote that "It is believed that Hauptbanfuhrer [Otto] Würschinger was also present." Ibid., 4.

26 See "Kinderhort," *Der Spiegel*, Issue 14, April 2, 1949. Note that the CIC report erroneously lists Hauptbannführer Heinrich Hartmann as the head of the entire Culture Bureau (*Chef des Kultur Amt*).

27 Reis, "Memorandum to the Officer in Charge," August 26, 1945, 2.

28 Reis, "Memorandum to the Officer in Charge," September 17, 1945, 6, Agents' Notes.

29 Note that I corrected the misspelling of the second letter from an "M" to an "N" but I did not put an umlaut over the first A as the CIC reports do not use German letters. It should be "SAMMLUNG DIE Anständigen."

30 Ibid.

31 Ibid.

32 Ibid., 7.

33 Ibid.

34 Reis, "Memorandum to the Officer in Charge," September 27, 1945, 2.

35 Reis, "Memorandum to the Officer in Charge," September 17, 1945, 4.

CHAPTER ELEVEN

1   Stephen Ambrose, *To America: Personal Reflections of an Historian* (Waterville, ME: Thorndike Press, 2003), 149–150.

2   Reis, "Memorandum to the Officer in Charge," September 17, 1945, 4.

3   Reis, unpublished memo.

4   A famous example was Sophie Scholl, who was executed on February 22, 1943, at the tender age of twenty-one. As a girl, she had been in the BDM, but she eventually turned against the Nazi regime. She was executed for being part of a small group, calling itself the White Rose, that wrote, printed, and distributed anti-Nazi pamphlets.

5   Reis, unpublished memo.

6   Reis, "Memorandum to the Officer in Charge," September 23, 1945, 1.

7   Reis, "Memorandum to the Officer in Charge," September 27, 1945, 2.

8   Reis, "Memorandum to the Officer in Charge," September 23, 1945, 2.

9   Ibid., 3.

10 Reis, "Memorandum to the Officer in Charge," September 27, 1945, 2.

11 Ibid., 4.

12 USFET Release No. 1406, March 31, 1946.

13 Reis, "Memorandum to the Officer in Charge," September 27, 1945, 4.

14 Ibid. Note that I corrected the misspelling of the second letter from an "M" to an "N" but I did not put an umlaut over the first "A" as the CIC reports do not use German letters. In German, it would be "SAMMLUNG DIE ANSTÄNDIGEN."

15 Anecdote provided to author by a confidential source, 2011. Hunter also mentioned in some of his unpublished writings that his car was sabotaged.

16 Anecdote provided to author by a confidential source, 2010.

17 Artur Axmann, *Das kann doch nicht das Ende sein: Hitlers letzter Reichsjugendführer erinnert sich* (Schnellbach, Germany: Verlag Siegfried Bublies, 1995), 462. Axmann thought the Russians would likely send him to Lubyanka or Siberia.

18 Ibid., 259.

19 USFET, "Interrogation Notes on NURSERY Case No. 1," January 2, 1946, (Top Secret) 1.

20 Ibid.

21 Axmann claimed this in both his memoir and during his interrogations by Allied authorities. As Axmann had just been in Bavaria, it is possible that he had secretly made contact with HJ figures there and arranged this meeting in Lübeck. Or he could have been telling the truth and had avoided contacting old comrades in order to minimize his chances of getting caught.

22 Axmann, *Das kann doch nicht*, 463.

23 A history of the American occupation of Germany stated that "eight million refugees were to come in from the East [to West Germany] between 1945 and the end of 1946." Eugene Davidson, *The Death and Life of Germany: An Account of the American Occupation* (Columbia, MO: University of Missouri Press, 1999), 131.

CHAPTER TWELVE

1 *Shanghai* (2010). Film written by Hossein Amini.

2 Reis referred to Kulas as Max in an effort to continue to protect his identity. He used Helmut for Heidemann and Bringmann for Bergemann. I have changed these aliases to their respective real names in brackets in quotes from this memo (Reis, unpublished memo, 1979).

3 Reis, unpublished memo.

4 Ibid.

5 Ibid.

6 Ibid.

7 Ibid., cover page. This is from the cover page to the memo; this cover page is dated June 10, 1979. Reis used Kulas's actual first name as the cover page uses real names while the memo proper uses codenames for certain individuals.

8 Reis, unpublished memo.

9 "The 17th Century," Passion Play at Oberammergau, accessed August 5, 2011, http://www.passionplay-oberammergau.com/index.php?id=127.

10 George Hochschild, interview with author, October 25, 2010.

11 The "computational knowledge engine" WolframAlpha came up with 2.457 million U.S. dollars as the 2011 value of $200,000 from 1945. This used an average rate of inflation of 3.87 percent per year. There are a number of other ways to calculate what $200,000 from 1945 would be worth in 2011. This almost 2.5 million figure should be seen as just one of a number of possibilities, but it is useful as a way to illustrate that this was a large amount of money.

12 George Hochschild, interview with author, October 25, 2010.

13 Ibid.

14 Ibid.

15 While the famous Nietzsche scholar Walter Kaufmann also was in the CIC during

World War II, this was not him. The Rosenheim agent spelled his last name with a single "n," while the famous scholar used two.

16 Reis, unpublished memo.

17 When interrogated, Memminger said that "EBELING was considered OVER-BECK's friend." USFET, "Interrogation notes on NURSERY case No. 1," January 2, 1946 (Top Secret), 4.

18 The indictment was issued on October 18, 1945. Final report to the Secretary of the Army on Nuernberg war crimes trials under Control Council Law, Issue 93, United States Government Printing Office, 1950, 143. It was served to the defendants the following day. Philippe Sands, *From Nuremberg to the Hague: the Future of International Criminal Justice* (Cambridge University Press, 2003), 1.

19 Baldur von Schirach was found guilty on count IV and not guilty on count I.

20 Gerda Fromme, email to author, April 25, 2012.

21 Ibid.

22 Ibid.

23 Artur Axmann, *Das kann doch nicht das Ende sein: Hitlers letzter Reichsjugendführer erinnert sich* (Schnellbach, Germany: Verlag Siegfried Bublies, 1995), 466.

24 Irving J. Lewis, "Memorandum to the Officer in Charge," March 8, 1946, CIC, Rosenheim, Bavaria (Top Secret), 1.

25 William L. Shirer, *End of a Berlin Diary* (New York: Alfred A. Knopf, 1947), 140.

26 Leo Barton, Military Intelligence Service Center, USFET, "Interrogation notes on NURSERY case No 2," January 20, 1946 (Top Secret), 8.

27 Melita Maschmann, *Account Rendered: A Dossier on my Former Self*, trans. Geoffrey Strachan (New York: Abelard-Schuman, 1965), 148.

28 "Kinderhort," *Der Spiegel* (Hamburg), issue 49, April 2, 1949.

29 Barton, "Interrogation notes on NURSERY case No 2," 8.

30 Irving J. Lewis, "Memorandum to the Officer in Charge," March 8, 1946, CIC, Rosenheim, Bavaria (Top Secret), 1.

31 Although people writing in English often use this term just to refer to the German Army, it compromised the army (*Heer*), navy (*Kriegsmarine*), and air force (*Luftwaffe*).

CHAPTER THIRTEEN

1 Jack Hunter, *The Terror Alliance* (New York: Dorchester Publishing Company, 1980), 154.

2 Irving J. Lewis, "Memorandum to the Officer in Charge," March 8, 1946, CIC, Rosenheim, Bavaria (Top Secret), 2.

3 Reis, unpublished memo.

4 Lewis, "Memorandum to the Officer in Charge," March 8, 1946, 3.

5 Ibid.

6 Ibid.

7 Ibid. Note that the time was referred to as 2:15 P.M. elsewhere in the same memo (page 1). This though is just a five-minute difference.

8 Reis, unpublished memo.

9 Bob Hunter, emails to author, August 28–29, 2011.

10 Reis, unpublished memo.

11 Ibid.

12 Artur Axmann, *Das kann doch nicht das Ende sein: Hitlers letzter Reichsjugendführer erinnert sich* (Schnellbach, Germany: Verlag Siegfried Bublies, 1995), 467.

13 Ibid., 469.

14 Porter War, "Operation Youth: or The Story of Tim Reis and His Legion of Merit," *Lewiston Morning Tribune* (Lewiston, Idaho), February 23, 1947, 1.

15 Lewis, "Memorandum to the Officer in Charge," March 8, 1946, 3.

16 Reis, unpublished memo.

17 Lewis, "Memorandum to the Officer in Charge," March 8, 1946, 4.

18 Ibid., 5.

CHAPTER FOURTEEN

1 George Santayana, *Soliloquies in England and Later Soliloquies* (New York: C. Scribner's Sons, 1923), 102. This quote is commonly misattributed to Plato. See Andrew Fiala, *Public War, Private Conscience: The Ethics of Political Violence* (New York: Continuum International Publishing Group, 2010), 31.

2 Artur Axmann, *Das kann doch nicht das Ende sein: Hitlers letzter Reichsjugendführer erinnert sich* (Schnellbach, Germany: Verlag Siegfried Bublies, 1995), 469. See also the notes from interrogations of Artur Axmann.

3 Axmann, *Das kann doch nicht*, 469, and Message from USFET to BAOR, "Subject is Operation Nursery," December 21, 1945 (Top Secret).

4 Message from USFET to 3rd U.S. Army for G-2, "Reference Plan Nursery," January 18, 1945, (Top Secret).

5 It later was officially named Camp King.

6 Axmann, *Das kann doch nicht*, 469.

7 Ibid., 469-470.

8 George Hochschild, email to author, August 17, 2011.

9 This does not include earlier prisoners, such as the head of BDM, nor does it include low-level arrestees. The list is in Message from USFET to EXFOR for GSI, "Subject is Nursery case," January 9, 1946 (Top Secret). The names are: "AXMANN, MEMMINGER, OVERBECK, PAUL MUELLER, OTTI HABERMEHL, ERNST GABRIEL, EDMOND BERTSGH, HEIDEMANN, WALTER BERGEMANN, ERAN PRANTZ, OTTO THOMAS, ERIKA KISCHKAT, KURT SCHOELLKOPF, FRANK OTTO STRASSEL, PAULA FUEHRER, GEORG THEIL, HENTSCHKE, BOKU, UNZE, HELTMANN, SIMON WINTER."

10 Leo Barton, Military Intelligence Service Center, USFET, "Interrogation notes on NURSERY case No 2," January 20, 1946, (Top Secret), 3.

11 "German Raised Fresh Voice for Socialism," *Los Angeles Times*, December 17, 1979, B22.

12 Axmann, *Das kann doch nicht*, 472.

13 Ibid.

14 Baldur von Schirach testimony on May 24, 1946, International Military Tribunal, The Trial of German Major War Criminals: Proceedings of the International Military Tribunal Sitting at Nuremberg, Germany, Part 14 (London: H. M. Stationery Off., 1946), 369.

15 USFET, "Interrogation notes on NURSERY case No. 1," January 2, 1946 (Top Secret), 1.

16 Ibid., 3.

17 Ibid., 4.

18 Ibid.

19 Ibid., 5.

20 Ibid., 10.

21 Barton, "Interrogation notes on NURSERY case No 2," 1. Note that he used the British spelling of the word "realised"; in American English it is "realized."

22 Ibid., 2.

23 Ibid., 4.

24 Ibid.

25 Ibid.

26 Ibid., 5.

27 Ibid.

28 Ibid. Note that he used the British spelling of the word "organisation"; in American English it is "organization."

29 Ibid.

30 Ibid.

31 Ibid., 9.

32 William T. Salzmann, email to author, September 21, 2011.

33 Message from USFET to BAOR, "Subject is Operation Nursery," December 21, 1945 (Top Secret).

34 Reis, unpublished memo.

35 Bruce Haywood, *Bremerhaven: A Memoir of Germany, 1945–1947,* (Raleigh, NC: Lulu, 2010), 154–155.

36 Bruce Haywood explained that the CIC then occupied a former police building and the briefing was on the second floor. Bruce Haywood, email to author, November 14, 2010.

37 Haywood, *Bremerhaven*, 155–156.

38 Bruce Haywood, email to author, November 14, 2010.

39 Haywood, *Bremerhaven*, 156.

40 Ibid.

41 Ibid., 157.

42 Ibid., 158.

43 Ibid.

44 Ibid., 159.

45 Bruce Haywood, email to author, November 14, 2010.

46 USFET Release No. 1406, March 31, 1946, 3.

47 See Richard Oregon, "Raids Stop Plots of Nazi Fanatics," AP, *Stars and Stripes*, USFET (German Edition), Volume 1, Number 353, March 31, 1946, 1.

48 "Hitler Fanatics Battle Allies," AP, *Los Angeles Times*, volume LXV, Sunday, March 31, 1946.

49 Ibid.

50 Ibid.

51 Original version (as kept by Jack Hunter) of USFET Release No. 1406, March 31, 1946, 3.

52 Hunter, unpublished material. Hunter went on to explain why and how he held on to the original version of the release.

EPILOGUE

1   Don DeLillo, *White Noise* (New York: Penguin, 1986), 287.

2   Bruce Haywood, *Bremerhaven: A Memoir Of Germany, 1945–1947*, (Raleigh, NC: Lulu, 2010), 162.

3   Haywood later wrote, "I knew I had arrested the wrong Inge. It was the mother I should have taken in." Ibid., 163.

4   Ibid.

5   USFET Release No. 1406, March 31, 1946, 3.

6   Artur Axmann, *Das kann doch nicht das Ende sein: Hitlers letzter Reichsjugendführer erinnert sich* (Schnellbach, Germany: Verlag Siegfried Bublies, 1995), 478.

7   Ibid.

8   Ibid., 475–476.

9   Schilde, *"Artur Axmann auf der Spur,"* 103.

10 April 29, 1949, Denazification Proceeding of Artur Axmann, Nuremberg, Germany.

11 Professor Toby Thacker, email to author, July 4, 2011. Professor Thacker is the author of the book *The End of the Third Reich: Defeat, Denazification and Nuremberg* (Stroud, U.K.: The History Press, 2009).

12 UPI, "Ex-Nazi Leader Fined," *The Times Recorder* (Zanesville, Ohio), August 20, 1958, 1.

13 Professor Schaar Torsten, *"Artur Axmann—Vom Hitlerjungen zum Reichsjugendführer der NSDAP—eine nationalsozialistische Karriere,"* 1997, a revised version of his PhD dissertation (University of Rostock, 1994), Section 4, *"Zur Nachkriegsentwicklung Artur Axmanns*, quoting the 1958 denazification proceeding's judgment regarding Artur Axmann.

14 Alfons Heck, *The Burden of Hitler's Legacy* (Phoenix, AZ: American Traveler Press, 1988), 89. Alfons Heck had felt "elated" after hearing a speech that Axmann gave during the war; his feelings toward Axmann changed after the war.

15 Ib Melchior and Frank Brandenburg, *Quest: Searching for the Truth of Germany's Nazi Past* (New York: Presidio Press, 1994), 256.

16 Axmann, *Das kann doch nicht*, dedication page.

17 Ibid, 483. Although this quote comes in the context of Axmann refusing to criticize Hitler while during questioning, it appears to apply to his mindset toward criticizing Hitler in his memoirs. *Der Spiegel* also interpreted it that way, writing that "the son refused, even recently in his memoirs to say 'bad things about his father.'" "Am Rande: Hitlers Sohn," *Der Spiegel* (Hamburg), November 11, 1996.

18 Dagmar Reese, *Growing Up Female in Nazi Germany* (Ann Arbor, MI: University of Michigan Press, 2006), trans. William Templer, 1 fn2.

19 Alan Cowell, "Artur Axmann, 83, a Top Nazi Who Headed the Hitler Youth," *New York Times*, November 7, 1996.

20 *Frankfurter Allgemeine Zeitung* (Frankfurt, Germany), October 27, 1996.

21 Ibid.

22 "Am Rande: Hitlers Sohn," *Der Spiegel* (Hamburg), November 11, 1996.

23 Hunter, unpublished material.

24 Ibid.

25 Jack Hunter, email to a confidential source, who provided it to the author.

26 Ibid.

27 Although the name of the award ("Pour le Mérite") was French, it was a German award. The award had its origins in Prussia, and it was fashionable among the Prussian elite at the time to use French.

28 Jack Hunter, "The Blue Max Revisited," *Over the Front 13*, no. 3 (Fall 1998).

29 "The Nation's Oldest City," City of St. Augustine, accessed June 11, 2011, http://www.staugustinegovernment.com/visitors/nations-oldest-city.cfm.

30 Ibid.

31 The Immigration and Nationality Act as amended October 30, 1978 (later renumbered in 1990). See INA 212(a)(3)(E). Kulas was a member of the SS, which is considered a criminal organization in accordance with the IMT. This creates a rebuttable presumption that he should not be let into the United States. Given Kulas's activities in Latvia, it seems highly unlikely that he would be able to overcome this presumption. See 9 FAM 40.35(A) "N1 Background and Summary of INA 212(A)(3)(E)(I)," (TL:VISA-77; 03-30-1993). U.S. Department of State Foreign Affairs Manual Volume 9—Visas.

32 Jack Hunter, "Treason's Payoff," from his blog, January 5, 2008. He refers to Kulas as "Karl" to protect Kulas's identity even after all this time.

33 Ibid.

34   The decision in the West German criminal trial of Siegfried Kulas can be found at
     the following cite: Einzelausfertigung der Gerichtsentscheidungen des Verfahrens
     Lfd.Nr.526: LG Karlsruhe vom 20.12.1961, VI Ks 1/60; BGH vom 28.5.1963, 1 StR
     540/62.

35   "Hans Garms," *Der Spiegel* (Hamburg), November 18, 1948.

36   "Timothy M. Reis, 92, Cottonwood," *Lewiston Tribune*, June 27, 2007.

37   Ibid. Note: The newspaper referred to it as "Gamble's"; the correct name is "Gam-
     bles."

INDEX

ABOUT THE AUTHOR

Scott Andrew Selby is a graduate of UC Berkeley and Harvard Law School. He also has a master's degree in Human Rights and Intellectual Property Law from Sweden's Lund University. He is the coauthor of *Flawless: Inside the Largest Diamond Heist in History* and is licensed to practice law in California and New York.

The website for this book is www.TheAxmannConspiracy.com.